The
Musical
Maverick

Also by the author

Louiz Banks: A Symphony of Love

The Musical Maverick

The Authorized Biography of
SHANKAR MAHADEVAN

Ashis Ghatak

RUPA

Published by
Rupa Publications India Pvt. Ltd 2024
7/16, Ansari Road, Daryaganj
New Delhi 110002

Sales centres:
Bengaluru Chennai
Hyderabad Jaipur Kathmandu
Kolkata Mumbai Prayagraj

P-ISBN: 978-93-5702-672-7
E-ISBN: 978-93-5702-948-3

First impression 2024

10 9 8 7 6 5 4 3 2 1

The moral right of the author has been asserted.

Printed in India

To those who value childhood friends the most...

Contents

Foreword
by Javed Akhtar

Let me begin by saying what I will say at the end too—Shankar Mahadevan is a musical genius. Reflecting on my journey with Shankar, it all began through the creative Imtiaz Dharker—a cherished friend and renowned painter. She reached out to me to write the lyrics for her documentary that focussed on Mumbai's street children. She was aiming to capture their essence through a singular song rather than conventional commentary. I happily agreed.

Guided by Imtiaz, I found myself at a studio to meet Ehsaan Noorani. Soon after, his partner Shankar Mahadevan arrived. It was a brief yet defining interaction. In just minutes, he composed a musical masterpiece, leaving a lasting impression on me.

Later, I called Ehsaan, asking if they would be interested in composing for films. He said he would get back but never did. Later, I learnt that he became so flustered and nervous that he couldn't muster the courage to return my call!

Despite that, I kept telling my producers about these exceptionally talented young individuals. However, it is ironic that anything that's different faces resistance from the market.

Besides the music of Shankar-Ehsaan-Loy, there was another idea I had been trying to sell for almost seven years. Many singers and composers found it interesting, amusing and new, but I suppose most people believe that nothing should be done for the first time.

One day, incidentally, I met Shankar at Saregama and narrated the musical idea to him. He instantly agreed to collaborate. We titled it 'Breathless'. By the way, the music video for 'Breathless' marked the first directorial attempt of Zoya and Farhan, as they teamed up on it. This is how two of my 'convictions', which were not widely shared, came together, giving birth to 'Breathless'.

Meanwhile, doors began opening for them in the industry. The trio's versatility and range were evident in Farhan's *Dil Chahta Hai*, Nikkhil Advani's *Kal Ho Naa Ho* and Vidhu Vinod Chopra's *Mission Kashmir* proving them to be a force to reckon with.

In addition to being an excellent composer, Shankar is an exceptional singer. The way he sings, most people can't even speak with such ease. I've seen him in the recording studio; while rummaging through a pile of papers for the second stanza of a song, he effortlessly continued to sing into the mic.

There's also this memorable incident. At an event, Shankar was singing on the stage when Yesudas arrived and sat in the front row. Just then, the interlude started. Shankar, with his cordless mic, came down the steps to pay his respects by touching Yesudas' feet. As he was returning, the interlude concluded and Shankar immediately started singing the *sargam* while climbing the steps back to the stage. His singing is as effortless as breathing is for you and me.

I would be undermining his talent if I mentioned only his work in films. Shankar is an esteemed member of the highly respected international musical group Shakti. Being one of the busiest people with an overpacked schedule, it's obvious that he has no time for any *riyaaz*. However, I have watched him engage in *jugalbandi* with maestros like Ustad Rashid Khan and it is truly amazing.

I've known him for almost 30 years now, yet he hasn't stopped surprising me. Artists are often associated with mood swings, careless attitudes and narcissism. But none of these 'qualities' have ever shown in him, not even from miles away. Throughout our association, I have never seen him flustered, irritated or self-praising. But perhaps, it's these qualities that make him a great friend, a perfect husband and a wonderful father. Although, I must also give equal credit to his wife, Sangeeta, and their sons, Siddharth and Shivam, both of whom are exceptional singers.

Without any exaggeration, the Mahadevans are the most closely-knit, loving and happy family I have seen in my life. Perhaps what keeps them even closer is that all of them are serious foodies.

Do I even have to tell you that I have thoroughly enjoyed working with Shankar and quite often with great results? In all these years, besides music and lyrics, we have shared millions of jokes and tons of vanilla ice cream! He is much younger than I am. I not only love him but also respect him because he is a musical genius.

Prelude

The big, round, crimson disc is hanging enchantingly over the rippling horizon of the Arabian Sea. The skyscrapers along the coastline are gradually coming alive in twinkles. The BMW swivels into the fleet of cars, moving like a streaming line of ants on the imposing tarmac of the Bandra–Worli sea link. The person sitting inside the car lifts his eyes from his iPad to gaze at the scarlet evening sky and starts humming a tune. This happens almost every time he crosses this stretch. Along the way, the happy and carefree faces of the lovers courting each other by the shore often inspire a new tune in him. Looking at this, he gets a sense of déjà vu. He instantly decides to include his age-old favourite song in tonight's song list, 'Abhi Na Jao Chor Kar, Yeh Dil Abhi Bhara Nahin'. Strains of the Yaman Raga start resonating inside him. He picks up his iPad once again to have a look at the lyrics of a song, yet unborn. Suddenly, the still words begin grooving to the tune forming in his mind.

The man closes his eyes and leans back on his seat as he tries to visualize the notes that seem to unravel inside his brain. The car staggers and halts in the perennially backed-up traffic of Mumbai. The concert would start in the next couple of hours. The man escapes the thoughts of the night's song list. Even the snarling traffic and the unending red signals could not break the rhythm forming in his mind. He is in the middle of composing a new tune that is slowly taking shape. He turns the sound recorder on and keeping the beats on his thigh, he voices out the tunes running inside his mind. By the time the car enters the rear gate of the auditorium, a new song has been born.

People in and around the auditorium are slowly growing in number. The crowd is huddling on the road. The traffic police are frantically manning the vehicles to clear them out of the bottleneck in front of the auditorium. The overwhelming presence of a youthful crowd brings along an air of vibrancy and mirthfulness. Sound check was in progress and the sound of a familiar guitar riff or drum roll would often spill out of the hall, making the cohorts of college goers go berserk. The hysterical and high-pitched screaming only gets louder as they enter the auditorium.

The crisscross laser rays instantly make the atmosphere intense. From the teenyboppers to the raucous youths flaunting their 'Jim Morrison' and 'Che Guevera' T-shirts; from the ladies looking soignée and chic to the middle-aged family men excitedly waiting for the concert to start—the ambience in the auditorium is pulsating with anticipation. The sprawling stage presents an exciting spectacle of three guitars placed in three corners, with the one at the front gleaming and reflecting the radiant shafts from the spotlights. The crowd is already imagining the riff of 'Haan Yehi Rasta Hai Tera' coming from its strings. The grand, white piano at the left of the stage looks sedate, just like the person about to play it. The drums and other percussion instruments are kept on a pedestal at the back of the stage, overlooking the arena.

A lady in a trendy outfit and stilettos appears from behind the wings with a cordless microphone. She shimmies on the stage as the kaleidoscopic light spots her. With an effete spontaneity, she tries to rev up the audience and employs a few hackneyed ways to charge up the already excited crowd. After all this, she finally makes the most important announcement. The musicians standing behind their instruments start playing them. The sound of drum rolls and loud guitars slowly climaxes towards a crescendo, heralding the arrival of the masters on the stage.

The man, relaxing in his BMW some time back, now gets into a completely different groove. Shankar Mahadevan steps into the arena, and greets his audience with open arms and a trademark broad grin. He then closes his eyes to focus on the first song of the evening. The keyboard player gives a chord. The gentle sound of a shaker comes from a man sitting in the partially-lit area of the stage. Soon, the ambience of the auditorium changes as the spiritual strains of 'Ganesh Vandana' oozes out of the maestro's voice. The excited audience is silenced into a meditative calmness. The man starts his chant with complete devotion to his gods,

Shree Vakratunda Mahakaya Suryakoti Samaprabha
Nirvighnam Kuru Me Deva Sarva-Kaaryeshu Sarvada...

The song, with 108 names of Lord Ganesha, is articulated with the deepest reverence. It feels like the maestro is establishing a divine connection before entertaining a crowd of about 3,000 people for the next two hours. As the song ends, he bows before the cheering crowd and says, 'Ladies and gentlemen, I started the show with a prayer as a sincere wish for the happiness and prosperity of all of you lovely people.'

Ehsaan picks up his guitar, Loy starts playing intro notes on the piano and Shankar braces up to enthral the crowd. The evening of euphoria is underway.

One

Jugnu jaise hain armaan...

Childhood in Chembur

Days in Chembur began with the chirp of sparrows and martins, the chug of early-morning local trains in and out of the station, the mumble of the morning walkers sauntering by the nearby park, vegetable sellers crying their wares and the chime of bells from the neighbourhood temple. Then there would be the incantatory note of sacred Sanskrit *shlokas*. Unlike the disconcerting hammer blows of the table clock, the shlokas acted like a gentle wake-up call. Be it during the dripping monsoon rain, the lazy-hazy winter or the sun-laced warm summer, the wake-up calls of the shlokas were unmissable and inevitable. Every morning, as early as 4.00 a.m., Shankar's father would start the day by cleaning the portraits of the gods—neatly aligned on one side of the kitchen wall, giving the house the feel of a divine temple—and chant shlokas. The stale *mogra* garlands and the flowers, offered to the gods the previous day, would be replaced by fresh ones every morning. The portraits included those of Lord Ganesha, Ayyappa, Krishna, Murugan, Rama and Venkateswara.

Shankar would be hypnotized by the sound of his father chanting shlokas every morning, and would listen intently. This sound was like an imperceptible preceptor that instilled in Shankar's psyche the vibrations of the transcendental chants. Strains of 'Bhaja Govindam' by M.S. Subbulakshmi or Lata Mangeshkar's Marathi *bhakti geet* would also be playing in the background at the serene hour. All of these sounds were absorbed into Shankar's subconscious. Whether he was asleep or half-awake, these chants would continue to play in his mind.

The happiest and most musical time of the year, especially for the young kids, would be when the entire neighbourhood would get decked up for Ganesh Chaturthi. There would be the droning sound of *aarti*; the energetic rhythm of people's claps; the sound of *dhol* and *taasha*; and the loudspeakers blaring Ganpati *bhajans*. All of this created an atmosphere of mirth and merriment, a sense of festivity. The food was another irresistible attraction. Maharashtrian neighbours would pamper the kids of the locality with lip-smacking *ukadiche modaks*, ghee-smeared *puranpolis* and mouth-watering *laddus*. A group of lezim dancers in colourful garbs would display spectacular callisthenics, while also jingling cymbals and playing *dholaks*. A wide array of cultural programmes would be held in the *pandals*. Following the temple traditions, during the Ayyappa puja, there would be regular nagaswaram performances where nagaswaram artists played extensive *raaga alapanas*, scintillating *pallavis* and rapid *swaras*. Tamil *vidwaans* would keep pace with that using their percussion. The auspicious sound of the programmes would create an ambience of revelry.

Chembur holds a special place in the heart of the South Indian community in Bombay (now Mumbai). Apart from making him rooted in his own culture, the cosmopolitan identity of the place got Shankar acquainted with a culturally syncretic neighbourhood. One could see boys carrying their violins or tablas to learn music, and middle-aged gentlemen—with their *vibhuti*-covered foreheads and crisply ironed white *veshtis*—would be engaged in deep conversations in Tamil about arrangements for the upcoming *kutcheris*. Girls decked up in half sarees would go for Bharatnatyam classes. Women wearing South cotton sarees with temple-border designs; with long braids adorned with jasmine flowers; and diamonds glittering from their nose pins and earrings, were a common sight. Shankar grew up soaking in the energy of these sights and sounds around him.

While Shankar's mother Seetha Narayan hailed from Coimbatore, his father R. Narayan hailed from the beautiful hill town of Coonoor. Soon after their marriage, they migrated from South India to Bombay. Shankar's friends from school would often visit the house and Seetha would feed them Tamil delicacies like idli, dosai, rasam and sambhar served on plantain leaves. Shankar also had Marathi friends in the neighbourhood, from whom he got a taste of *kande pohe* and *sabudana khichadi*.

Among the Tamil Brahmins, Palakkad Iyers had an identity of their own. In every household, atleast one kid would be taking lessons on Carnatic music. There would either be a violinist playing the Kalyani Raga, or someone learning the beats of a mridangam or kanjira.

Shankar's family was no exception. Mani, Shankar's brother (older to him by seven years), was the first one in the family to take formal lessons on Carnatic music from an eminent Carnatic musician, Shivaramakrishna Bhagwat (Bhagwat Sir). Shankar was very young at that time. When Mani was having his music lessons, Shankar would be busy playing around in the adjacent room. But even then, the notes that the old man played on the harmonium made an impact on Shankar's mind. Surprisingly enough, he could decipher whenever his elder brother faltered. On many occasions, Shankar would toddle inside the room when Mani struggled to find the right key. He would easily fill up those gaps. The teacher would ask Shankar to sit with his brother when he would teach Mani the inflexions of Carnatic ragas. One particular song called 'Na Danu Manisham', based on the Chittaranjani Raga, was one of Shankar's favourites and he would often find himself humming it. The teacher had a strange way of taking snuff, and it never failed to amuse Shankar. At the end of the class, the two brothers would often mimic the teacher's snuff-taking when they found some snuff on the floor of the house.

As a kid, Shankar was a bundle of endless energy who could not sit still for even a minute. Many Carnatic classical *sabhas* would be organized in Chembur at that time and his mother would take him along. In one such sabha, a three-year-old Shankar got so fascinated by the harmonium the artist was playing, that he cried and insisted on going and touching the instrument. Much to the embarrassment of his mother, the artist obliged and when Shankar fiddled with the black and white keys and heard the sound coming from it, he gave a triumphant smile. The whole sabha, including the artist, was amused seeing his innocent smile. The magic of music and musical instruments had already taken him over.

Once, the family had taken a trip to Coimbatore to visit Shankar's maternal uncle's home. As in almost every Tamil household, there was a harmonium kept in the corner of a room. Shankar was instantly drawn to it and to everyone's delight, he started playing the tune of the popular Hindi film song, 'Chal Chal Chal Mere Sathi'. Listeners in the room were quite taken aback by such a marvel, and they started requesting the kid to play tunes of other popular songs and bhajans as well. And the kid immediately decoded the sargam and effortlessly replicated the tunes on the harmonium.

Shankar's parents noticed his uncanny ability. Like his brother, they decided to let Shankar take formal lessons from Bhagwat Sir. However, quite surprisingly, Shankar wanted to learn something else. When they went to buy a new harmonium for him, another instrument appealed to him more than the simple harmonium. He was particularly attracted by the hollow and large part of that instrument, which resembled the head of a dragon in the young kid's imagination. But at that point, the instrument was too big for him to play. Even normally, the instrument was already played with three pillows under it, and Shankar had to add an additional pillow to reach up to its fretboard. This instrument was the veena. It was quite uncommon for a three-year-old to start taking his Carnatic music lessons on it.

He started learning the veena at the age of five and his first veena teacher was Rajam Venkataraman, daughter of the eminent musician Lalitha Venkatraman. Slowly he picked up other musical instruments as well, like the harmonium and flute. Everywhere he went, Shankar showed his proclivity for replicating tunes he had heard on the radio, or on the vinyls that his father would bring. Later, he was sent to take classes from Lalitha as well. He would attend classes at her residence at 11th Road Shabari Sarayu in Chembur, along with a few other students. Once he realized that he could master any tune given by his teacher, Shankar started playing truant. He unknowingly developed the confidence that given a chance, he could play anything and everything on the instrument. He believed that to do that, he did not need any rigorous riyaaz. His exceptional ability to play with tunes and push his own limits was not necessarily guided by rigorous riyaaz but was something instinctive and unbidden.

The Ultimate Teacher

Shankar belonged to a traditional, middle-class Tamil family. His father had a very simple background of working in Hindustan Petroleum, where he held the humble post of an executive. But within his limited means the man was very content. There was an inherent feeling of happiness that would exude out of his personality. Even though in a normal South Indian family education is given priority, Shankar had the liberty to pursue his passion for music. The happy-go-lucky personality of this man influenced both Mani and Shankar. The children also imbibed their father's easy-going approach to life. However, the person who held all of them together by making a very cohesive and close-knit home was Shankar's mother. The lady with her calm and loving, yet disciplined, constitution instilled a sense of order in the family. The children's education went hand-in-hand with the training in Carnatic classical music and the two domains thrived within their respective territories. In their household, the children got strength from the boundless affection of their parents.

Shankar would always accompany Mani when the latter took part in cultural shows and competitions held by the Tamil community in different parts of the city. The energy of playing in front of the crowds and the words of appreciation that Mani received from the audience made Shankar happy too. Soon after, Shankar himself started taking part in such competitions and got used to winning them. He would compete either in sub-junior or junior categories and would win almost every time. Soon, it was a foregone conclusion that no matter how tough the competition was, Shankar would invariably emerge victorious. Other participants of his age would start crying and whining the moment they found out that Shankar was a fellow participant. Shankar's father had to employ all his loving ways to placate those kids. He always tried to instil in Shankar his philosophy of excellence. He told Shankar, 'You should not only be the first in any competition, but the difference between the first and the second should be significant. There has to be a large gap to prove that you are excellent.' Lalitha would teach Shankar the range of traditional Carnatic ragas. She would ask him to not just play the ragas on his instruments but to sing those notes as well— sometimes in sargam, or sometimes just in swaras (expressed through simplified *taans*). Slowly, Shankar began to decode and analyse all binaries of music, and it became a game for him to decipher the musical notations.

Carnatic music competitions would be held in smaller gatherings like Nadanjali Sabha and Nada Brahma Sabha. These would sometimes be held in small garages with very few participants. The participants performed in front of a handful of people cheering them up. Acclaimed personalities from other parts of the city would often chair the judges' panel. Some of them were very kind and loving even with their criticism, and others would be so stern that the kids wouldn't dare to hold their gaze. However, the advice of the judges was valuable enough for the kids to attend these competitions and feel inspired. There used to be some competitions that were held in memory of great composers. These included the Thyagaraja Competition, Swathi Thirunal Competition, Dikshitar Competition, Subramania Bharathi Competition and the like. The competitors were meant to sing the tunes composed by these legendary composers. By attending those small yet significant competitions, Shankar developed his mastery in Carnatic classical music.

Shankar's father would be his constant companion in all such events. He was more conscious and anxious than Shankar before any performance. Whenever Shankar went anywhere to perform, his father carried flasks filled with hot water and hot milk. He would index all songs that Shankar performed in a green-coloured copy. Though he had faith that Shankar would not falter in remembering the lines, he made sure that the lyrics were handy in case Shankar needed them. In such small gatherings, the audience would mostly be sitting on the floor or on rough carpets. His father would be standing right at the back and observing the responses of the audience, in apprehension that his son might goof up the notes and lyrics.

∽

Mani kept taking home lessons from Bhagwat Sir, and Shankar went to learn veena at Lalitha Ma'am's home. This routine continued for a few years before old age restricted Bhagwat Sir's movement. Then Mani started taking lessons from the doyen of Carnatic classical music, T.R. Balamani. Shankar often accompanied his mother when she went to pick Mani up after the classes were over. That opened up a whole new world for Shankar. Balamani knew of Shankar's interest in Carnatic music. One day, she playfully decided to test his skills. She sang a few taans and asked Shankar to croon the same. To her delight, the little boy rendered it effortlessly. She was so impressed that she told his mother to send him for classes, once he was old enough to travel by himself to her residence in Matunga.

It was only a matter of time before Shankar was allowed to travel alone by bus. He got the company of two talented girls who were almost his age—Mala Iyengar and Bombay Jayashri—and the three friends used to travel by '8 Ltd BEST' bus to reach Balamani's residence. It was a small, 150 sq. ft, one-room-kitchen flat with the most modest means imaginable. Even then, the students would excitedly huddle in front of their teacher. Balamani was a worshipper of music and wanted to instil in all her students the clandestine musical energy that remained unrealized within them. It was beyond the children's cognitive ability to recognize the celestial energy then, but they could feel it all the same. They would listen to their teacher with absolute awe and veneration. For Shankar, the augustness of mornings at her place was quite unlike any other. He would always take the seat beside her fridge. She would sing one *kriti* based on Yaman or Todi Raga, and the students sitting around her would repeat it. Except Shankar, everyone would complete their tasks diligently. Shankar would always trust his innate ability to sing at a moment's notice. Others might have slogged for hours to learn a raga, but Shankar would internalize it while playfully chatting with Mani or with his friends. So, the trend of Shankar playing hooky and skipping the riyaaz continued in Balamani's classes as well. This incurred the anger of his teacher very often. As a punishment, she would ask him to replicate a complicated *sruti*. But Shankar remained unfazed and replicated it to perfection. The moment Shankar would start singing, her heart would melt and her anger would fade away. The strict teacher only reserved her taciturn gaze of appreciation for Shankar. Sometimes, she would give a slight smile of appreciation and pride in the direction of her husband or daughter. While nothing was said verbally, Shankar knew that the smile was meant for him. He remembered every single expression of appreciation as a token of his success.

Even years later, Shankar remembers with utmost fondness that even though he was reprimanded quite often for his naughtiness and irregularities in practising, he was also the most loved student. As he had confidence in his talent, he was hardly assiduous in doing riyaaz. Shankar knew music was part of his being and would never desert him. He felt that Balamani was opening up the universe of music for him. Balamani's presence in Shankar's life was an assurance of support and strength.

Even with all the laurels and accolades Shankar earned later in life, those lessons he had learnt from Balamani remained the most abiding source of influence for him. Respect and admiration flow out in every word when he speaks about his Guru. Shankar says:

> T.R. Balamani was and will remain the ultimate teacher for music for me. (sic) She taught me everything I am capable of today. She taught me that the knowledge of music is boundless. It is like a vast ocean where each time one takes a dip he comes up with invaluable, distinct beautiful gems. She taught me the little principles and formulas of music which were like magic potions and gave me a Pandora's Box which when opened one could find innumerable ways to use music. (sic) Her methodology was such that she would not teach me how to sing Kalyani Aravi or Mohanam ragas but talk about how to structure, develop and embellish an alapana whatever the raga is. I dedicate all the music in me to her.

The foundation that Shankar got from Balamani was so strong that it became a part of his system. It gave him the ability to be comfortable with any form of music.

಴

Shankar's excellence in Carnatic classical music was confined only to his home, religious gatherings and kutcheris. None of Shankar's friends in Our Lady of Perpetual Succour High School had any inkling of the musical ability that he possessed. He remained a detached and silent observer during the cultural festivals in his school. He could analyse and decode where the singers did well and where they went off-key. But he would just be reserved and reticent. It was only in Class V that Shankar's musical skill was brought to the notice of others. One of his schoolmates lived on the ground floor of his building. His name was John Marcelin. John was part of a *qawwali* group in the school. On the day of a musical programme at school, their music teacher, Victor Sir, fell ill. He was supposed to play the harmonium for their qawwali

performance of the song 'Hain Agar Dushman' from the film
Hum Kisise Kum Naheen. The interlude of the song had a long
harmonium solo which no one but Victor Sir could play. Owing
to his absence during the final rehearsal, they decided to scrap the
performance. At this point, John saw Shankar hanging around the
rehearsal room and, to everybody's surprise, he dragged Shankar
in front of others. Then, at the top of his voice, John very excitedly
declared that Shankar could play the harmonium. Shankar was
quite taken aback and embarrassed when everyone's eyes fell on
him. At first, he was feeling a bit shy. But once he was in front
of the harmonium and played the piece in his usual effortless
manner, it left all his friends and teachers agape in wonder. They
were amazed by the prowess of the 10-year-old boy who generally
remained aloof. That was the day Shankar was initiated to a bigger
circle of listeners.

Word spread everywhere in the school. He was called to play
harmonium in all musical functions like Teachers' Day, Parents'
Day and Annual Show Days. Some months later, the teachers
discovered that their harmonium player could also sing any song
at a moment's notice. So, while on one occasion he was asked
to sing 'Gurur Brahma, Gurur Vishnu', on another he would be
singing 'Yeh Dosti'. However his most excellent performances
were on Republic Day and Independence Day when he would
sing 'Chhodo Kal Ki Batein' or 'Jahan Daal Daal Par Sone Ki
Chidiya'.

Every year, once the dates of the annual function were
announced, Shankar would be out of his class and practise
playing the harmonium, while the other kids would sing or
play other instruments. On one occasion, when he was in Class
VIII, Shankar asked his friend Sudarshan to accompany him to
these rehearsals. They were to perform the qawwali 'Dekh Lo
Ishq ka Martaba', originally sung by Yesudas and Aziz Naza.
Shankar was to sing the lead part, with his friend in the chorus.
But Shankar went up to their most formidable teacher, Kailaja

Ma'am, and convinced her to allow Sudarshan to sing as one of the two leads. Sumeet Saigal, who later became a Bollywood actor, was also a part of that qawwali band.

While singing hits from old Hindi films brought Shankar into the limelight at school, participation in Carnatic music concerts in the neighbourhood won him accolades there as well. This made him all the more popular and confident in doing music of all genres.

Katta, Kishore and The Originals

Shankar was growing up with a bunch of like-minded boys in his school and neighbourhood. His neighbourhood had the aroma of curry leaves and mustard seeds crackling in coconut oil, mixed with the heady smell of freshly ground coffee wafting out of a few houses. Shankar would often sit by the window with his books open, but his mind would be pulsating to the tune of a particular Kishore Kumar song. He would sit by the window and often, a voice would call him out from below: 'Jaadya'. Evenings would glide by immersed in play and laughter. After sunset, they would sit over the *katta* near their playground. Someone would be cracking a rib-tickling joke and someone else would be sniffling over a petty squabble with their parents. These post-play chat sessions would make their days complete. There, they would often share the petty frets of life, seeking solace and support—all the while making memories together.

The boys especially looked forward to the day after the term-end exam results were declared. On those days, their happy hunting ground would be the beautiful church and the field adjacent to it. Some of them would top the list, while some others would flunk. Sudarshan would come with his sorrowful story of failing in Maths and the draconian ire of his father. Some friends would say some sympathetic words of comfort, and someone else would mimic Sudarshan's father, making others laugh as a result.

They would talk about another friend, Manoj, getting a severe dressing down when he was caught taking a puff from the cigarettes kept inside his father's kurta. The sweet and sour tales of adolescent crushes, the hilarious chain of events following misplaced love letters, the invariable rebuttal of the scared unwinnable girls or even a nudge of approval was part of their evening chats. They would have fun all the time. Their philosophy of life was to laugh about their problems, instead of sulking over them. These moments were part of their brief adolescence filled with laughter and limitless lunacy.

Shankar believed that Kishore Kumar sang songs for every occasion in one's life. Once in school, Shankar and his friend were asked to sing 'Bane Chahe Dushman Zamana Hamara'. Even then, Shankar fought to sing Kishore Kumar's part of the duet. Kishore Kumar was Shankar's shelter. In Shankar's own words: 'Kishore Kumar connected to the heart. He was above songs and rhythm. He was the one who drew me to music. If I am asked to rank Hindi film singers, I will give the first 10 places to Kishore Kumar and the rest will come later.'

∽

The camaraderie Shankar shared with his friends was reaffirming and reassuring for him. Their bond grew stronger over time and they decided to call their group 'The Originals'. This group included Sudarshan Rao, Umesh Pradhan, Rajesh Pradhan, Mohan Vijayan, Suresh Ramalingam, Murli Venkatraman, Manoj Sonalkar and of course, Shankar Mahadevan. Later in life, their paths diverged, and now each one of them is in a different part of the globe, separated by time and distance. But all of them remember with great pleasure and pride how they stood by each other through thick and thin.

Even after they became successful professionals in their respective fields, what still matters the most to them is their friendship. Money, fame, popularity and success—nothing could snub their identity as old friends. Shankar says:

The only thing that you make in life are memories. Rest everything is all temporary and memories are the only thing that is going to stay with you permanently. I believe in creating wonderful memories and those memories are going to remain with you. Nothing else matters to me. The beauty of this group was that they don't take you for the success you have, they don't take you for the money you have made, they don't take you because you are a famous personality and they want to attach themselves to you. They don't care a bit about that. Half of them still call me Jaadya. That's how it has always been and it is the same to this day.

Ram Shyam Gungan

Rajesh was Shankar's closest friend and also his partner-in-crime. They would talk about everything, except studies of course. Even when they would meet in their neighbourhood, they would only speak about games and music. Knowing Shankar's innate ability to sing spontaneously in any situation, Rajesh wanted Shankar to talk to his uncle. Rajesh's uncle was someone who was always preoccupied with music. Every time Shankar visited him, the sanctified ambience of the man's house would fascinate him. The bespectacled man with grey hair, dressed in a white *kurta-pyjama,* had a sublime poise. The songs that he would play on his harmonium would strike a chord with Shankar. Nowhere else had he heard such great depth and variety of music. The man would always greet the young kids with a smile. Rajesh would coax Shankar to hum a tune in front of his uncle. Listening to Shankar's singing, the man would always pat Shankar's back and say something encouraging like, '*Kabhi kabhi yaha par aya karo* (You can come to me at times).' The man loved the innocent, naughty energy of the boy and saw a spark in him.

Shankar didn't know then that this man—with whom he shared such an informal relationship—was the doyen of Marathi music, Srinivas Khale. It took Shankar some time to realize that a person of such great stature stayed in his neighbourhood. Srinivas Khale was one person everyone wanted to meet, and here he was trying to meet Shankar. One day, Shankar was called in by Khale Kaka (as he was popularly known). However, Shankar was hesitant as his mind was preoccupied with the marble game his friends would be playing at their regular haunt. Rajesh almost dragged his friend by force. Khale Kaka was looking for a veena player for a music piece in his new album, *Ram Shyam Gungan*.

'*Toh tum veena bhi bajate ho* (So, you play the veena as well)?' Khale Kaka asked Shankar, when Rajesh very excitedly and proudly revealed this facet of his friend. The 13-year-old kid just smiled.

'*Toh veena leke ao abhi. Bajake sunao kuch raaga taana* (Then bring your veena and play a tune or two).' Shankar couldn't let the man down. He rushed out to get his veena from his home and came back excitedly. He played the raga that he had learnt just a day back. Khale Kaka marvelled at the swiftness and precision with which Shankar played. Then he played a tune on his harmonium and asked Shankar to replicate the same on his veena. Shankar wasn't prepared for this and asked Khale Kaka to repeat the tune. He played it once more. This time Shankar was prompt, and instantly played the piece. Khale Kaka was amazed and expressed his glee in his reserved way, '*Bahot badhiya. Kal aa jao recording me. Yehi music kal tum wahan bajaoge. Theek hai* (Excellent. Come over tomorrow for the recording. You will play this very tune tomorrow, ok)?'

∽

That was the first time Shankar entered a recording studio. Rajesh accompanied him. The soundproof rooms, the glass cubicle for the singers, a bigger hall for the orchestra, the wires and microphones, the strange imposing silence in the room and the sound of musical instruments in the air seized Shankar's attention. Shankar thought that, perhaps, it was places like this where Kishore Kumar sang the songs that he loved so much. But soon he came to terms with reality, as Khale Kaka took him inside the recording room. Two other singers were sitting there and speaking very softly. Khale Kaka introduced Shankar to a lady dressed very simply in a white saree. Shankar could not believe his eyes; he felt like he was dreaming. She was none other than Lata Mangeshkar. With her was a gentleman, dressed in a white *dhoti-kurta* with a black jacket. Shankar later got to know that this man was Pt Bhimsen Joshi. As Shankar was very young, he was hardly aware of the magnanimity of the whole situation. He simply took their blessings and played the part Khale Kaka had taught him the other day.

In one of our interviews, Rajesh narrated what had happened that day and how it remained a red-lettered day for them. He said:

> We took a taxi and went to the studio. Shankar finished each recording in one single take. Everyone present there was stunned beyond imagination. Dubey ji, the owner of the studio was flabbergasted. We were kids at that time and were taken by surprise by the amount of remuneration received along with reimbursement of the taxi fare. This was his first recording and we got 600 rupees for that which was a fortune for us in those days. That is how his training and association with Khale Kaka grew. Because of this, he was influenced by Marathi music, especially bhaav geet.

Shankar was yet to realize the gravity of the events of that day, and he was too immature to figure out its impact on his life. For him, that day just came and went by like countless others. But from then onwards, Shankar started frequenting Khale Kaka's home a little more.

For a 13-year-old, learning music as an extra-curricular activity or playing a small musical piece was considered regular. The opportunity just came to him suddenly, and the hurried events did not allow him time to reflect on its significance. While he kept taking formal lessons from his other gurus, everything that Khale Kaka did became a learning experience for him. He could not understand how pleasantly the musical notes fell when Khale Kaka sang. Shankar would just sit and listen to him, observing his way of selecting the notes. After returning home, he would close his eyes and sit in front of his veena, remembering the melody that Khale Kaka had created. Later, he observed people visiting Khale Kaka's home. From their attitude he could tell that they were the heavyweights in the music industry. Khale Kaka would remain ever so gentle with all of them, irrespective of their stature. He was equally warm with Shankar and Rajesh as if they were as precious as those luminaries visiting his house. Owing to his regular visits to Khale Kaka's house, Shankar was introduced to another fascinating world. A new musical life was awaiting Shankar and Khale Kaka led him into it. Khale Kaka's way of composing music would always inspire Shankar, and he would often wonder why he couldn't do the same. Shankar recalled:

> I was Khale Kaka's live recorder. Khale Kaka composed tunes sitting in front of me. It was so beautiful to observe how a song would gradually take shape. How a life was being created. He would compose and then forget. Then some days after he would grope for the tune he had once composed. I would recollect and tell him the inflexions he made. This is how I saw how a song was born every day when I used to visit him. A composition was like his baby. That might have stayed with me even now. I am so fortunate to have met him.

The education that Shankar got by being around him was a gift. Khale Kaka had tremendous love for Shankar. Apart from his musical knowledge, Khale Kaka also taught him the value of humility. Shankar observed that Kaka's humbleness was on another level. He possessed almost a child-like mentality that was beyond one's imagination.

Shankar realized quite early in life that while singing Kishore Kumar numbers would earn him more popularity and love, to reach musical heights he needed to strengthen the rudiments. He needed to imbibe and assimilate the lessons learnt from great gurus like T.R. Balamani and Srinivas Khale.

Sangeeta

Once the school days were over, Shankar had to face the unavoidable separation from close friends. He was admitted in the South Indian Education Society (SIES) College, as most Tamil immigrants staying in Bombay would be back then. Some boys took admission with Shankar, and some others got dispersed in other institutions like the Khalsa College. Those who had taken science as their subject, got to meet at the famous Agarwal Classes at Dadar for advanced coaching for their engineering entrance exam. For Shankar, those were the most monotonous days filled with the dull theories of quantum physics and cryptic, bizarre equations of inorganic chemistry. Their patience would fail them after two hours of non-stop lectures. The other friends, who did not have coaching classes, waited for them at Umesh's house. As Umesh's mother was a school teacher, there was no one at the house during the day and they would while the day away chatting, listening to songs or simply doing nothing.

The Originals had a 'special whistle' to call each other when they wanted to meet and play. Rajesh and Umesh were first cousins and they were close to Shankar's family. As Rajesh was learning to play the tabla, there used to be hours of music practice at his place. One set of tabla and harmonium were kept at his place, and one at Shankar's place as well. They would have a great time singing ghazals, Hindi film songs or Marathi bhaav geet. Shankar had the uncanny ability to play any musical instrument he could get a hold of like guitar, bongo, tabla and flute. He could even create a musical rhythm by merely hitting a storage *dabba* with sticks. Often, during Rakesh's tabla class, Shankar used to come to Rajesh's house and quietly observe the teacher and his techniques. Rajesh recalled:

> In tabla, there is a very difficult rhythm to play that is *dhire dhire* or *dhirakita* which uses the power of the whole palm. This takes a lot of practice to get it done perfectly. (sic) One day Guruji taught me this particular rhythm and left saying that I should practice it. The moment Guruji left, Shankar excitedly sat in front of the tabla and had a go. And to my surprise Shankar could play it instantly, almost as good as Guruji.

Shankar could play the *kaayda*s taught by the teacher and would recreate it with a twist of his own. His grasp on the rudiments of music was amazingly fast, even in the early days of his life.

Every day, as Shankar walked through the gates of his college towards the large corridors of the building, his attention would instinctively move towards the buzz coming from the corner room. The rhythmic thumping of desks, the snapping of fingers and the offbeat claps would become louder as he inched towards the room. Shankar felt an instinctive pull to join the jamboree in the canteen. The sight of self-absorbed groups of students, swaying to their own tune, felt welcoming. There was an air of abandoned gaiety. In the canteen, time seemed to be frozen. The clinking of tea cups and bottles of colas filled the air. Attending classes gradually became more of an aberration, and college became a jubilant hunting ground to make new friends while participating in inter-college music competitions and various college programmes as well. The pigments in test tubes and glass beakers in the chemistry laboratory paled in comparison. The pungent smell of formalin in the biology laboratory started stinking in comparison to the aroma of *misal pav* and *vada sambar* emitting from the canteen. Lolling on the stairs in a delightful disorder felt far more enjoyable than the sombre classrooms. The memories of time spent 'studying' in SIES College would not even fill up the copy of a kindergarten kid, but the fun memories made there could be written about for a lifetime.

While crossing the threshold of school, when for the first time the boys went to pursue higher education, there was a breezy entry of a girl in Shankar's life who became the sole lady member in the close-knit group of eight friends. This girl was Sangeeta, and it was not long before the first vernal showers of love took to a heady romance and life took a beautiful turn for him.

∽

For Shankar, the days of adolescence were ever so fleeting. The excitement of staying together as a bunch of happy-go-lucky boys—experiencing the joys of liberty after the routine-bound life of school days—was so strong that trivial matters could never be a deterrent to their joys of life. In winter of that year, something exciting turned up. When these teenage boys gathered in the badminton court, a bunch of school-going girls (all in Class VIII or IX) would join them. Their friendship grew. Often, they would scatter on the ground and chit-chat casually. At other times, they walked the streets of Chembur, lined with beautiful pink blossoms of bougainvillea. Sometimes they would form two teams among themselves, and sit with an imaginary line between them and play *antakshari* and dumb charades.

In that group of around 14 boys and girls, there was a particular girl who used to stay diagonally opposite to Shankar's building. Shankar stayed on the first floor of that building, named Anand Bhavan. The rest were all standalone, small independent bungalows in the locality. She was in Class IX, while Shankar was in junior college (Class XI). Her family had come over from Gujarat two years prior. Her father was posted in the Gulf and her only brother was an engineering student in Baroda. She was the youngest of three sisters who stayed in Bombay with their mother. Her reticence and taciturn gaze was immensely pleasant for Shankar. While chatting, whenever his eyes fell on hers for a flitting moment, he felt an instinctive beckoning to steal another glance.

At that point, they could not meet every day. For a girl of 15, it wasn't easy to make hanging out with friends a regular affair. However, staying in the same neighbourhood had its advantages. She would run the household errands for her family. They also had the ritual of going and coming back from school at a fixed time every day. And then, there would be stray evenings of badminton, till a call from her elder sisters would drag her back to the study table. With these invaluable moments, that came intertwined with the everyday regular affairs, two hearts grew fonder. An unspoken assurance from both sides, nudged them to go with the flow of life while remaining unafraid of the uncertain future. With the quick passage of winter, an unpronounced pledge of togetherness was exchanged between the two.

The thought of the humblest upbringing of a middle-class family of four huddling in a 500 ft flat never bothered him. But the image of an elfin kept hovering around him in the mundane surroundings and sat like a plume on his palm when at the day's end he would retire to his own thoughts.

೧

It was the evening of Makar Sankranti, the festival of kite flying and distributing *teelgul* among friends and relatives. Maharashtrian ladies were decked in beautiful black sarees to get ready for *haldi kumkum*. Many young teenage girls would also be excited to take this opportunity to wear a saree. That evening, Shankar was with his friends in one of their regular haunts when Sangeeta came in with nimble steps. The girl, whom Shankar saw almost every day, was looking so beautifully different in a saree. The air of domesticity that enveloped her that evening brought out an added charm in her. She came to Shankar with a teelgul hidden in her palm. She fed Shankar some teelgul and mumbled, '*Teelgul ghya god god bola* (Take teelgul and talk sweetly).' When Shankar returned home, a cassette of Kishore Kumar's rare songs was being played on a tape recorder. While the lyrics could not cast any telling impression on the young boy's mind, the soulful tunes and the maestro's unparalleled singing imbibed the rapture of budding love and all the uncharted emotions that Shankar had felt for the first time. Even years later, when those songs would play on any radio station or at a tea shop, a smile would light up his face. He would reminisce the days when he was going through the pristine feelings of being in love.

On 13 January 1983, two days after that memorable evening, the boys and girls formed two groups as usual and started playing dumb charades. The titles of the films that Shankar and Sangeeta chose to whisper in each other's ears were *Tere Ghar Ke Samne, Dil Deke Dekho, Aa Gale Lag Ja* and *Mere Jeevan Saathi*. Subtle vows of love were exchanged throughout the game. The proposal and acceptance, the exuberance, the joy and the blushing made all the friends ecstatic. There was laughing, rejoicing, playful taunting and a rush of precious emotions and feelings.

The Originals grew in number that day from eight to nine. Sangeeta became the first lady in an all-boys group.

ↄ

That was the onset of a new voyage for Shankar. In this voyage, the main compatriots were not just Sangeeta but every member of The Originals. They took a silent vow to always be there for one another and stand as pillars for their dearest 'Jaadya'. Though the thoughts of future adversities didn't come to their tender minds, both Shankar and Sangeeta knew that the path they had chosen would one day lead to the altar. There was no complication in the intent of the two young hearts. The girl never thought whether the boy could give her a secure future, and the boy did not care if the girl was mature enough to protect a family. It was a pure and pristine beginning to a beautiful future. Both of them were committed to each other.

Obviously, it was not smooth sailing for two young people in love. It was not easy to meet frequently, as these decisions were largely determined by the conventions of that time and by the fear of one's family members. This was a typical middle-class neighbourhood, and it was the early 1980s when dating was unheard of. Shankar was happy-go-lucky as ever, but he too knew that people in his family would not welcome his hanging around with a girl at that age. So, it had to be a surreptitious affair. They had to find stolen moments of togetherness, be it at the grocery or vegetable shop. Shankar would be waiting at the crossroads just to get a glance of her when she was walking to school or tuitions. Sometimes, Shankar would even jump over the wall at the back of her school to meet her. The Originals came to action to make these flitting trysts as frequent as possible.

College Days and Midnight Mehfils

One day, as Shankar was sitting in his college canteen, his friends informed him that the Golden Voice Award Competition was going to be held in Shanmukhananda Hall and that he must take part in it. Shankar felt a rush of magic and excitement run through him. The song that instinctively came to his mind was the one he would always sing when taking his friends for a car or bike ride—'Musafir Hoon Yaaron, Na Ghar Hai Na Thikana'. Shankar would always marvel at how his idol Kishore Kumar had sung the lines that glorified the bohemianism that every traveller feels.

That afternoon, he rushed to Sangeeta to express his wish to participate. He wanted to see the look of approval gleaming in her eyes. Every time Shankar spoke about music, Sangeeta would sense something deeper in his words, his exuberance and the way he kept waving his arms to mark the flow of the melody he was singing.

In his childhood, winning the first prize in any music competition had been a cakewalk for Shankar, but he had always visualized himself singing Kishore Kumar songs in front of a huge crowd (maybe even a full auditorium). But he didn't know the route to realize this dream. He would only switch among learning Carnatic classical in T.R. Balamani's house; singing in kutcheris and sabhas; or recording a small veena piece in any song which he never cared to listen to after. The competition in Shanmukhananda Hall triggered in him the dream he had always chased. Practice started with his friends clapping for him, together in rhythm. But it was the stage rehearsal that took him to a different world altogether.

The backstage of Shanmukhananda Hall boasted of the presence of music legends, as this was the very auditorium where grand events like Filmfare awards or concerts by music stalwarts were held. But what boggled Shankar's mind was the huge structure of the auditorium. Layers of ascending seats, the vastness of the ceiling and the photographs of the great Carnatic classical musicians like M.S. Subbulakshmi adorning the walls made him feel a surge of emotions. This was the place where Kishore Kumar used to sing songs in sold-out concerts. For once, Shankar stood stupefied at the centre of the hall.

On the day of the rehearsal, he was transported to a different world when the earlier empty stage started filling up with musicians and musical instruments; wires and sound accessories; and the 'dith' and 'din' coming out of the instruments. Musicians screaming for sound check; the resonant bass from the tabla; a small piece of familiar tune from the rehearsing flautist; the sudden bursts of rhythm from the practising dholak player; the constant thumping of bass drums from the curly-haired drummer who was rolling his arms on cymbals and tapping the pedals simultaneously; the glistening lights on the bright red, imposing keyboard from where the opening bars of the iconic 'Yeh Mera Dil Pyar Ka Diwana' were coming; and the sheer energy emanating from the presence of so many musicians, simply fascinated the young boy. He saw some of the most talked about musicians assembling to accompany the singers participating in the competition. The man behind the shining keyboard was none other than Chitti Pillai—the pianist and accordion player who accompanied almost all legendary Hindi film music directors. The one who drew Shankar's attention the most was the charismatic Aadesh Shrivastava, who used to play for R.D. Burman and Rajesh Roshan. People whom he had never even imagined seeing or meeting in his wildest dreams were there around him, waiting for him to sing! These people were the *real* creators of the music that he heard on radio, TV and cassettes. Shankar was overwhelmed by the very presence of such stars. Even though music was a part of his life since childhood, he never imagined that such a day would come in his life. When narrating this moment, Shankar gave a funny comparison to his situation, 'It is like if you are working as a clerk in a bank, you cannot think of buying a Mercedes S class. The maximum you can think is that maybe some time in my life I might have a bike of my own.'

On D-Day, there was an even larger number of musicians. It was simply astonishing for Shankar that these musicians didn't even need many rehearsals to get things perfectly in sync with the singers. They just came, saw, played and delivered. With much appreciation from these accomplished artists and to the cheering from his friends, Shankar sang 'Musafir Hoon Yaaron' with trademark effortlessness. His friends' encore knew no bounds when his name was announced as the Golden Voice contest winner. That was the beginning for Shankar—the start of dreaming the seemingly impossible dream. It was here that he realized that come what may, his mind belonged only to this sound of music and not in the theories of physics or chemistry, or the numerics of mathematics and economics.

The day before the final exam, a long-faced Shankar was sitting beside his window. His father noticed the absence of the frequent whistles from down below the street, hearing which his son would leap out of his chair and rush outside to meet his friends. He came and stood closer to his sulking child and asked the reason for the unnatural blues in his demeanour. 'Tomorrow is our exam and I don't think I will do well,' Shankar replied sheepishly. The man smiled at his son and without any words, gave a light shrug. This silent reassurance and the smile from his Appa helped Shankar get back his lost confidence. This is the kind of support that every erring student seeks. His report card didn't boast of any flashy marks, but he crossed the threshold of junior college days and overcame all probable hiccups. Like all his friends, he also joined the beeline to collect forms for engineering institutes and got entry into another new world of academics. He was yet unaware of the powerful whirlwind approaching him—the wind that would change the course of his life forever.

☙

Around that time, Shankar was introduced to another world of music by Ranjini Balamani, T.R. Balamani's daughter. Once, during his class with T.R. Balamani, Shankar heard a voice singing an *alaap* in a very unique way. The song was very distinct from the regular ones he had heard. The way of articulating the lines was extremely unique. It was Ghulam Ali's ghazal that Ranjini was playing on a tiny cassette player in the adjacent room.

When he heard the strains of 'Chupke Chupke Raat Din' he was mesmerized—as if under a magical spell. It was part of Shankar's psyche that whenever he heard something unique that fascinated him, he would start learning that art form. Before he realized it, he got pulled towards this world of ghazals through the magnetic voice of Ghulam Ali. Ranjini was more than happy to play one ghazal after another for Shankar as he tried to fathom the depth of Ghulam Ali's singing. Gradually, he introduced Ghulam Ali's songs to all his friends and soon they also became a part of the 'Ghulam Ali Fan Club'. Ali helped Shankar discover a world of his own during his time of self-discovery and the turbulent passions of early youth.

Shankar was eager to sing everywhere, except when he was told to practise music at home. His mother would lose patience and often declare a ban on him going out unless he sang a *varnam* or *kriti*. The wily Shankar would pick the smallest kriti, finish it up fast and before even anyone would realize his beguiling ways, he would rush to meet his friends. In the meantime, kutcheris of Carnatic classical music would also keep happening where Shankar used to participate regularly. By then, Shankar had become a proud owner of a small synthesizer—the MT70, more popularly called by the generic name 'casio'. Soon this became Shankar's regular instrument for his performances in the cultural programmes organized by various *saarvajanik Ganeshotsav* groups.

During this time, Shankar was the most sought-after musician in all nearby neighbourhood events. This was also where all his diverse musical skills came to the fore. First, he would sing devotional songs or Marathi bhav geet; second, he would improvise with Carnatic classical music; and finally, he would finish his performance with super hit songs of Kishore Kumar. He was a complete package and so both the audience and the organizers were happy when he performed. Once, a disciple of Shri Shankaracharya had come to Bombay from Sringeri Math. During the disciple's travel within Bombay, Shankar was given the charge of accompanying him with his keyboard to play bhajans with the group.

However, the most coveted time for Shankar was when he would sing a Ghulam Ali ghazal, with Rajesh accompanying him on the tabla. These kinds of *baithaks* at Shankar's place would have all their friends in full attendance, along with Sangeeta and her friends as well. The Ghulam Ali mania was at its peak. Shankar was so deeply enamoured with these ghazals that in many inter-college ghazal competitions he would invariably be singing them to win the competition. In many cultural programmes, Rajesh would take over the role that Shankar's father played earlier by sitting on the stage with a green copy which had all the lyrics written down meticulously. If Shankar would falter during the performance, Rajesh would promptly open the page where the lyrics were written. These musical soirée evenings were held at Shankar's place where all his friends would join in. Quite often, the *mehfils* would continue well past midnight. Among the frequent guests were Durga Jasraj (daughter of Pt Jasraj) and a young talented singer by the name of Rattan Mohan Sharma, who later became a classical singer of great repute.

Once, Shankar sang in the presence of the maestro Pt Jasraj. The show was for a foundation initiated by Durga Jasraj. When the performance was over, Shankar very humbly said that he would like to pay a tribute to Pandit ji by singing one of his compositions. Pandit ji was very happy. After the show, he said that his daughter had brought Shankar to him many years ago requesting Pandit ji to teach him. Pandit ji had refused to teach Shankar because he could teach only those who had dedicated their lives to music and Shankar's priority at that time was engineering. However, that day, on the stage, he declared without any hesitation that it was his bad luck that he missed the opportunity to teach him. Pandit ji said that Shankar had grasped knowledge just by hearing his music, and that he had sung Pandit ji's composition with such a unique take that it had opened his eyes. Shankar was floored by such a huge compliment.

಄

There was an abundance of musical talents in SIES College, as it had a large number of South Indian students. A talented young man, two years senior to Shankar and whose mother was a Carnatic vocalist, was one of the key mridangam players. At that time, Kumar Krishnan, the secretary, asked that mridangam player to invite his mother to judge a singing competition. Shankar was one of the participants and as expected, he floored everybody, right from the judges to the audience. Seeing Shankar's performance and his friendly nature, the boy immediately felt the desire to talk to him. He introduced himself as Sridhar Parthasarathy. Soon, the conversation veered into their likes and dislikes and they were ecstatic to find out that both of them were huge Ghulam Ali fans. Within no time, their friendship grew stronger. They started meeting in many concerts happening in and around Chembur. One of the earliest major concerts Shankar remembers was in Goregaon (in Ram Mandir), where along with Sridhar and Jayashankar Balan, Shankar had also participated. After junior college, Sridhar pursued graduation in science while Shankar moved to engineering. But they kept in touch and their friendship only got stronger as time passed by.

Two

Choone hai taare ise
Chahiye...saare ise

The Boy Bands

Once, Sridhar came in the evening to a friendly *majlish* at Shankar's place and spoke of a music band of which he was a part. He told Shankar that it was a jazz fusion band called 'Divya', and that the band members had been rehearsing for a tour to Europe. At that time, the band was looking for a male vocalist, as they only had a female vocalist Sandhya (who was also the wife of the band's founder Dinshah Sanjana). When they were looking for a new vocalist, Sridhar suggested Shankar's name to Dinshah.

Shankar went and instantly fell in love with the whole atmosphere. It was a band with a few players. Dinshah was the keyboard player and the band leader. Though all the songs were written down, Shankar was intrigued by the improvisations that the musicians made during the rehearsals. With the improvised passages, keyboard runs or a solo mridangam passage, the songs got a new life and sounded so exciting. Shankar felt at ease with the bonhomie among the band members. He started frequenting the rehearsals and one day he couldn't resist and sang a short impromptu *alaap* along with a guitar riff played by a guy named Roy Venkatraman. Seeing this, the young man on the tabla started adding a slow rhythm and together they jammed excellently. The young man was Fazal Qureshi—the youngest brother of Ustad Zakir Hussain. This impromptu jam made Dinshah want to use Shankar's voice within this jazz fusion framework. He then asked Shankar to join the band for an upcoming Europe tour. Shankar leapt in joy and excitement and then, reality hit him. It was his first year of engineering and a three-month-long tour meant missing a whole semester. He was pretty sure that he would not get approval from home. However, Shankar's eyes filled with tears of joy when he heard his father say, 'Your engineering can wait for a few more months but a chance like this may not come again.' Not only this, Shankar's father assured him that he would get whatever financial help he needed for this tour.

With his father's unconditional support, he jumped onto the bandwagon of a bunch of highly energetic musicians with his veena by his side. There was Sridhar on the mridangam, Roy Venkatraman on the guitar, Fazal on the tabla, Bondo Fernandes as the drummer and percussionist, Shernol Mathias on the bass and Sandhya as the vocalist. They were rehearsing for the recording of their first album (*Madras Café*) which was to be done in Belgium. Shankar didn't feature in the original recording, but they made a demo cassette in order to participate in various jazz festivals. The cassette had to be sent to the organizers of the jazz fests. Their fate depended on these organizers. Everything worked out and the Europe trip turned out to be a stroke of luck for Shankar. Those three months in Europe became a turning point in his life and proved to be a stepping stone on his way to becoming a professional singer. Destiny played its part and things happened in such a way that it opened up many new avenues for him. This young computer engineering student was about to embark on a journey of self-discovery.

৩

Shankar was bubbling over with excitement when the plane crossed the Indian peninsula and flew west. For a middle-class person, the first ever experience of taking a flight (that too for an international trip) is a historic event. He was exhilarated about going abroad with a great bunch of musicians. The thought that the upcoming three months would be spent solely focussing on music, instead of attending the insipid lectures in college, was irresistible for Shankar. A sojourn in music is all the more attractive than the fear of uncertainties. He was elated when the flight touched down in Amsterdam.

Everything in the city appeared straight out of the pages of a fiction novel. The waterways, the lush green parks, the vivacious squares, the huge sprawling museums, lovely buildings in beautiful shades of pastel lined on both sides of the canals and the colourful leafy avenues cast a spell on him. And of course, there was music everywhere. There was an arena in central Amsterdam where a podium was set up for music performances. There were also music halls to host electronic dance music performances. The city was peppered with opera houses to host opera, ballet and pop concerts. The terraced cafés on the squares were leisurely places, where people would bask in the sun with beer and wine. The city wore a carnival robe. Shankar was overjoyed at the thought of performing there, but everything reminded him that he had left a piece of his heart in his city, and the three months seemed like an eternity. With no luxury of international calls available, Shankar filled his heart with countless memories and stories that he would take back for his sweetheart Sangeeta.

Contrary to the picturesque landscape, the boys were housed in a ramshackle building which was to be renovated later. Within a few days of their stay, the organizers and the lead band members just vanished. In a relatively small room, all these boys were left alone without a clue about anything. But they took it quite sportingly, as keeping their stomachs full and staying calm were their priority then. And above all, their music filled these days of uncertainty and fear with abundant joy.

Once the concerts began, each member got together again and there was no complaint. They hopped from one city to another in buses and felt like the rock bands from the West touring in their caravan. They had concerts in all major cities of Europe. The band Divya represented Indian jazz fusion in several jazz festivals. Bringing in improvised alaaps in Dinshah's Westernized compositions, Shankar caught the attention of the audience and critics as well. Dinshah thought of him as a powerhouse of talent. The way Shankar unified a variety of elements with his alaaps gave a new edge to the compositions. Of the many fellow bands taking part in those jazz fests, a Swedish band named 'Mynta' took an active interest in Shankar's singing and invited him to join them for the recording of their album. Along with him, Fazal was also asked to be a part of the team. That became Shankar's first collaborative effort with an international band. Mynta described themselves as 'Nordic ice and Indian spice'. Mynta graduated from being a jazz-rock and funk band to one of the most authentic world-music bands. They blended Swedish folk with Indian classical; Cuban music with African beats; North American Jazz with Middle Eastern music. Mynta released nine albums with Shankar singing many songs, and they also performed at all the prestigious music festivals worldwide.

∽

Before the trip, when they were recording the demo version of *Madras Café* in Bombay, there was another man who used to come and observe them with great pleasure. He was Taufiq Qureshi, Fazal's elder brother. Taufiq particularly loved the way Shankar improvised the tunes in a jazz framework. The two young boys connected right away and started to dream of working together in the future. Soon, Taufiq and Fazal became regulars at the mehfils in Shankar's house. Very often, the mehfils would continue till late at night, or would begin with the doorbell ringing at 2.00 a.m. Shankar's mother would dish out hot crisp dosas in a jiffy with his father making his special filter coffee. This comfortable atmosphere, along with the music, brought all of them closer day by day.

Sometimes people learn from adversities. This tour with Divya taught Shankar some lessons. By staying with the bandmates for so many months, he learnt the virtues of bonhomie in a musical band. He learnt how to be cautious while also not becoming deceptive in life. He learnt everything about band ethics. He learnt that music is just a natural offshoot of the vibes that are felt when there is an intimate connection between every single band member. Later on, he found this sense of belonging and affection in all of his collaborations.

After Divya returned home, they formed small bands and started performing at different levels. The group of musicians comprised Sridhar, Shankar, Fazal and Sriram Iyer (the violin player). It became a regular event for them to get together and perform at small family functions—be it a puja or a marriage anniversary. Coincidentally, Durga Jasraj and Rattan were regulars in the evening musical soirées at Shankar's place and it was only a matter of time before they started trying out jugalbandis between Rattan and Shankar. Gradually, this diverse group of musicians started exploring various genres and moved into fusion music. Jugalbandis with various combinations like Shankar and Fazal, or Fazal and Sridhar helped them improve their skills. That opened up a whole new world of innovative music for all of them. With their confidence growing by leaps and bounds, they needed a stage to perform and soon an opportunity came their way.

∽

Malhar was the prestigious inter-college festival organized by one of the oldest and finest colleges in Bombay—the St Xavier's College. This festival was held on a grand scale and included various cultural contests from performing arts to fine arts. It was around 1986–87 that Taufiq participated in the competition with his band of percussionist trio—Nitin, Shankar and Sridhar. While enlisting their names, they realized that they had not thought of the name of the band. Without the name, they would not be allowed to participate and each of them started racking their brains. They were almost in panic mode when Taufiq glanced up and was almost blinded by the sun rays falling on his eyes. He almost jumped with joy shouting, 'Surya! Surya! That's the name!' Though they didn't win the competition, Taufiq was excited about his new band Surya. He wanted to develop this percussion band into a more versatile one. He chose Piyush Kanojia for the keyboard and a very young teenager as a second keyboardist. This kid was none other than Salim Merchant.

The compositions of Surya were primarily free-flowing but within a structure. Each of the members would have a passage where they could improvise. It was primarily a college band which was slowly gaining popularity in various college and university fests. Sometimes the *konakkol* between the three master musicians—Shankar, Taufiq and Sridhar—would be a great draw. In some concerts, even Fazal would join. The infectious vitality of the band members was key to the band's joyous presence in the musical gigs. That was the time when each one of them was exploring their potential as composers and players. Shankar was also beginning to discover the composer in him. He was proficient in Hindustani classical, Carnatic classical, ghazals and bhajans. Apart from that, he was a kanjira and veena player as well. They could connect with the young audience. Shankar was realizing his potential as a singer as well. Surya became very popular and, in some shows, they had Ustad Sultan Khan and Ustad Zakir Hussain as guests.

This special bond among them is still there. Whenever Shankar meets Taufiq or Fazal, they end up laughing over silly jokes. With Fazal, the bond grew stronger when he started singing professionally. Shankar's bond with Taufiq is even more abiding, since they have participated in jazz and fusion concerts and even recorded various albums together. Even today, whenever they meet, they greet each other by names like 'Taufiq-e-Hastaba' and 'Shankar-e-Mustafa' and guffaw in childlike glee. Shankar said that the whole interest of doing fusion music started with Surya.

Days of Love

Alongside music, the clandestine affair of two star-crossed lovers kept going on with furtive glance exchanges and occasional trysts. Things went downhill when one of Shankar's love letters got intercepted by Sangeeta's family members. The fact that a school-going girl was moving around with a boy in junior college who had no idea of his future plans caused resentment in her family. There were lot of arguments and showdowns at her place. All of this resulted in Sangeeta getting grounded. The thought that they might not see each other ever made their young hearts cry.

The pain, anxiety and restlessness used to take a toll on Shankar and he used to talk animatedly for hours with The Originals about never wanting to leave her side even for a minute. If one of The Originals saw her sitting in her small verandah, they would run to Shankar. He would slowly walk past her house controlling every urge to look up lest someone else saw him. By doing this, he knew that Sangeeta would get a brief glimpse of him and feel a bit happy. There was a small food joint opposite her house, and from there he could see her window. Shankar and the group used to sit there for hours hoping to get a glimpse of her.

During those days, the ghazal by Ahmed Faraz would constantly come to his mind:

Ranjish hi sahi dil hi dukhane ke liye aa
Aa phir se mujhe chod ke jaane ke liye aa

Please come to me even if it is to cause pain or torture
Come to me to leave me again.

Sangeeta's family had been wanting to move to a bigger house in Vashi in New Bombay for quite some time. And now they wanted to hasten the shift on the pretext of keeping Sangeeta away from meeting her paramour. The packing of furniture and winding up of things started, and Shankar's heart started sinking. All the family members were busy with the loading of the goods. At that time, The Originals struck and whisked Sangeeta one block away where Shankar was waiting for her. He could not let her go away without a last meeting. While copious tears were shed, vows of reassurance were also exchanged while The Originals stood guard.

On the day that Sangeeta was shifting to Vashi, The Originals instinctively took a decision. They hired a cab and before the tempo with all of Sangeeta's family's belongings reached the new address, Shankar and the group were already waiting there. They positioned themselves like artilleries at war and during the process of unloading furniture, they furtively took Sangeeta once again for a brief yet cherished rendezvous with Shankar. He was waiting a little away at Sagar Vihar, a little rocky backwater area in Vashi. Rajesh stayed on guard to warn them in case of any danger.

The lovers were filled with mixed feelings of sadness and excitement because though they were to part, there were also promises of a new beginning. They discovered newer ways to dodge the guardians and kept meeting on the sly. Sangeeta's movements became less restricted. Shankar pounced on every opportunity and would cherish the brief meetings. These meetings would last only a few minutes, even though he would travel for more than an hour to reach there. When Sangeeta's tuition was about to end, a melodious whistle would come from the road and she would smile hiding behind her books. Who else but Shankar could whistle in such a perfect tune! These moments of young, unpretentious love were so precious.

∿

Whistling was their medium of communication on many different occasions. A very common feature in the friend groups of the typical Bombay middle-class neighbourhood was that any vehicle, especially a personal bike, became public property; it became a *saarvajanik* vehicle. When Shankar would be busy with his work in his first-floor flat, someone would whistle from the street. This was a sign that they wanted the keys to Shankar's bike. Without even looking out, Shankar would throw the keys from his window. Later, the keys would be promptly returned to the *dhobi* who was present on the ground floor of Shankar's building. Apart from Shankar, Rajesh could also whistle very well but his whistle was used as a sound of caution for the lovers. Rajesh would trail Shankar and Sangeeta whenever they met, and he would keep an eye out for any familiar face. If he happened to see someone, he would urgently whistle in a different pattern and the very next second the lovers would go their separate ways. The restrictions on Sangeeta loosened once she finished her school and joined Shankar's college for higher education.

∿

The Originals were not much into drinking, but they did smoke occasionally. Whenever they did this, Shankar would pay for the smokes out of his pocket money. Be it the college canteen or the roadside stalls, Shankar would be the first one to fish out money from his pocket. In the late 1980s, a vada pao would cost around 50 paisa. Each time they ate out, Shankar would end up spending around ₹7–8. As Umesh delightfully recalls,

> It was like *sabka saath sabka vikaas* in those days with Shankar. It was not that he would get a lot of pocket money but whatever he got he would share it with everyone. He is the same till date. Recently, on his marriage anniversary, Shankar and his family were going to Greece and he was

constantly convincing me to accompany them. He likes to take people along with him. For him, it is still, the more the merrier, as he always proclaims [himself] to be a 'people's person'.

After Sangeeta joined SIES, their days were full of joy, laughter, mischief and enjoyment. Sometimes they would hop into Gurukripa for chaat, samosas and lassi, or they would go to the Udupi Ramdev restaurant for onion uttapam and coffee. Many joyrides would be taken in the Maruti 800 that Shankar's father owned. The diminutive car became a magic chariot for the gang of 10 as they drove it through narrow alleys and broad highways. This was their time to laugh away the uncertainties of the future. The laughter of that bunch of carefree revellers had the power to surmount all the bumps that they faced along the way.

Occasionally, Shankar and Sangeeta would spend some moments of solitude together. Shankar remembers with great fondness the first time they entered a movie hall together. Theirs was a love with commitment—they were each other's one and only and they were filled with innocent, pure and pristine feelings of love. Their intimacy was more in the mind and even holding hands was a very beautiful feeling. It was while watching the movie *Gandhi* that the two lovers held hands for the first time.

After the film, both of them were walking hand in hand in a world of their own. Suddenly, they were jolted back to reality. A little ahead of them, Sangeeta spotted a gentleman who stayed in a building adjacent to hers. They feared that he must have seen them together. She started walking ahead towards the bus stop, with Shankar following her at a distance. They got into the same bus and Shankar got down a stop earlier to be on the safe side. Much to their relief, it was a false alarm and they were not discovered.

Though the freedom of college days allowed them to spend time alone, Shankar and Sangeeta loved hanging out more with their friends. Many times, when they decided to have a house party, Shankar would don the chef's cap. A complete foodie right from childhood, he would make his way to the kitchen and chat with Rajesh's mother showing keen interest in whatever she was cooking. At home, he had seen his father helping his mother in the kitchen and he would even whip up delicacies for his sons. While planning one such party, the adventurous Shankar declared that he would cook egg biryani for them. Being the 'chief chef', he would delegate all the sundry chores to his commies. Everyone would be grumbling while working, but the outcome would be so delicious that they would forget everything and would be left licking their fingers.

If there was one thing that Shankar lacked, it was a sense of direction while driving. While moving around on two-wheelers with his friends or during his occasional trips by car, he used to depend on his friends for directions. Umesh had an open Jeep in which they would drive around together. All of them were devotees of Lord Ganesha and they would often go to the famous Siddhivinayak Temple every Tuesday to attend the *aarti*. Shankar was the only person in the group to have a driving licence. Hence, he would be behind the wheels of that open Jeep. On one such trip to the Temple, his friends decided to pull his leg. They planned to not give him any directions while driving back home. He also didn't ask the directions and confidently relied on his instincts. He kept driving in the dark till he felt the ocean breeze. Everyone burst out laughing when he looked around and realized they had ended up reaching the western suburb of Bandra—almost in the opposite direction of Chembur. Such extended detours only added to their fun-filled days.

One of Shankar's friends, Sudarshan, said that even now Shankar is exactly how he was years before. Success never got to his head. And most importantly, his rapport with his friends never got an added appendage even as name and fame chased him. Sudarshan said:

Shankar remains so detached from his success. He loves to live life. He is still a great chef. He still loves to cook and feed us. He is so full of life. We never discuss work when our group meets. Even today to unwind and relax he listens to the ghazals. At our informal get-togethers, we still sing those ghazals and we are all in the same zone that we were years back. Both as a human being and a musician he is the best. Shankar's story is not only about music. It is about Sangeeta. She means the world to him. Their story is an inspiration, a living proof of how unconditional love and understanding are the foundations of a happy marriage and family. Shankar's life is a celebration of music, love and of course, food.

∽

As mentioned earlier, by her college days, Sangeeta's family had got pretty lenient with her, as they were sure that Shankar was not in the picture. Shankar would accompany Sangeeta to Vashi every day and would then take the bus back to Chembur. Once, while the two were chatting at the Vashi bus stop, a very close friend of Sangeeta's brother saw them together. The day which they always dreaded had arrived, and on being asked, Sangeeta tried very hard to deny the relationship. At that time things were different, as she was no longer a school-going kid. She was now in the first year of graduation, and he was in the third year of engineering. Dinesh acted maturely and insisted on meeting this boy who had by then already been in his sister's life for more than three years.

A meeting was fixed at the Cactus Restaurant in Vashi, where Shankar was summoned by Dinesh. He was accompanied by his wife Deepika. Shankar had spent many sleepless nights rehearsing this crucial meeting with his friends. He had reached before time and was standing near the restaurant's gate when he saw the couple walking towards him. He took a deep breath, while muttering prayers, and gave them a small nervous smile. Dinesh nodded awkwardly and they took a seat. This was followed by a deadly silence for about three minutes. Dinesh kept on smoking cigarettes while Shankar felt the pressure mounting on him. Finally, Deepika broke the ice and a formal conversation followed.

The inevitable question regarding future plans came up. As Shankar was pursuing computer engineering, he promptly answered that he would join a software company once he completed his studies. He earnestly told Dinesh that he was very serious about the relationship and wanted to eventually marry Sangeeta with the blessings of both their parents. He said that he would never do anything to hurt Sangeeta's parents and would come over and meet them before taking any step. Deepika instantly took a liking towards him owing to his honesty. After patiently hearing Shankar, Dinesh asked him, 'What if our parents don't agree to this match?' Shankar replied coolly and confidently, 'Then that would be too sad for your parents.'

The last statement had a deep impact on Deepika. She saw his honesty, sincerity and determination for the relationship and expressed her liking for him within their family. Sangeeta's father was to come over to Mumbai from his workplace Muscat and everyone at home was a bit worried about breaking the news of this relationship to him. It did cause a flutter when the family members spilled the beans to him, but finally he succumbed to their collective plea and agreed to meet Shankar.

The musical aspect of his personality was still hidden from them. The way it was introduced to their family makes for a highly amusing story. When Shankar performed at musical gatherings, or participated in inter-college competitions and closed-door small informal gatherings, he would invariably sing ghazals of his favourite, Ghulam Ali. He had once voice-recorded several ghazals. The recording was one of those scratchy ones with a lot of disturbance in it. He had lovingly gifted it to Sangeeta who used to play it repeatedly at home. When asked about the artist, she would confidently say that it was Ghulam Ali performing in one of his informal gatherings. Shankar's flawless singing never brought even an iota of doubt in her family's mind.

When their relationship was out in the open, Sangeeta revealed the truth about the cassette. Maharashtrians are also very musically inclined, so the prospect of their future son-in-law being such a good singer made them extremely happy and they overlooked Sangeeta's white lie. After that, all they wanted was to hear Shankar sing.

Though her family had approved, Dinesh was still sceptical and would not speak much to both Shankar and Sangeeta. At a family gathering with Shankar present, Deepika requested him to sing and the song that he chose happened to be Dinesh's favourite—'Apni Tasveer Ko Aankhon Se Lagata Kya Hai'. Dinesh was immensely touched by his singing. This is how slowly and steadily, through his music, Shankar made his way into Sangeeta's family. Owing to his music, the family that was fiercely protective of their younger daughter started opening up to him. It was music that swept away all the obstacles in their path.

The two families started coming closer, and it was finally decided that Shankar and Sangeeta would soon tie the knot in a South Indian marriage ceremony. People whose first love manifests into a lifelong relationship are truly blessed, and these two were on their way to a beautiful life together.

Jingle Bells

In 1987, Shankar had one more year to go till he became a software engineer. Those were the days of the software boom and it was only a matter of time before Shankar would get a lucrative job offer and have a secure future. As soon as he finished college, he landed a job in a software company called Leading Edge in Bandra. The carefree and happy-go-lucky Shankar started his professional corporate career with dreams of marrying his childhood sweetheart and leading a beautiful and simple life. Working with a bunch of promising professionals; attending client meets in spick and span conference rooms; working inside the slick office that highlighted the squeaky-clean corporate culture; and drawing a decent salary were all the things that the young men from middle-class families dreamt of in the 1990s. The most important advantage of being a computer engineer in the '90s was the lure of settling abroad. For Shankar, everything was going as expected. But then, destiny made a sudden change in the simple script of his life.

☙

As mentioned earlier, after coming back to India from his first international tour with Divya, Shankar became further occupied with other music bands like Surya. At that point, Surya used to travel for various concerts all over India. Salim Merchant, the then-teenage keyboardist for the band, spoke of his much-cherished association with Surya. He recalled:

> I was 17 or 18 when Taufiq bhai noticed me at a recording with Piyush Kanoria. My brother was learning from Abbaji

[the great Indian tabla exponent, Ustad Allah Rakha]. I started rehearsing with them in Abbaji's garage and that is where I met Shankar for the first time. We used to spend a lot of time rehearsing there and of course, we had shows in college fests and other places. My first show outside Mumbai was at the Madras Music Academy in Chennai. Those days we could not afford the luxury of a flight. So, me, Taufiq bhai, Shankar, the mridangam player Sriram and the flautist Rajeev Raja boarded the train to Chennai. There were different rhythms when the train was moving and the musicians were counting the rhythm in 5 beats [or] 4 beats and so on. It was quite crazy and I found it so amusing. I was like 'Give it a break man!!' Leave music alone in the journey at least! But what a great time it was!

Shankar's friendship with Fazal, Taufiq and Sridhar grew as they were always with each other in their free time rehearsing in the Shimla House garage. The residence of the Qureshi brothers was no less than a place of worship for musicians with the presence of two music maestros, Ustad Zakir Hussain and 'Abbaji' Ustad Allah Rakha. While Zakir was mostly travelling abroad for his shows, the assuring presence of Abbaji made everyone feel happy. Shankar fondly remembers him having a childlike innocence. Abbaji was a person who would be entirely immersed in music. The rest of the world never really mattered to this apostle of music. In between rehearsals, Ammaji would treat them with authentic mouth-watering Awadhi cuisine complete with *keema*, *karela gosht* and the soft and fluffy *khamiri rotis*. Very often Abbaji would smile and tell them very fondly, '*Bacchon, aaramse khao. Rajma bahut acche bane hain, zaroor khana* (Eat well, children. The Rajma has been made exceptionally well, please eat).' Such simplicity and humility in such a great artist left a deep impression on Shankar. Zakir's empty room would be the band's place for *adda*. Shankar had always been fascinated by Zakir's personality and charisma. For him, Zakir bhai was a huge hero—someone who was way beyond his reach. Entering his room, seeing the various awards and touching his tabla would make Shankar feel closer to his hero. On many occasions, the band members would spread newspapers on Zakir's bed, sit cross-legged and have dinner.

Making music with Surya made Shankar fall in love with fusion music. This young, enthusiastic gang of musicians was very open to new elements, sounds and improvisations. In various fusion concerts, Shankar would improvise raga and alaap, bring in elements of thumri and Carnatic classical music and keep experimenting with ensemble sound. He often brought his classical elements into the framework of funk and fusion.

One of the most crucial persons to give Shankar's musical journey a new direction was Ranjit Barot—an ace drummer and musician who also happened to be associated with legendary music directors and several fusion bands of international repute. Sometimes, Ranjit used to play music for Divya. Shankar and him got acquainted with each other, stuck together and played at small gigs here and there. At that time, Ronnie Screwvala had formed an association named Culture Club which had its base in Bombay and was slowly spreading its wings to second-tier cities like Pune. Sridhar and Ranjit performed in many of their events together.

The circle at Shimla House got extended, with Ranjit also joining them during rehearsals. Ranjit had forayed into the advertising industry by then. Through Ranjit, this musical gang got a chance to witness many such small gigs and concerts of these advertising bigwigs. Sometimes, they would get a chance to perform as well. On one such occasion, an impromptu Carnatic performance by Shankar and Sridhar made a lasting impression on Ranjit. He was just itching to use Shankar's alaap somewhere. Finally, he got an opportunity to do that in the form of a jingle which eventually brought about a revolution in the jingle industry. Lady Luck was all dressed up for Shankar, and the road to fame was almost open!

A Rollercoaster Ride to the Altar

PepsiCo, the cola company, was about to enter the Indian market, and as per the law, they were only allowed to use hybrid names for their products in India. The name 'Lehar Pepsi' was given to the cola. The ads of Lehar Pepsi, with the slogan 'choice of a new generation', caught the fancy of the public. In one of the earliest Pepsi ads, Remo's hushed-up vocal was followed by his flute piece and then the gradual crescendo with Ranjit's drumming climaxes in an electrifying *sawal jawab* of distorted guitar and sitar. The tune revs up with Remo's histrionics with electric guitar in a stadium, amid a loud encore that gets juxtaposed with Juhi Chawla pirouetting in a Kathak-style classical dance. It brought along a great fusion of Eastern and Western strains in tandem with Lehar Pepsi.

Ranjit took this ad forward and conceived a wonderful and equally scintillating sequel, where Shankar's soulful alaap and a brief and brisk *tarana* ('ni dha ma pa ni sa') got fused with Remo's vocals. The sweet, little Penny Vaz is seen playing the already familiar and popular note of the jingle on the piano when Remo joins in with his tongue-in-cheek remark, 'Hey Penny, what is all this magic about?' Together they chime in with the familiar slogan—'hold it, taste it, know that is right.' The tempo shifts gear and then from almost nowhere, Shankar's vocal stuns the listeners and carries them to a different groove. Finally, the thumping hookline that drove the nation crazy was: *'Yehi hai right choice baby, ahaa* (This is the right choice baby, ahaa).' This is how a new voice stormed in the jingle industry.

∽

Around 40 years back, an ad set the country on fire. Emboldened by India's Men's Cricket World Cup victory in 1983, the nation started aspiring for a repeat feat four years later when India hosted the tournament. Reliance came on board as the main sponsor and the Prudential Cup got rechristened as the Reliance World Cup. Vimal, the textile brand of Reliance, decided to rope in the Caribbean legend Sir Vivian Richards to endorse their brand. He was seen relaxing on a pool float, walking with a majestic gait while wearing a dapper suit, shaking his leg by the poolside and jigging with a reggae tune in the background with a voiceover—'Now Vivian found a new love.' With 'Only Vimal' and the 'Looks of a Winner' flashing on the TV screen, the advertisement took the country by storm. Soon, Reliance decided to promote its principal brand—the identity with which it remained one of the torchbearers of the country's textile industry—Vimal Sarees.

Reliance industries was becoming bigger day by day and the simple homely look of Vimal Sarees needed a makeover into a classy, rich look to target the upper class and the high society. The mantle of making this shift rested on the shoulders of the experienced Kailash Surendranath. Ranjit Barot was roped in as the music composer. The canvas had to be vast and impactful. The gardens of Bombay's Chota Kashmir (where the old ads were shot) were replaced by the rambling forts and beautiful temples of Rajasthan and Gujarat. The presence of top-of-the-class models like Mehr Jesia and Deepti Bhatnagar gave a sophisticated look to the brand.

Ranjit Barot brought in Shankar's vocals to deliver an ethnic touch, a feeling of Indianness and a raw, earthy appeal to the ads. A brief alaap, a tarana, folk-style singing and an added echo delay created a larger-than-life imagery. This was exactly what was needed to project the grandeur and style that the brand wanted to represent. To appear in sync with the age-old practices of Rajasthan, Shankar had floated his alaap in Rajasthani folk style. The visuals of a man wearing those colourful turbans while running the bows of the sarangi, along with Shankar's voice, gelled brilliantly with the ad film. Ads came in different lengths and the husky, sonorous and Westernized ditty of 'Only Vimal' was blended with Shankar's alaaps.

In those days, Indian TV serials were also on a roll. As the TV sets were few, these serials became daily community events or happy gatherings in relatives' or neighbours' homes. The popular and familiar tunes of the serial's title track would act as the clarion call for mothers to quickly put off the stove, and children would take a break from their homework and huddle in front of the TV sets. The title track of these serials played a crucial role in popularizing them.

Durga Jasraj, one of the regular attendees in the musical soirées at Shankar's place, as mentioned earlier, had once introduced him to the veteran Marathi music composer Ashok Patki (who had also composed the title tracks of various popular tele serials). When he heard Shankar singing Khale Kaka's compositions so effortlessly, he was overwhelmed with joy. He gave Shankar a chance to sing an alaap in the title track of an upcoming tele-serial, *Commander*. The serial went on to become one of the most popular ones of the time, and the catchy tune of the title song was an added attraction.

One show he composed for was *Ek Se Badhkar Ek,* whose title song was sung by Mahalakshmi Iyer. The show was sponsored by BPL under the direction of noted filmmaker Mukul Anand. On Mukul's insistence, Shankar acted for the first time, enacting the role of a funny character named Leeladhar Cyclone who is always seen talking to his neighbour in a musical language.[1] Shankar used to compose a lot of songs for other artists. Zee had the most popular reality show *Sa Re Ga Ma Pa* where they would do

---

[1]Information courtesy: Kalpana Swamy and the magazine *Nostalgiaana*

an album for their winning contestant. Shankar would compose for some of them.

Gradually, with various opportunities like these, Shankar became a familiar name in the industry and his skill in churning out improvised alaaps became an effective means of showcasing various products and shows.

∽

Soon, the advertising fraternity—the small, closed clan of Western musicians comprising the likes of Louiz Banks, Leslie Lewis and a few more—discovered a rare talent. They found an artist who was innately Indian in his take and whose voice stood out with its strikingly disparate texture amid the chic, elegant and modernized Western sounds. In addition to this unique voice, the chief draw was the way he would make the director's vision his own and give out something unique with unparalleled spontaneity. As a South Indian brought up in Bombay, Shankar could easily dub in all four South Indian languages. So, in a single day, four different jingles would be done and that too, most of the time, in one single take. He was the producer's delight, for their time and money were not wasted on innumerable takes. He was also the jingle composer's favourite, as he would sing in most of the languages. The only people somewhat unhappy when Shankar recorded were the studio owners, as a day's work would often get over in some hours.

Soon, Shankar became the most sought-after voice in the cash-rich advertising industry. Hopping from one studio to another in his Bajaj Chetak was immensely fun for him. The ambience of the studio attracted Shankar like nothing else. His desire to think, discuss and make music all day was gradually turning into a reality. And on top of it, he was discovering the value of having his own money. His job as a computer engineer got him a handsome salary of ₹2,600 per month, whereas one single jingle would fetch him ₹2,000. Managing his professional job and the jingle world was not easy. He says he was very lucky to have supportive colleagues. In his absence, they used to hold the fort at the office. On a single day, he would be at a studio in Andheri in the morning and would have to rush to another part of the city to work. He would try to resist the recordings often but there would be repeated requests to do a small dubbing in a studio. Bombay traffic was eponymously notorious and many times he could not come back to the office in time. His immediate boss would also never chide him, as when in office Shankar would give his best.

One fine day, his boss called Shankar to his chamber. Shankar was sure that he was going to be reprimanded for his irregularity. He was pleasantly surprised when he was told that they wanted to give him an opportunity to work for Oracle in the US. Here was an opportunity of a lifetime, served to him on a silver platter. However, he was caught in a dilemma. Though there was a dollar-paying, structured and secure job of a computer professional waiting for him, his heart yearned to brave the sweltering and sultry summer or the relentless rain of the Bombay monsoon while flying on his bike from one studio to another.

Ranjit was the one who asked Shankar to give up his job, as he felt that Shankar belonged in the studio with his music. Shankar had the belief of The Originals—the people who knew him better than he knew himself. They were the ones who, even with a generous sprinkling of expletives, always gave him an honest opinion and guided him through this restlessness of mind. Their lovable Jaadya had music flowing through his veins, and they knew that he would never be happy without music.

Finally, Sangeeta's words cleared the cloud of confusion in Shankar's mind. She lovingly held his hand, looked into his eyes, smiled confidently and said, 'There may be hundreds of computer engineers but there will only be one Shankar Mahadevan.' His eyes shone with newfound confidence and determination. She understood very well that his future lay not in the swanky apartments of Los Angeles but in the lilting reverbs of recording studios. His boss had a heart-to-heart chat with him, and told him to give himself a year and follow his dreams. He assured him that the doors of his office were always open for him if ever he wanted to come back.

∽

Shankar has no qualms about acknowledging how much he owes to his friends for staying beside him, helping him recognize his potential and supporting him in every walk of life. But the person whom he missed the most at that critical juncture was his father. But he knew in his heart that had his father been there he would have smiled and said, 'Go ahead!'

Shankar's father had passed away when he was in his teens. Shankar had to grow up overnight. His father had been his silent voice of reason. Having to live without his father's support was one of the hardest realizations that Shankar ever had. The man did not have any physical ailments. He never needed to visit a doctor all his life, so much so that they could not think of a physician's name to even get a death certificate. A sudden cardiac arrest and everything was over. It took time for Shankar to come to terms with his father not being there. His presence was felt in every corner of the house—be it the kitchen where he would whip up delicacies for them, or the living room where he would pamper the kids with toffees and candies. His chanting of the mantras during the early morning puja still echoed in Shankar's ears. He was about to retire and was looking forward to a peaceful life with his wife and family. This picture of togetherness between his parents remained the most abiding memory in Shankar's mind. This value of closeness with one's life partner was inculcated in Shankar by his parents, and he recreated the same when he stepped into the most august phase of his life with Sangeeta.

When the two star-crossed lovers stood at the altar, Sangeeta had dreams of a wonderful future and Shankar had a belief that come what may, they could win over any adversity of life together. On 30 April 1992, in a simple and modest South Indian ceremony, two childhood sweethearts became Mr and Mrs Mahadevan. A new phase arrived in their life and a new horizon beckoned them.

During the grand celebration of their twenty-fifth wedding anniversary, they acknowledged the vital importance of all The Originals by calling them on stage. It was an emotional moment when the couple said, 'We are here together today because you were there for us then.' All the friends and family members had a hearty laugh when Rajesh recreated the whistle with which he used to warn the lovebirds during the courtship period. Shankar said, 'These friends, my family and these priceless moments make my life complete.'

A Star Is Born

The city of dreams, Bombay, runs at a pulsating pace with the gigantic towers piercing the sky and the bedazzled Queen's Necklace adorning the bay. However, the heart of the city is the culture and tradtitions kept alive by its middle-class population. They are the ones who give life to this city; they are the ones who hope and dream of a better tomorrow. Life is a daily struggle for them, yet they have this ability to find happiness in small moments.

The reasons of joy for a middle-class Mumbaikar comes from the simple pleasures of catching a lucky fourth seat in the crowded local or a glimpse of one's beloved through the crowd; people at the footboard of a speeding bus helping a running boy get hold of the steps; or a smiling rickshaw wala refusing to accept the extra change.

The newly married young couple, Shankar and Sangeeta, who hailed from two middle-class families had simple dreams about their future. Living in a small house with many family members hardly gave them any privacy at home, and they did not pine for that either. They could adapt to all situations and find ways to be happy in a typical Bombay *jugaad* style. In the early days of their marriage, the bedroom door was broken and Shankar didn't have the money to fix it for almost six months. Life was simple, wants were not many and happiness was in abundance.

Neither of them had any fear or uncertainty about Shankar's earnings. Sometimes, frequent calls for dubbing or recording would fetch him a decent amount at the end of the day. And sometimes, he would go days without any work. This is the norm of any freelancing job, and especially for a rookie it was more lows than highs. But whatever the earnings were at the end of the month, they knew that there wouldn't ever be any scarcity. However unpredictable the future appeared, for them the most comforting thing was being there for each other. Life had been a roller-coaster ride ever since their marriage. Every call for a recording filled them with excitement and Sangeeta would eagerly wait for Shankar to come home, so that she could listen to his stories about meeting new people and having new experiences. Kishore Kumar's song with the lyrics, '*Thoda hai thode ke zarurat hai, Zindagi phir bhi yahan khoobsurat hai* (We have less and the need is less too. Yet, life is still so beautiful),' was the theme song of their lives. For the newly married couple, every small joyous occasion was momentous. The day Shankar got a cheque with five figures, they celebrated by treating themselves at a Chinese restaurant. Returning home by the double-decker bus, they held on to each other firmly. They were approaching the cusp of success and prosperity and building their world.

They went on their honeymoon a few months after their marriage. Their first trip together was to Mauritius and it was like a dream. They had to do quite a bit of financial planning and saving for the trip due to limited resources. Shankar had got a cheque for an amount of ₹10,000 as remuneration from an ad agency, and they decided to spend their savings and go to Mauritius. He was relieved that when they returned, this cheque could easily take care of the expenses of the next two to three months. However, after their return, when he went to deposit the cheque, it bounced. As always, The Originals were there to lessen his worries with a good dose of laughter. All of them had a good laugh, maybe with an extra chuckle that day.

Be it in their early struggling days, or now when Shankar owns a huge mansion with cars donning the gates and a vast farmhouse on the outskirts—life at his home was always about the little things that the two of them did together. Though he can easily afford to live in the plush swanky suburbs of Bandra or Juhu, where most of the stars have their homes, he still chooses to live in Vashi in Navi Mumbai.

∽

The whole family, including The Originals, were extremely happy and excited when they heard about Sangeeta's pregnancy. Shankar was over the moon when he got the news that he was going to be a father. On 16 April 1993, Siddharth was born. The Originals along with the family were at the hospital to celebrate.

For an average, middle-class man, there are certain events that remain etched in memory. Buying a four-wheeler for the first time for his family is one such memory. They bought their first car, a Maruti 800, within a year of Siddharth's birth. Shankar remembers that landmark event of his life with huge contentment. He says:

> We went to the showroom in Navi Mumbai. We took Siddhu with us and he was in all white—white dress, white cap and white socks, looking so beautiful. We were happy with our two-wheeler but with Siddharth, like every parent who dreams of giving that extra to their child, we thought of booking a car. We had booked a red one as children are attracted to bright colours. I can never forget that feeling when I sat behind the wheels of my own car and drove back home with Sangeeta and Siddhu beside me. Today we have so many cars and we are still equally happy as we were on that day. The feelings haven't changed a bit. And this happened only because of Sangeeta. She is the one who has kept all of us grounded.

From Tara Devi to Ehsaan Noorani...

Ranjit used to call Shankar whenever he would record any kind of music. Shankar would regularly go to his house to record jingles or to plan for some fusion gigs. Every day he saw an old lady, who appeared to be more than 85. She was Tara Devi, the elder sister of Ranjit's mother, the famous Kathak dancer Sitara Devi. Due to an eye problem, Tara Devi used to wear dark glasses and hardly went out of the house. Except for a customary namaste, Shankar hardly interacted with her, as he would always get busy with work.

One day, Ranjit had gone out somewhere. Shankar was sitting alone in the music room and was just dabbling with the computer. The door opened and this old lady walked in. She was 4 ft 5 inches with *mehndi*-dyed hair, and fully wrinkled skin. Shankar did not realize that she had walked in, as he was facing the other side. She came and tapped him from behind. He looked back, smiled and greeted her with a namaste. She asked him in her frail, thin voice, '*Gaana sikhoge* (Will you learn music)?' Shankar instantly agreed and she told him to get the harmonium.

The moment she sang her first note, Shankar's jaw dropped in awe. He had never in his life heard anything like this and he was quite sure he would never hear it in the future either. The clarity, the pitch and the throw in her voice were unbelievable, especially for a person of her age. She stopped for a moment and told Shankar, 'You have that special quality and I would love to teach you.' Shankar was overwhelmed and sat beside her like an awestruck kid. She taught him the song 'Ab Radhe Rani

De Daaro Bansi Mori'—a traditional bhajan on Lord Krishna. From that day, whenever Shankar used to go there, she would teach him one thumri or sometimes she used to sing an *azaan*. Shankar, in all his life, had never heard anybody sing an azaan like her. Sitting beside her, listening to her songs and learning the nuances were incredible experiences for him.

Soon, he started getting busy and became the most popular jingle singer. He used to do 10–12 jingles every day. In that period, Tara Devi used to ask him to come over. Unfortunately, due to such a busy schedule, he just did not get the time to go there often. She would tell him sometimes in a sad reprimanding tone, 'When I die, I will take whatever I have with me. You won't get anything.'

Many times, it so happens that one does not realize the importance of certain persons or words at that particular time. That was the time when Shankar was earning around ₹2,000 an hour for his jingles. He had never experienced earning so much money a day. Most importantly, he was living the dream life that he had always thought of. Some years back, when the Marathi music director Anil Mohile had called him to sing a Marathi song, he had been acquainted with Vinay Mandke—the man who sang the iconic jingle of VIP Suitcase, Hamara Bajaj and many other ad films. Vinay walked into the Radio Vani Studio and everybody just stood up and greeted him. Shankar was watching all this and asked his co-singer about this man. He came to know that this was a man who would start his day at 10 in the morning, record about 8 to 10 jingles in almost 10 studios and take back a whopping amount by the end of the day. On that day, Shankar was blown away. Subconsciously, he had started dreaming of a day when he would have that kind of life, and now he was living it.

Due to his busy work life, Shankar kept procrastinating meeting her, until one day he got the news that she had passed away. Shankar was shaken from within and that's when he realized the importance of her words. He realized that she had gone forever.

She had an invaluable treasure trove of knowledge and she had taken it with her. At that young age, one does not realize the importance of these things, but he feels the pain and regret to this day. He says that he was fortunate to get the opportunity to arrange her final rites.

For him, the one bhajan, 'Ab Radhe Rani', taught by Tara Devi was equal to a thousand bhajans. Later, Shankar recorded the bhajan, and on his US trip with Zakir Hussain's Cross Currents band he sang the same song with Dave Holland (the English jazz double-bassist), Chris Potter (the American jazz saxophonist) and Louiz Banks in a unique blend of Western harmony and traditional Indian bhajan.

∽

Ranjit's contribution in giving a direction to Shankar's career was immense. Ranjit's house was almost like a second home for him. One day, during one of their music and chill sessions, Shankar met a guitarist who was a regular in the jingle industry. Having had taken lessons under the expertise of noted guitarist Bismarck Rodrigues from his teens, he had grown into a remarkable guitarist. Steeped in the influences of legends like Robben Ford, Larry Carlton, Roger Waters, Andy Summers, Michael Landau, B.B. King and many others, he had left India to study music in Los Angeles. When he returned to his homeland, he groped his way and found a vast world of music lying ahead of him in the jingle industry. He met people like Louiz Banks, Ranjit, Vaidyanathan, Shiv Mathur, Zubin Ballaporia and others. Soon, he too became an independent music composer of jingles by his own rights. This low-profile, gentle, ever smiling and extremely talented guitarist was Ehsaan Noorani.

...and Louiz Banks to Loy Mendonsa

Indian advertising was undergoing a transition in those days. Presentation in the advertisements was all very Western and the look was airbrushed. The advertising industry relied more on fashion models and it still had the impact of the colonial and occidental culture in it. Even the ads that had Hindi as the medium of expression upheld a society that included way more English-speaking gentries. The mantle was gradually handed down to the next generation of ad filmmakers who were more Indian in their approach. They sourced materials from everyday India—people at the country's grassroots level and the large section of Indian middle class whose language of communication was mostly Hindi. It was during this time, that two of the most illustrious names of this industry—Piyush and Prasoon Panday—stormed into the advertising scene. They spearheaded the industry with their rebelliously innovative ideas and the industry got a new language that was quintessentially Indian.

Around that time, Cadbury came up with an ad that blew the nation away with its freshness and innocence. Piyush Pandey conceptualized an advertisement driving home the point that chocolate was not only the favourite of the kids but was also a source of childlike pleasure in the adult mind. In the now iconic ad, the spontaneity of Shimona Rashi (the girl in the stadium who broke into an impromptu jig) as her lover Arvin Tucker (the batsman on the pitch) scored the winning run fascinated people of all ages. The unbridled enthusiasm of the lady and the young boy blushing at the juvenile antics of his beloved exude warmth and love. Mahesh Mathai gave shape to Piyush's imagination and the film rode on the waves of Louiz Banks' musical score. Gary Lawyer sang the English version of the song and the Hindi version was made immortal by Shankar. An instant bonhomie was struck between Shankar and Louiz. Shankar's voice added a lot of depth to the ad. Shankar recalls:

> When I heard the English song sung by Gary Lawyer, I thought if I sang it exactly as it was sung in English, the essence of our language and culture would somehow be lost. With much hesitation, I asked Louiz if he didn't mind if I could just Indianize it a bit. A man of few words that he is, he very calmly told me to go ahead and do whatever I felt was right. He loved my singing and had total faith in me. The jingle became a raging hit and people took notice of my voice.

Shankar was a huge admirer of Louiz Banks and it was a big fanboy moment for him when they first met. After the Cadbury ad, within two days, he was called to the Digital Domain Studio to record another ad. As usual, he took just 10 minutes to record the jingle. Loiuz smiled and came close to him. When Shankar heard what he said next, he could not believe his ears. In his trademark gentle and soft voice he said, 'I'm looking for a singer to join my band. Would you like to join us?'

Shankar was so overwhelmed that he didn't think twice and immediately agreed to the proposal. He would never think of losing such a golden opportunity. It was a defining moment when Shankar became a part of the band SILK which truly catapulted him to another league and he became the voice of India in the Indo jazz fusion world.

∽

The people from the ad film industry were much more open to new ideas and suggestions. When Shankar used to collaborate with these talented ad filmmakers, he used to give a few inputs that would interest them. These tiny yet significant changes gave a different feel and freshness to the originally conceived jingle.

The jingle composers were majorly into Western music and had a parallel life where they would do what they loved the most, performing at live gigs in restaurants and clubs. One such place was 'Just Desserts'—a quaint little place for coffee, conversations and desserts. It was slowly becoming the hub of live music artists like Ranjit, Karl Peters, Ehsaan and many others who used to perform there. Shankar used to frequent this place, as he loved the vibe and music created there. Once, when Ranjit was performing, a new face accompanied him on the keyboard and he was creating magic through his tunes. Shankar had never seen him before in this circle, and he got to know that this artist had just relocated to the city from Delhi where he used to work as a music teacher. His playing left Shankar spellbound. The tall, fair musician, sporting a tiny ponytail, had a quiet gentle air around him. After the concert, they met and hung out for some time. Shankar realized that apart from being a wonderful musician, he was a warm and lovely person. That was the day when Shankar was introduced to Loy Mendonsa.

Three

Tere liye nayi hai zameen naya aasmaan...

Jazzing up with SILK

Shankar kept on absorbing musical knowledge from his mentors, peers and even from the people he worked with. Starting from the indigenous South Indian Carnatic classical form to the array of musical forms of Hindustani classical music; and from the popular Bollywood fares to the more modernistic sound of non-film Indi-pop variants, Shankar's ears were attuned to the large mosaic of music. However, the brand of music that fascinated him to his deepest core was the music that defied the constraints of any country, region or mores of tradition. With its uninhibited expanse and limitless scope of traversing beyond any barriers was the Indo jazz fusion music. Jazz and its more modern inflexions were not for everyone. It never aimed to woo the masses and neither did it enjoy the patronage of all because of its intellectual complexities and niche appeal. But the snare of its freedom, to go beyond the written norms of conventional music, tantalized young Shankar. Rubbing shoulders with the likes of Ranjit and Louiz in the advertising industry exposed Shankar to a new doorway of music—vast and immensely captivating in approach. Like many of his more haloed predecessors, he was quite instinctively drawn to the melange of fusion sounds that belong to a starkly different league altogether.

When Louiz invited Shankar to be a part of SILK, it was like the wave of a magic wand that beckoned him to move into a realm beyond his cognitive power. Shankar had no inkling that the proposal for singing would come from someone as great as Louiz, that too after he sang just two jingles for him. He took time to come to terms with this most pleasant surprise. SILK belonged to a glorious tradition that had been started years back, when the music of India was characterized as a melting pot of diverse cultures.

Musicians in India could not stay out of the immense influence of Shakti. So, when Louiz Banks and Braz Gonsalvez conceived the formation of the first Indo jazz fusion band Sangam, it took immediate influence from Shakti, the Mahavishnu Orchestra and Weather Report—all bands of international repute. Unlike Shakti, Sangam was an all-Indian band where Western jazz harmonies were blended with the Carnatic singing of Rama Mani.

In the 1990s, SILK started exactly where Sangam had left off. Louiz was again at the helm of it. Shankar carried the baton of singing Carnatic vocals from Rama Mani and also blended light Hindustani classical music. Along with Shankar, there were also Sridhar and Karl. Louis named the band 'SILK' with the first letter of each member's name—'S' stood for Siva, Shankar and Sridhar; 'I' for India; 'L' for Louiz and 'K' for Karl. The band's first show was staged on the banks of the Ganga at Banaras (now Varanasi). The magic of Shankar and Siva enthralled the audience. They went ecstatic when Siva fused his raw unusual rhythms with Shankar's vocal motifs.

SILK gave repeated performances at various college festivals. To a generation that thrived on rock, pop and funk, SILK was a welcome variation. There was zing and yet it was deeply rooted to the traditions. Shankar was infallible in his sense of timing. His vast knowledge of Indian raga and jazz harmonic progression drew awe among the listeners, and also among the other band members. The vocals carried forward the notes in a myriad of different layers. The musicians trusted the mood of a particular evening and the music was created on the stage. It was spontaneous and instinctive. Shankar summed up the essence of the band, saying:

It is as if there are five painters and just one canvas. Each stroke is perceived differently by the others who respond to it and a magical painting was created. (sic) We would just take cues from each other. We wanted our audience to appreciate classical music and know their roots. While we know they cannot sit through a three-hour Carnatic concert we thought a fusion of jazz and classical would have their attention. SILK comprised emancipated free-thinking individuals who tried to think differently, feel different and sound different. Performances with this band have always been of high standard and high calibre and there have been so many on-the-edge moments not only for the audience but also for us, the band members. We were unaware of how we perform, and how the music comes across. There have been moments of instant composition where with just a look at one another, we have picked up notes interpreted and just played them. This is the reason why every time we played; it was different.

SILK was much unlike most other fusion outfits with vocalists. In a fusion band, generally, a vocalist brings others in his zone. The sound of the band weaves around him. But with Shankar, it often happened just the other way around. Shankar's malleability was such that he would glide in within the existing format. Sheldon, who often played bass when Karl was unavailable during certain gigs, pointed out:

Shankar would be bringing his own zone into our zone which was more jazz, funk or fusion. At the same time, he was not manipulating us to play what he could do. He was the first guy I saw who could sit and learn any kind of unison or instrumental part written by Uncle Louiz which is not written for Carnatic music. It's written in a jazz format, like writing an instrumental line. Uncle would sometimes branch out from the raga-based stuff into these very harmonic jazz changes which have inflexions which are not studied by Indian singers. Shankar would just pick them up like that in a jiffy. He would be just singing these lines and replicating them in sargam flawlessly and I was like, 'Man!! That stuff, that's like a different school of thought!'

The most striking characteristic that Shankar brought to the band was the improvisations over jazz harmony. Obviously, there was a precedence of Rama Mani doing the same in Sangam, but Shankar might have gone further in improvising different chord changes. Louiz, the man at the helm of SILK, spoke on how he wrote the compositions keeping Shankar in mind:

> Shankar was the first singer and the only singer in SILK and when SILK performs it is always Shankar. No one can take his place. I give him the melody, decide on the raga then he improvises on the raga. I arranged it so that the improvisation part is open. It has to be open so that he can sing and develop his solos, take it to a height and then he would give us a cue and then we come in. We don't know where he is going to give us a cue to do our thing, what is in his mind, the mood he is in. That's the great thing about jazz. Creativity happens all the time.

No wonder, despite many individual commitments, whenever there is a SILK show, the members still try to get together and recreate the magic that began decades back. Shankar attributes the success of this group largely to Louiz and the way he allowed Shankar to apply his own styles in the band. Notwithstanding Divya or Mynta, SILK was the first significant musical band where Shankar's unparalleled tour de force of classical music was exposed not only in India but to a wider audience abroad. SILK shows, home and abroad, gave Shankar the confidence to go beyond the barriers.

Recently, in 2021, the band had travelled to London. Sheldon has shared his experience of the same, saying:

The music is very complex in this band. Shankar as a singer also needs to carry a lot of weight as this is not as simple as Bollywood because he himself doesn't know what is coming. Singers are like the pilot and the plane is like a supersonic jet because all the guys are at full pace. So, to fly a plane that powerful, is difficult, because you don't know which way it is moving. But when it is going smoothly it means that the singer is flying it well. That is very difficult to put in words, as we just know he has got your back. You can do anything behind, he is picking it up. Whatever storms or turbulence we are creating, he is handling the turbulence. That is why he is a great singer. This experience was amazing.

Camaraderie with Qureshi Brothers and the Pandeys

At one point in his life, Shankar was undergoing a phase when many things were happening simultaneously. Along with recording jingles, he was performing at musical gigs with different outfits like SILK, Surya and several independent fusion bands. With Mynta and Surya, he had occasional foreign trips as well.

Once, he had gone to Dubai. The band was put up in a lavish hotel, and Shankar was sharing a room with Taufiq. Staying in a luxury accommodation meant nothing short of exploring an altogether different world of fantasy for the young boys. The hotel had a glass capsule lift, which was not a common sight in Indian hotels in those days. It amused them so much that they kept on going up and down like kids on a joyride.

Once, Surya got an opportunity to go to Ahmedabad and perform in Vishala, the dance school founded by Mallika Sarabhai. Shankar and Taufiq decided to go shopping in Ahmedabad—famous for its *bandhani* sarees and ended up going to the prestigious Bandhej shop. As Shankar was newly married at that time, he went on a shopping spree for Sangeeta without realizing that he didn't have enough cash in hand. Credit cards were also a rarity in those days. Thankfully, Taufiq used to own one and came to Shankar's rescue. They had developed this wonderful friendship and had become very close. Together they had many memorable moments, but one thing in Shankar's life was made possible only because of Taufiq and Fazal.

For many years he had frequented Shimla House, but meeting his idol Ustad Zakir Hussain had remained elusive for long. Zakir was to perform in the Malhar festival at St Xavier's College that year. Shankar was very excited and had taken Sangeeta along to experience the live performance of the legend. Shankar was simply blown away by the maestro's skill and mastery of his craft. During the break, Taufiq and Fazal took Shankar backstage and introduced him to Zakir, almost showing off their friend proudly as a very good singer. Shankar says that the moment when Zakir blessed him and gave him the coveted autograph is etched in his memory forever. He was over the moon, grinning like a child. Throughout the journey home, he was constantly raving over how great an artist and how cool a person Zakir was.

At that time, Zakir was doing the music for a film named *In Custody*, produced by the prestigious Merchant Ivory Productions. For one of his compositions, which was an old classic ghazal, he wanted to try out a new voice. Time and again he had heard his brothers praising Shankar, his voice and his incredible range of singing. After meeting Shankar at the Malhar festival, Zakir expressed his desire to hear him sing. Shankar had been to their house many times before, but when he was going there to sing for Zakir, it felt so special. The fact that Zakir wanted to hear him sing seemed unbelievable. He was a bundle of nerves but was very excited at the same time. He walked into the huge hall and found Abbaji and all his three sons waiting for him. He was a bit anxious but the moment he looked at Abbaji, the stalwart who smiled so lovingly, he forgot all his fears. He chose to sing a ghazal by his all-time favourite, Ghulam Ali. He rendered it flawlessly. Fazal and Taufiq glanced at Zakir with the 'we told you so' look all over their face. Abbaji lovingly blessed Shankar. Zakir decided that Shankar would be the voice for his composition. That opened up the most significant gateway of Shankar's life. That is how Shankar stepped into mainstream film music.

The recording was scheduled at Sangam Studio and on that

very day, Shankar's voice just cracked. He had no clue what to do. Before the recording, Zakir calmly asked someone to get some sliced raw onions from a neighbouring restaurant. He comforted Shankar by sharing an experience with him. He said whenever Pt Bhimsen Joshi's voice used to have any problem, he would eat raw onions. To Shankar's relief, by evening his voice was back and he was ready to go. In the first-ever recording with so many musicians, including the legendary sarangi player Sultan Khan, Shankar was able to impress Zakir at the very first take. Not many people had attempted to sing the ghazal 'Naseeb Azmaane Ke Din Aa Gaye Hain', written by the renowned poet Faiz Ahmad Faiz. Ghazal was a genre always close to Shankar's heart. Quite interestingly, the lyrics of this beautiful ghazal resonated with what was going on in Shankar's life: '*Naseeb Azmaane Din Aa Rahe hain/Kareeb unke Ane ke Din aa Rahe Hai* (The days are coming to try your luck/ The days of his arrival are coming closer).'

∽

Around 1994–95, Walt Disney came up with a project of dubbing their animation film *Aladdin* in several Indian languages, with Lalit Modi being the Indian franchisee. He approached the Pandey brothers (Piyush and Prasoon) to write the dialogues and songs for the Hindi version. They were huge admirers of Disney films, as they believed that nothing rejuvenates the child in us like these films do. Ranjit was in charge of the songs and music. Though they had Shankar in mind for the song 'Sapnon Ka Jahan'—the Hindi version of 'A Whole New World'—it was Sonu Nigam who got the song and did a splendid job. Shankar sang the song, 'Arabian Nights'.

The Pandey brothers were an immensely talented and respected duo in the advertising field. Shankar sang for them in innumerable ad films. They touched the sentiments and emotions of people irrespective of their differences, and were purely Indian to the core. In the Asian Paints ad film, they visualized an ideal home of conjugal bliss. Shankar brought out the feeling of togetherness with his gentle and expressive singing of '*Har ghar chupchap se yah kahta hai, ki andar iske kaun rahata hai* (Every house silently says who lives inside it)'. The voice had that element that brought out the dreams associated with every new home.

'*Har Khushi Mein Rang Laye* (Bring colour to every happiness)' was the popular slogan of Asian Paints, in a series of ads that upheld the Indian joint-family system. The 2-minute ad film captures the story of a traditional Indian wedding with all its opulence and elaborate paraphernalia—from *sangeet* to *bidai*. Shankar effectively brought to the forefront the deep sentiments associated with the most important occasion of anybody's life in any Indian wedding. The ad has a sequel too. It speaks of another happy occasion, the birth of a child and the prosperity it brings to Indian households. Shankar's singing has an affection and tenderness befitting the occasion shown in the ad.

That was the time when Shankar was particularly close with the younger of the Pandey brothers, Prasoon Pandey. In a collaborative career, spanning more than three decades, Prasoon and Shankar jointly took part in so many projects. Prasoon underlined this quintessential childlike simplicity and freshness in Shankar. They could laugh at the silliest of things and it happened many times that Shankar would even fall off the chair laughing. Sometimes, a simple, silly thing would act as a trigger, and they would be rolling with laughter. The best part was that amid all this laughter, they would also be doing some amazing work together. As reported by Prasoon:

> Apart from work we would do some totally weird things together like I may write a parody on a thumri which may be silly and nonsensical and send it to him. Shankar would laugh hysterically but then sing the same very seriously with all the required alaaps and send it back to me. This is not work but still, Shankar is interested in it. He loves life, fun

and what is happening around him. That child in him is fresh, curious, wants to have fun and that is what gives him the ability to experiment.

Prasoon found similarities between Kishore Kumar and Shankar, as both of them were curious about life and felt the urge to do the regular things unconventionally. Prasoon added, 'As we grow up, we lose our bravado, we start having thoughts saying what if it doesn't sound right, but a child is free from all such thoughts. Shankar has retained that and he is not scared.'

Prasoon shared an incident from one of the many music sittings they had together. He was doing one commercial for the Kelvinator fridge. The concept was of a music teacher teaching a *besura* student to sing. The Guru ji sings one note and immediately closes his ears when the student starts singing off-tune. In the background, there is a Kelvinator fridge which gives out chilly air when opened. Owing to the cold air from the fridge, the besura student starts shivering and manages to hit the right notes. Prasoon said that Shankar was to sing the complete jingle but getting Shankar to sing besura was impossible. The shiver part he sang impeccably with all the *murkis*. But singing the besura part was just not possible for him. So finally, they got someone else to sing that part.

Sridhar recalls another such incident that points out the flashes of talent that Shankar showed. He said:

Aditya Birla group wanted to do an anthem kind of song to be played in the office premises. They wanted to do a shloka which was a long one. Shankar went into that recording and you have these language overseers who make sure that the words are as they should be. It was not just the music but also the words. Shankar made a few markings on the paper like where the alphabet is stretched or it is kind of shortened. The overseer had come from Bharatiya Vidya Bhavan for Sanskrit and he was a really tough person to satisfy actually. But Shankar goes in. The overseer said that if there was a glitch at any point they would stop then only. Shankar sings the whole set in one shot without any stop. That was Shankar. It was amazing to have found all these qualities in one person.

Shankar's habit of dabbling in jingles stayed with him for a long time. With all the different avenues his talent flowered in, he kept coming back to sing jingles or anthems. However, at this time a more glitzy and glamorous showbiz was beckoning to him. The young kid who had once heard the names of the famous music directors and thought that they were mythical characters of a fictional world started sounding real. People whom he had seen and heard only from a distance in many inter-college music competitions and the names he saw on the TV screen and in the title credits of the films he watched, were now calling to work with them. Names like Anu Malik, Jatin–Lalit, Nadeem–Shravan and Anand–Milind, who once held the young boy's fancy, slowly seemed so real and close. If Zakir Hussain was the man who introduced Shankar to this whole new world, the man who took him a step forward was the prodigy from the South, A.R. Rahman.

Lying Low and Singing Small

Mani Ratnam's *Bombay*, originally made in Tamil, centred around one of the most defining and significant chapters of modern Indian history—the events surrounding the demolition of Babri Masjid and the subsequent unrest that gripped the nation. The film's soundtrack acted as a testimony to the prodigious talent of the Chennai-born, and also left the audience gaping in wonder using the chilling background scores. Against the visuals of the newspaper headlines on the Babri Masjid demolition and the symbolic barbed wire, a deeply evocative human voice added to the chill of the melange of some shocking visuals. Shankar sang the high-pitched alaap that gave everyone goosebumps when juxtaposed with the ominous cawing of crows. Rahman still remembers the impact Shankar's alaaps had created in the cinema halls.

When Shaad Ali got to know that Shankar had done the background vocals for *Bombay*, he was thrilled. When Shaad saw the movie for the third time in Kanpur, he took a cassette player and recorded the full background score mainly because of Shankar's alaaps.

Shankar caught Rahman's fancy and was immediately called to sing for the film *Humse Hai Muqabla*, which was originally a Tamil film, *Kaadhalan*. The song 'Urvashi Urvashi' became a rage, topping every music chart and featuring every week in Doordarshan's weekly film music shows *Superhit Muqabla* and *Chitrahaar*.

The unheard style of music, the eye-popping choreography

and gravity-defying dance moves of Prabhu Deva were the top draw. Shankar's voice is quite prominent here, as he sings two lines of each *antara* of this song. Being a Tamilian, it was a sort of a homecoming when he sang 'Vennilave' for a big-budget Rajiv Menon film *Minsara Kanavu* in 1997. The movie was dubbed in Hindi by the name *Sapnay*. Even though he did not sing the sad version of 'Chanda Re' (the Hindi counterpart of 'Vennilave'), he got the opportunity to sing in the foot-tapping 'Ek Bagiya Mein' which was an instant hit. The industry got a whiff of a new voice slowly making its presence felt. His voice caught the attention of the music moguls of Bollywood.

Shankar's journey into mainstream Hindi film songs was running parallel to his dabbling in other genres of music. Bollywood film music became the melting point of all the diverse forms of music he experimented with. So, from the repertoire of Indo jazz fusion songs to one-minute melody of jingles; and from folk-rock language of modern-day variant to his deeply ingrained classical music, Shankar employed his entire range of versatility when he stepped into this new arena.

౧

At the beginning of his career in Hindi film music, his identity was mostly confined to the singing of alaaps, sargams or one-liners. Like a budding artist singing in a neighbourhood soirée, he would stick his neck out among a host of popular artists of the time. As his focus was on the parallel domains of music, Hindi film songs were just like some practice or consignment matches to earn some fast bucks. The music directors of the time would seek his cameo presence in their songs to decorate the melody, or to add some lyric-less improvised singing to enrich the tapestry of the compositions. But those significant cameo sections in the songs made him an invariable choice for almost all the music directors. They knew that only his incredible range of singing could do justice to their vision.

Anu Malik used Shankar's voice for a 10-second vocal adlib prelude for a very popular Udit Narayan number 'Aisa Zakhm Diya Hai' for the Indian version of the Hollywood classic *Kramer vs Kramer*—Mansoor Khan's *Akele Hum Akele Tum*. That was the time when Shankar was increasing his proficiency as a programmer as well. In 1995, Ranjit Barot was composing music for the film *Oh Darling Yeh Hai India*, where besides singing all the songs, Shankar also assisted Ranjit as the programmer.

In one of many conversations, Sridhar pointed out an incident to me where Shankar's brilliance as a programmer came out quite instinctively:

> Ranjit Barot was very fast at programming and on one such occasion with Shankar they did a song with an Arabic feel. Ranjit said that the melody though good, wasn't sounding to be coming from the Middle East. Shankar immediately proposed to change the piano melody and then select[ed] the kind of tuning on the keys. Ranjit selected the Arabic tune and everything fell in line because the way they tuned their keys was slightly different from the rest. This led to a sound change. When Shankar heard the track, he analysed all the instruments used and discerned why they were sounding like that. He could break down each sound in no time. In later days, good programmers could also do that but Shankar was able to do that much before all of them came in. Just by listening he could say everything.

In 1996, Shankar's voice featured in several Hindi film soundtracks. Under Anand–Milind, he sang in *Daanveer* and *Muqadar*; and Anu Malik used his voice in *Daraar*, *Ghatak: Lethal* and *Auzaar*. In all these films, Shankar has a tertiary presence besides the more formidable names like Kumar Sanu, Abhijeet or Udit Narayan. While others were given all the songs, the kitschy leftovers were meant for him to sing. Additionally, the songs had the most derisive, inane and asinine lyrics like: '*Kya hai chemistry pyar ki/Dil ke iss tube mein/Pyar ka oxigen dalo/Kya hai zaroorat pyar ki* (What is the chemistry of love/ In this tube of my heart/ Pour oxygen of love/ What is the need of love)'.

This was the time when the choreography with crass and sexually titillating expressions and atrocious lyrics had become a torment for the audience. The trend of using Shankar's voice to sing high-pitched sargams continued for the next few years. Dilip Sen–Samir Sen composed a lilting melody in 'Ja Ja Udd Ja Re Panchhi' in *Itihaas*. The song sounds extremely sonorous in a well-choreographed scene. But Shankar only sang the background alaap at the beginning of the song. Nadeem–Shravan used the same technique of bringing in an additional emotional quotient to the song by making Shankar sing with Jaspinder Narula in 'Meri Zindagi Ek Pyaas' for *Judaai* and multiple songs in *Pardes*. Among such melee of songs, where Shankar's presence was just blink-and-miss, he got to sing in the film *Auzaar*. Anu Malik sampled the great sufi number 'Allah Hoo' by Nusrat Fateh Ali Khan and made an electronica-based version. Shankar got a complete song for himself without being a supporting singer to any other lead.

A year later, when Anu Malik composed for the blockbuster hit *Border*, he used Shankar's voice as supporting vocals of Kulbhushan Kharbanda's inspiring recitation, 'Hindustan Hindustan'. This was a rip-off from Bill Conti's *Rocky* theme 'Gonna Fly Now'. 'Hindustan Hindustan' didn't work that much in comparison to other songs of the film, but it only presaged the fact that Shankar would be the invariable choice when any music director needed songs having some patriotic fervour. Music composers of the time only reaffirmed the faith that his school teachers had in young Shankar, when he was the only choice for singing patriotic songs on the school's Annual Day, Republic Day and Independence Day celebrations.

∽

Between 1992–98, two significant things happened in Shankar's career. For the first time in the history of Hindi films, a team of music directors comprised of three men instead of the iconic duos like Laxmikant–Pyarelal, Kalyanji–Anandji and Shankar–Jaikishan or their modern counterparts like Nadeem–Shravan or Anand–Milind happened. With Ehsaan and Loy, Shankar became the third arm of a triangle. Their acronym 'SEL' reflects them as a singular entity instead of three separate individuals. Then, something phenomenal happened in the contemporary music scene that left the listeners gasping for breath in awe. Shankar reached every corner of the country, when his album *Breathless* was released and created an unprecedented sensation all over.

Breathless

In those days, TV commercials and ad films often turned out to be quite attractive and alluring. They would either precede the weekend film shows or would get broadcasted in between daily serials. In a quick span of 30 to 60 seconds, they would promptly resonate with the viewers' psyche while strategically promoting consumer items. By syncing chic visuals, catchy story lines and refined music, they presented an entire gamut of emotions that would transport the viewers to a familiar or desired world altogether. Be it the kid jumping in glee at the sight of his favourite food; or a young man savouring the pleasures of finding his dream woman walking down the promenade with oomph; or the stadium cheering the candid lady as she flouts the rules by dancing on the cricket field when her boyfriend hits the winning sixer—the commercials would come up with stories that would subtly and delicately encapsulate the essence of life.

The concepts of these ad films were set on a larger, almost 5-minute long canvas. The symbiosis of visuals and the audio of these films portrayed an array of emotions. The stories embedded in these films captured the imagination of the young crowd. This multiverse of new sound and music concoctions turned out to be something of a grand phenomenon in the 1990s and came to be known as a separate genre of songs—Indi-pop music. These non-film repertoires of songs started enjoying a personal space.

The music videos of the Indi-pop songs were equally fascinating to watch. The universal wanderer of Mahesh Mathai's epic film on Lucky Ali's 'O Sanam'; Pradip Sarkar's wonderfully crafted love story on Euphoria's 'Maeeri'; Ken Ghosh's cult music video for Alisha Chinai's 'Made In India'; or Baba Sehgal's 'Dil Dhadke' were the stories each one could relate to. Divas like Alisha Chinai, Suneeta Rao, Sharon Prabhakar and Shweta Shetty; and male counterparts like the rap exponent Baba Sehgal, Bhangra king Daler Mehndi and the groovy Lucky Ali; and the music bands like Euphoria, Aryans and Strings created a rage in the music industry.

Channels like MTV and Channel V were the chief promoters of this music. Music labels like Magnasound Records, BMG Crescendo and Sony Music were instrumental in churning out these albums which were becoming more and more popular. The look of the box audio cassettes and audio CDs, with extended inlays containing lyrics and colourful photos, had style written all over them. Looking at this new trend of music, music labels like HMV, Tips Industries and EMI Records—that were more associated with mainstream film music—also joined the party. EMI piped in the bard of delightful imageries, the one who was indefatigably trendy and modern in his poetry—Javed Akhtar. By bringing in the legend of Pakistan, Nusrat Fateh Ali Khan, and Javed together in an album named *Sangam*, they created waves. The music video of the song 'Afreen Afreen', featuring the stunning Lisa Ray walking in the desert with a mystic look and appearance became extremely popular. After the success of this project, HMV was very keen on doing another non-film album with Javed. The genius that the man is, Javed took this as a great opportunity to break free from the stereotypical functioning of Bollywood music and also the current trend of Westernized, frothy Indi-pop albums. He then ventured into doing something that was never experimented with before.

☙

Javed was toying with the idea of a different kind of classical composition and had spoken to several classical singers and musicians, but nobody showed any interest. One day, when Javed was at the HMV office, Shankar came and greeted him very warmly. Javed recognized Shankar and remembered meeting him and Ehsaan through the famous artist Imtiaz Dharker. She was making a film, *Shelter*, for a social cause under her company SOLO. Javed had written a theme song for the film and Shankar had sang it while Ehsaan had composed the music. Though it was a brief encounter, Javed had heard him sing before. So, without any hesitation, he told Shankar that he had an idea for a song. Shankar's heart stopped beating for a minute, and he was more shocked than surprised. Here was a man, a genius, the scriptwriter of cult classics like *Sholay*, *Deewar* and *Shaan*—the movies he had cheered, whistled and clapped for—wanting to share an idea of a song with him! Javed's friendly and witty demeanour slowly brought him to terms with reality and he keenly listened and tried to figure out what idea he had in mind.

Shankar recalls:

Javed saab wanted to explore a song having a strange parabola, a strange journey, sometimes slow, sometimes fast, sometimes high or sometimes low. This instantly attracted me. He had shared the idea with other singers but somehow, they could not understand it. He asked me if anything came to my mind when I heard the concept. I got an instant connection with the idea and very confidently said we shall start the album with this song. At that time, I did not know how I was going to do it or what I was going to do, but the challenge of doing something new fascinated me. There we decided after much deliberations that the whole song would be sung in one breath. Within a matter of 15 minutes, the name 'Breathless' was also chosen. I had no idea how it was going to be executed. I just hummed a tune and gave the metre to Javed saab to write on it. A week passed and I got a call from him, asking me to come over as he had finished writing the song. I was very eager and excited to go to his house for the first time and also see what the word wizard had in store for me. When I reached there, he gave me a bunch of full scape sheets filled with words from top to bottom. I was startled and was trying to figure it out. Very slowly I asked him whether it was an article he had given me to read. He replied that this was the song—'Breathless'. I was shocked beyond words.

Shankar was getting the seething excitement of doing something unprecedented. He asked Javed to read out the lines that he had scribbled. These words instantly created a rhythm in his brain. The continuity of the lines and the sound started creating ripples in his mind. He collected the bunch of papers and took leave of Javed saying that he would be back with the song soon. During those days, he was staying with his in-laws in Vashi. He came out, hailed a taxi, put on the digital recorder he always carried, took the lines one by one and started composing the tune in the Yaman Raga. The base of the song was classical. By the time he reached Vashi, 'Breathless' was born. The sequencing and arranging were done in the one-bedroom flat in Dadar where his brother-in-law stayed. Javed was extremely impressed with Shankar's work and was also very happy that his vision of doing something different had come out in such a splendid way.

'Breathless' earmarked two significant events. Firstly, Shankar Mahadevan became a star. The music video featuring the singer himself started beaming on numerous TV channels and took the song to every corner of the country. Indi-pop music got a new fillip as experimentation reached unimaginable heights. Secondly, it was the start of a bond, a beginning of a cherishing relationship between two talented artists that kept on getting closer and more affectionate with mutual respect and love.

The music video of 'Breathless' went a long way in establishing Shankar's immense popularity. It was again Javed's idea to employ his son Farhan and daughter Zoya to collaborate with Shankar to direct the music video of some songs of the album. When Javed played the 'Breathless' number for Farhan, Shankar was not present there. Farhan had earlier heard Shankar during a Shakti concert and he was completely aware of Shankar's immense skill. Upon hearing the song for the first time Farhan was flabbergasted, to say the least, because it was something that he had never heard before. Apart from Shankar's incredible singing, what intrigued Farhan was the mind that conceptualized something like this. Farhan remembered his initial impressions of the song. He said,

> The genius of the singer lies in the way he thought it because Shankar can sing any song, but to think that 'let me do something from the start to finish without any break of breath' was unique. I remember when I heard it for the first time, I told Dad to play it again because I wanted to hear where or whether he had taken a breath. I heard it a couple of times and naturally could not decipher it.

Soon, Farhan made a video that represented the basic idea of the song and showed it to Shankar. The idea was to do the video without any cuts and make it seamless as one line of the song glides onto the other. The whole idea of the music video was that the protagonist of that love story started walking from a room, went through a whole journey and ended back in the room again. It was as if he was singing out the thoughts that lay inside his mind. It was much unlike the outdoor videos being made at that time.

'Breathless' became a trendsetter. Its popularity and capacity to captivate the audience never really waned. Till date, many singers from reality shows attempt to sing it and many performances are choreographed on this number. Several film songs that came later were sourced on the basic idea of this song. A year later, Shankar himself recorded a devotional song 'Endrendrum Ayyappan' where he sang in a style similar to that of 'Breathless', though that song was a devotional number sung in praise of Lord Ayyappa.

Recently, on Hanuman Jayanti (16 April 2022), Shankar recreated the magic of 'Breathless' by singing the Hanuman Chalisa in the same manner. The song was recorded for *Shemaroo Bhakti* and became an instant hit on YouTube.

Though the myth of the song being sung in a single breath was busted millions of times, yet, a willing suspension of disbelief is at work each time one listens to the song or watches the music video. The speed at which the song's movement and Shankar's movements are synced shows a defiance of being rebuffed in love, and the end of the song leaves one breathless. Renu Desai shared the screen with Shankar in the video. Tubby played the keyboard and Sham, who passed away after a few years, played the mridangam in the track. The modern recording technology might have camouflaged his breaths that came in between the lines but one gets a taste of his mastery and unbelievable control of breath when he is found complying to the multiple requests to sing this song during his concerts. Taufiq, who performed innumerable stage shows with Shankar, said that each time Shankar sang it on stage, he would be watching him closely to note where he took breaths. He would be gasping in wonderment, as Shankar would invariably veil his breaths with subtle tricks that left one baffled.

In the music video of the song 'Tere Khayalon Mein' of the same album, Siddharth made his debut as a child actor and also as a mouth percussionist. In an interview, Siddharth later recalled this unforgettable event of his life, 'I was three years old then. I remember that I was very nervous and refused to sing. My father asked everyone to go out, switched off the lights and assured me that no one was there. I sang and that was recorded. It was a cute and innocent moment that will be etched in my memory.'

Breathless sold 300,000 copies and stayed at the top of the charts for weeks. Taufiq, one of the percussionists in the album, was in splits when he remembered an incident that happened soon after the album got released. Shankar had become a sensation and they had a series of *Breathless* shows all over India. Once Taufiq, Sivamani, Karl Peters, Sridhar and Shankar were travelling to Chandigarh for a concert. At the airport, a Sardarji kept staring at Shankar and kept on following them. Then, all of a sudden, he screamed with joy. The man was so excited that he started stammering. Pointing to Shankar, he shrieked, 'I know you, I know you.' He could not recollect Shankar's name at that time, so out of helplessness he blurted out, 'You...you are that non-stop singer. I saw you on TV.' Taufiq said, 'All of us just burst out laughing at this new name given to Shankar and for a good time this became a standing joke amongst us, sending us into fits of laughter.'

∽

In every middle-class extended family, a wife seeks the presence of her partner and it was the case with Sangeeta as well. But often the path to fame comes at the cost of precious family time. Shankar's household was no exception to the problems arising due to lack of time. But the gradual success and the beckoning of a brighter future made Sangeeta resilient. When *Breathless* hit the roof, she was extremely satisfied. She remembered the time when she had told him that there might be a thousand engineers but there will be just one Shankar Mahadevan. Within her heart of hearts, she realized once more that her husband is undefeatable and come what may, he would continue choosing the right way to success.

Years later, Shankar attributed the meeting with Javed Akhtar and the birth of the song 'Breathless' to divine intervention. He said, 'God has written the script beforehand. When he thinks time is ripe, he will press a switch and make someone famous. And when he does that, success is bound to come. I was blessed that he chose me and 'Breathless' happened with me.'

Interlude

Saturday night's verve turns the small octagonal pub into a place pulsating with life. All the waving arms have flashing beads and steel bangles. The small room with old-fashioned leather armchairs and bar stools is chock-a-block with a crowd of 100 people. The vibes of youthfulness can be felt in every corner of the room. The week-long toil seems to get washed off when these cheery folks grab a bottle of beer as if holding a trophy of their feats. They thrust them in the air with a scream as the corner of the room lights up.

A blue hue illuminates the stage, as it gets filled with musicians. The drummer seated behind gives the count and kicks the bass drum. Three men standing in the front beam at the cheering boys and girls. The highly animated atmosphere revs up with the first stroke of the guitar. The huge sound coming from the bass fills the air. The drummer is adding energy to the guitar strums with groove-laden beats. Listeners lose themselves in excitement.

Holding those pint-sized beer bottles, the audience starts swinging to the rhythm of the blues. The man at the centre guides them to a delirious world with his guitar that reminds everyone of the timeless string bending of B.B. King. While the guitarist to the left delivers the chops and the bassist shakes his long mane up and down, the man at the centre is quiet and wearing an unfading smile. It gets widened as the cymbal splashes and the guitarist gets a punch with a humbucker pickup. The excitement in the air thickens up. The man now closes his eyes as he feels the rhythm around him. Shrill screams fill the air as his solo journeys through different alleys. The man sitting quietly with his keyboard stands up, caresses the reeds and a beautiful dreamy tune emanates. Suddenly, the moment turns intimate. The audience comes out of the spell when the music fades, and the guitarist at the left shouts out amid roars:

'Ladies and gentlemen, that was "M.I. Blues" by the one and only Ehsaan Noorani.'

Ehsaan accepts the cheer with his unfading smile and a slight nod of his head, and moves to his right so that all eyes can fall on the pony-tailed bald musician who gets hidden partly by the guitarists in the front and partly by his keyboard.

'And the man whose fingers can peddle dreams, Loy Mendonsa.'

The Saturday Night blues band presents another evening to the vivacious crowd revelling in the diverse music. The gig ends and both of them come out, hail a taxi and get into it. The sultry Mumbai heat catches them offguard. Beads of sweat are on their faces. There is always a deep sense of contentment when a blues gig ends and they return home together. The city traffic and snarls from the streams of cars don't sound disconcerting when they start discussing music. The car gets stuck beside a music shop selling CDs, and a familiar tune flows in:

Here comes the sun, doo-doo-doo-doo
Here comes the sun, and I say
It's all right

'You know Loy this was one of the very first songs that brought me to the guitar. What lovely guitaring man,' Ehsaan reminisces with a smile.

'Oh really! I thought it was "Smoke on the Water".'

'Oh, that came a little later. I remember my dad getting me the first cassette player when I was travelling abroad and I heard stuff like *My Fair Lady* and Paul Mauriat... Then Ventures and Shadows and stuff like that. Lovely music! My sister introduced me to Abba, Boney M. Once I started listening to Deep Purple, I got into the whole rock thing completely. You remember I told you of a friend of mine who showed me how to play a few chords on the guitar?'

'Allen, no?' Loy replies with a smile.

'Yes, it was Allen. I think in our minds we always had some chords, we had our jet planes, and we were already touring with hordes of girlfriends. And everything. We hadn't even started playing guitar. Gradually, I took formal lessons and joined the bands.'

'Are you speaking of Mickey's New Home?' Loy enquires.

'Yes, what a great band it was. Full progressive pop stuff. There was Sanjay Divecha, Karl Peters and Ranjit with me. In fact, with Sanjay, I had another band, Crosswings.'

'Man, the hook line of the song "Autorickshaw Mambo" that you sang today is fantastic!' Loy guffaws.

'You know Loy, I learnt how to write hooks ever since I was in Mickey's New Home. I went to America to learn guitar. But once I returned to Mumbai, I thought I was a big zero. I know nothing that will fetch me a living. I remember the time Ronnie Desai called me up and asked me to play bass in a jingle. I knew nothing of bass guitar but I said I would play. You never know how small things in life teach you big lessons.'

The salty breeze cools down the heat as the taxi passes by the bay. There is a tone of contentment when Loy recounts his tale, 'Yeah, things fell in my lap too when I chucked my steady job in Delhi and landed here as a tyro. And suddenly that "World This Week" music brought me to the fore. With a horde of 15 to 17 cousins in the family, there used to be a birthday party almost every alternate week and I used to play the guitar while everyone else would break into songs. That was a sort of training for my ears to pick up the right tunes.'

'And one thing leads you to another and the learning curve continues to grow.'

'I loved the way you weaved your guitar in that jingle for the soap. It sounds so breezy and what a beautiful melody it is!'

'Oh that Lifebuoy commercial! You know I even played Chinese music in that Ching sauce commercial the other day.'

'Oh yes, you told me that you watched *The Last Emperor* all night to get into that space.'

'But you know what happened the other day Loy? The client wanted me to play the effect of thunder on my guitar. And when I played it, he puckered his eyebrows, shook his head and you know man what he said?'

'What?' Loy asks with a grin, expecting something funny.

'He said the thunder is like a British thunder and I want an Indian thunder! Now how can a thunder be British or Indian?'

Together they break out into peals of laughter. The two best buddies go on sharing tales of the past and present as the night rolls on in the by-lanes of Mumbai. Both of them are so passionate about their music. No matter what genre of music they were into, they put their heart and soul into it. Very often it happens that they couldn't get into the specific zone they were looking for. When this happens, they silently detach, hang out in the street, watch life going by outside the zone of music and then come back once again.

Before they part for the night, Ehsaan reminds Loy once more about the job at hand, 'Seeing you tomorrow at 4D then? Mukul gave me an urgent call yesterday and asked us to be present by 10 tomorrow.'

'Did you call and inform Shankar?' Loy asks.

'Oh yes. Today he had a Carnatic sabha somewhere in Chembur. I called up Shankar to be there on time tomorrow. See you there then.'

∽

Mumbai truly is the city of dream peddlers. In every street, there is a dream waiting to be discovered and lived. All you need is the right frame of mind to find it. And when you have friends that share your dream, realizing them doesn't feel like a distant reality.

The last empty double-decker bus leaves the depot. Street lamps keep glimmering beside the sidewalk where just an hour back, office workers were making their way through the copies of international brands of apparel. As the two part, their thoughts trail off. The empty street keeps reverberating the Don Williams song that is coming from somewhere:

Ain't it amazing, that miracles happen
Ain't it amazing, you can still find your dream
Ain't it amazing, it all comes true
When someone like you can happen to someone like me

Four

Iss zameen ka aur koi aasman hoga...

'Hai Naya Iss Dil Meh Ek Tarana'

When Shankar met the quiet and self-effacing Ehsaan at Ranjit's house, he had no clue as to who he was. Soon after, Ehsaan called him to sing a jingle for an ayurvedic tablet called Trishun—a medicine for cough and cold. The small ditty on the ayurvedic 'sardi zukham wala goli'—'Mausam badla din badla sardi zukam ka hamla'—is a fond memory for them. They did several jingles together, but the jingle scored for Baygon Power Mats, one of the first ones that Ehsaan composed for Shankar, has an interesting story attached to it. Ehsaan recalls, 'The original one was done by a rapper who had a tough time doing it. Shankar came in and did this jingle in all four South Indian languages just like that and walked out of the studio in just 20 minutes. That was the kind of talent he had.'

Together, they worked a lot in days to come but both of them fondly recall one ad in particular. It was the ever so melodious 'Kabhi Zindagi Se Bhare' for Cadbury's Perk which was first made memorable by Rajeshwari and then by a chirpy and nubile Preity Zinta.

When Shankar was entering the jingle industry, getting a chance to playback for films wasn't easy. The production houses were not liberal enough to try out new voices. On the contrary, the ad industry was more open. Shankar was known as a guy who would come, read the jingle, have a couple of takes and finish it off. Soon, he became the most sought-after jingle singer. Shankar was clubbed in many projects with Ehsaan and Loy. Slowly, the three formed a team of producing jingles. Ehsaan would compose and

Loy used to do the programming bit. Shankar would obviously be the singer. Once, they were doing an ad for a fabric company and Shankar was at the studio to sing. The set-up attracted Shankar so much that he ended up trying his hand at programming the sitar and tabla parts. People took notice of his ability to sing all kinds of songs in many languages, and also noticed that he could play various instruments.

That was the beginning of the three like-minded artists spending substantial time in the small interiors of various recording studios like Four D, Music Room, Western Outdoor, Radio Vani or Digital Domain. Ehsaan and Loy were extremely easy people to work with. They always welcomed Shankar's contribution to the track. There was no thought of forming a trio in those days, but the camaraderie helped forge a bond based on love, trust and shared experiences of music.

One day, Ehsaan got a call from Mukul Anand. This was for a Pepsi commercial with Ehsaan and Loy, and Shankar was called to sing. Mukul and Ehsaan were very close friends. During the making of that Pepsi commercial, Mukul asked him to compose the title track for the TV serial *Hum*. It was to be aired on Zee and Ehsaan chose Shankar as the singer. Though the serial was unfortunately shelved, Mukul heard the song and loved the track and the voice. He was planning to make a film, a magnum opus of a kind and he told Ehsaan that he would like him to join in as the music composer for the film. Instead of feeling excited, Ehsaan's first reaction was to shudder at the very thought of composing music for mainstream Hindi movies. He was too apprehensive of diving into it because he wasn't a big lover of contemporary Hindi film music. But Mukul was an endearing friend and on his insistence, Ehsaan gave it a thought. Finally, he came up with the condition that he could accept the proposal if he could bring in his two friends, Shankar and Loy, along with him. Mukul assured him that he could bring in 10 people if required.

Since they had been working in the advertising industry for

a long time, while writing the tune of the first song, they made use of certain components of jingles. Instead of the loud and orchestral music of Mukul's earlier feature films, they had in mind a composition with minimal orchestration. Their first film song had a soft and gentle ambient sound on which Shankar wrote the melody. Loy came up with the idea of using a little tinkling sound in between. He wanted the music to breathe life in-between the lyrics. They decided not to add any other instruments except that brief percussive sound in a loop. That little sound gave a different edge to the track. Shankar brought out the delicate nuances of the metaphors that the lyricist Sameer had used to describe an ethereal beauty, when he sang the song 'Chandni Roop Ki'. For the song, when Sameer wrote the word *'surmai'*, Ehsaan couldn't understand it. He thought that it was the surmai fish available in Goa. Shankar later told him that it was not the fish but the kohl put on eyes.

Mukul was ecstatic upon hearing the song. He had no questions to ask and decided that they would compose the remaining tracks as well. That marked the beginning of a glorious phase of their lives. It was in 1996 that an unsigned bond of exemplary togetherness was formed. The musical voyage of Shankar–Ehsaan–Loy (SEL) had begun.

ℭ

It was the dawn of a new day. The band of three young men barged into the living room with guitars, amplifiers, upright basses and microphones in hand. They entered like a breeze of fresh air. The monochrome frames instantly turned multi-coloured and Shankar started to croon: *'Hai naya is dil mein ek tarana, mujhe baadalon se unche unche hai jaana* (There is something new in this heart, I want to go higher than the clouds).'

The words reflect the yearning of the singer. This is how SEL heralded a new beginning for mainstream music. As the band jazzed up the caffeinated morning with strums of guitar and tugs at the double bass, the entire mood gets livened up. With their music comes a whiff of positivity, mirth and youthfulness. The lyrics of the Nescafé song that came 16 years after this are testament to the time when the three took the musical scene by storm: '*Sunke awaaz dil ki, Mujhe raaste nayee hai banana* (Listening to the voice of my heart, I want to create a new road).'

The slogan of the iconic Nescafé ad—'Good Music, Good Life'—echoes the hope that these three brought into the world of Hindi film music.

Dus

'Chandni Roop Ki' could have been the first and last song composed by SEL, if Mukul hadn't thought of having them on board for all the songs. The offer to enter the Bollywood movie industry had been served to them on a platter. Mukul Anand and his banner were huge and he had already made a name for himself as a highly respected and talented director. The trio couldn't have dreamt of anything bigger.

But unfortunately, destiny had something else in store and what they got was more of a catastrophic debut. The joy and enthusiasm of entering into an unchartered domain got nipped in the bud. The untimely demise of Mukul Anand broke the hearts of these three men who were donning the cap of being Hindi film music composers for the first time. The movie *Dus* got shelved. The songs were recorded and some parts of them had been picturized as well. The maiden film getting canned doesn't augur well for any debutant music composer. The phenomenal success of Mukul Anand's *Khuda Gawah* had inspired him to make yet another larger-than-life film with the backdrop of terrorism in Kashmir. The name of the film was *Dus*, symbolizing the grenade attack by terrorists on Charar-e-Sharief late night on 10 May 1995. Despite a successful musical streak of five super hit films with Laxmikant–Pyarelal, Mukul had picked the uncapped music director trio SEL. *Dus* was one significant starting block for SEL to push off. However, they carried on their work.

Shankar was catapulted to glory when the music video of the invigorating patriotic anthem 'Suno Gaur Se' was released. In front of a huge crowd, waving and cheering with the Indian tricolour reigning high, Shankar was seen singing the song sporting the coolest shades. The aggression and verve with which Shankar shared the stage with superstars Sanjay Dutt and Salman Khan unleashed an infectious energy. 'Suno Gaur Se' changed the pattern of patriotic songs in Hindi film music. In the same year, another milestone patriotic song, 'Sandese Aate Hain' from J.P. Dutta's magnum opus, *Border*, entered the chart of all-time hits.

During this time, one song from *Dus* was also released. This song was 'Sur Mile Hai'. While the *Border* song followed the line of classic Hindi film songs on the Indian army, this song from *Dus* broke new barriers, as it was moulded with rock music. The progression of tune on Ehsaan's finger-style acoustic guitar strumming builds up the crescendo. When it reaches the hookline, it sounds like a warning bell to the world that the Indians are marching forward to victory, bold and nonchalant, at a breakneck pace. It was in league with A.R. Rahman's epic 'Vande Mataram' which came out in the same year as part of an album named *Gurus of Peace*. These were the new age patriotic songs that found a permanent place in the playlists for any occasion celebrating the spirit of Indianness—be it a cricket match, Republic Day or Independence Day celebrations. Mukul thought highly of the song, as he felt that it could be turned into an anthem. And it was for this reason that he had thought of releasing the film on 26 January.

The song that Shankar sang with Asha Bhosle and Udit Narayan, sounds extremely refreshing even today. For rookie music directors, nothing could have been more cherishing than a collaborative effort with the greatest Asha Bhosle.

What seemed like an unsuccessful attempt of the talented trio, in retrospect, opened up greater prospects and huge possibilities for them. But they always had an ache in their heart, as the man who had believed in them and brought SEL out to the world was not there to see their rise and success.

Rockford and Early Movies

The first film to hit the screen with SEL as the official music composers was *Rockford* in 1999. But only some fleeting seconds of the song 'Aasman Ke Par Shayad' by SEL were picturized in the background of the title sequence. The teasing cameo of the brilliant tune that SEL had composed raised questions as to why it had a presence as flitting as a rainbow. The sequence focussed on the young boy's dreamy eyes as he kept looking yearningly at the passing vistas from the car window. The story is a cinematic bildungsroman, as the young sheepish Rajesh Naidu enters the threshold of his boarding school; experiences all those lovely 'firsts' of a teen's formative years; and leaves the boundary as a jovial, triumphant sophomore. The tune with which the theme is introduced seems to lean into the joys of exploring the unknown future. The film's music album had multiple music directors and this SEL composition along with Leslie Lewis and KK's ever so adorable college farewell-cum-reunion classic 'Yaaron' became an inevitable choice in all Sony Music compilations of that time. The film did not have the space to incorporate songs because, much like *Hyderabad Blues*, music and songs could not be the driving force for director Nagesh Kukunoor's narrative. The album of the film mentioned that the music of *Rockford* was 'inspired by the film'. After watching the film, when one listens to the album separately, one gets an idea that the songs are the lyrical and musical interpretation of the film's theme.

The idea of using the song in the title wasn't there at the beginning. After the completion of the film, Nagesh thought of incorporating a song and asked Shankar to compose and sing it. Shankar promptly recorded the tune in a cassette in just 20 minutes and sent it back to Nagesh. There was no immediate response from Nagesh and Shankar was a bit surprised. A call did come the next day, but it was not from Nagesh. Upon hearing the voice, the landline receiver almost fell off Shankar's hand, as the man on the opposite side of the wire spoke in his trademark baritone, 'My name is Gulzar. I loved your singing. *Aapne toh gaane me kamaal hi kar diya* (You did wonders with the song).' Shankar was speechless, as the appreciation had come from someone he had always admired and looked up to. He was thrilled to the extreme but except for a formal, sheepish 'thank you', he could not express his amazement. This interaction marked the beginning of a long and endearing association. They spent countless evenings in Gulzar's citadel of creativity, drinking copious amounts of a special tea flavoured with lemongrass.

Till then, only an antara of the song was picturized and that also came intertwined with intermediate dialogues. But the song was used in full in the music video that Nagesh made as part of the promotional material for the movie. It featured the trio singing on the stage, draped in traditional South Indian outfits with the backdrop of a school reunion of the alumni. Shankar, Ehsaan and Loy represented the journey of the three friends from their adolescence to adulthood. Through the passage of the song, there is a dreamlike coalescence of past and present. Ehsaan's guitar, played on the chords of Loy's keys, has a vibe that wonderfully takes one on a nostalgic journey. The use of Carnatic violin gives it a local feel that complements the birthplace of the protagonist—a chap from Hyderabad. Nagesh made the film keeping in mind his own boarding school, Montford. Gulzar's magic with his words transports any listener to the golden memories of school days.

The music video features the trio as a band named 'The

Machans'. They are seen taking the stage after 20 years at the reunion celebrations of their alma mater. During the sound check, Shankar is seen stubbing Ehsaan's complaint against some technical loopholes in the gadgets—'Macha stop complaining here, we are machans, let's go.' The character signifies the quintessential Shankar. The man in the music video was similar to Shankar in many ways. Shankar's memories of his own college days were mainly about his music and hanging out with friends.

☙

'Aasmaan Ke Paar Shayad' was made in the early days of the SEL collaboration. But in hindsight, the song stands for the long journey that Shankar, Ehsaan and Loy have shared. It had its share of smiles and sniffles, but it only reinforced the bond of old friendship and stood as a symbol of the supreme joy that friendship emits. It represented their journey of growing together musically—touching one '*aasman*' and dreaming of '*aur koi aasmaan*' where they aspire to take refuge in a '*barish ka makan*'. Gulzar's lyrics worked like a fortune-teller's reading for the three of them.

Indeed, the days did keep turning fast for them. The trio kept treading the long lane ahead. With his feet firmly on the ground, Shankar went from nowhere to everywhere and kept fulfilling his childhood dreams.

With hearty laughter, Ehsaan and Loy recounted a funny incident that happened in Hyderabad during Rockford:

> When we were shooting the video for *Rockford*, we were staying in a really small low-budget hotel, as that's all we could afford. We were so fed up with the fare served there and thought of going out to a fancy place for dinner. After a lot of deliberations, we thought of indulging ourselves and decided to go to the Banjara restaurant at the Taj. We took an auto and told the driver to take us to the Taj. We were

all super excited, chatting non-stop throughout the journey. We were so busy talking that we didn't even realize the auto had stopped. The driver in typical Hyderabadi Hindi said we have arrived at the destination. We hurriedly got down and were speechless for a minute. To our greatest surprise, we found that we were standing in front of a shady hotel that flashed the pink and green glow sign board with the name 'Taj Boarding and Lodging'. We burst out laughing so hard that we couldn't even speak for a minute. Hearing us laugh like maniacs the auto driver was so scared and he was almost ready to drive away. It was so hilarious that even today whenever we remember that incident, we just cannot control our laughter.

Within a few years, the SEL band came into being. Shankar became the performer extraordinaire on stage and ruled the hearts of millions all over the globe. One of the key musicians for SEL, Dibyajyoti Nath, narrated his experience of touring with them for more than 12 years:

> The difference between SEL and others is that Shankar bhai never expresses even if he is dissatisfied with anything. Sometimes it happens that in some places we get a little low-quality sound, maybe the mixer console is not working properly. But I have never seen him complaining. But when he is not getting some keyboard play, he takes out one side of his linear to hear the whole stage sound. So, he is just going on. Never on stage, he says 'increase this sound, lessen that one'. But he does mention very casually and politely after the show that 'this had happened so next time just see to it'.

ॐ

Within a month of *Rockford,* a film called *Bhopal Express,* directed by the noted ad filmmaker Mahesh Mathai, was released. Set in the background of the Bhopal gas leak tragedy, the film featured SEL as the composer of the background score. The scene with grotesque images of a catastrophe had organ-based music with sad violin and deep piano notes to bring out the sombre mood of the grim incident. Incidentally, that was the only film where the title card featured their name not as 'Shankar–Ehsaan–Loy' but as 'Ehsaan Noorani, Loy Mendonsa and Shankar Mahadevan'. That was the time when SEL were one of many music composers in any film. It only showed that the rookie music composers in mainstream movies were yet to find firm footing.

Dillagi was Sunny Deol's directorial debut under Dharmendra's production house. Sunny Deol wanted to mount the film on a vast canvas and go worldwide with something extravagant. He roped in four music directors. In two songs, 'Kya Yeh Sach Hai' and 'Rahon Mein Chhayee', SEL seemed to continue the trend of the '90s heavily orchestrated music. The songs are rollicking but the cliched situations like lovers dancing in exotic locales, or a hero jigging in nightclubs, needed that '90s foot-tapping music feel. The trio sounded more like a slight variation of Jatin–Lalit, who defined the sound of that decade. Riding on the popularity of the music director duo, the music label used only their names and only gave credit to them as the music composers of the album. The trio faced the harsh truth about the music companies. They learnt that companies trusted the big names to sell an album even though it meant side-lining newer talents.

The title song of the movie stands out from the rest. They followed Sunny Deol's idea of using multiple vocalists and assembled 10 different singers to make a homogeneous mélange of vocals. The use of multiple singers was in vogue in non-film anthem songs, but in mainstream Hindi film songs this phenomenon was hitherto unknown and untested. This song also has a 1990s hangover in its instrumentation. The Jaspinder Narula bit reminds one of the ecstatic 'Pyar To Hona Hi Tha'. But SEL leave their unique touches in employing blended vocals, changing scales, use of guitar layers and piano chord progression.

Something interesting happened during the making of the songs, when SEL's advertising experience came in handy. Ehsaan narrated the incident:

> *Dillagi* that we did with Sunny Deol had many singers. Also, he had already completed shooting two songs and they were visually in place. The antara of 'Raahon me Chhaye' had been shot and in 'Kya Ye Sach Hai' there was no sync. But he can't reshoot all that. We said we would do it backwards composing to the picture. We did the song backwards to the film and that was because of our advertising experience.

Within a couple of years after the unfortunate shelving of *Dus*, Nitin Manmohan, one of its co-producers, produced another movie with Ram Gopal Varma. The team of SEL and Sameer was given the responsibility of making music for the movie *Shool*. Having worked as Varma's assistant for several films, director E. Niwas quite understandably trod on the tested path of making a film on the regional politics of the Hindi heartland and its dark underbelly. A film dwelling on a lone man's quest to restore order and struggling against the bastion of political ruffians naturally did not have much scope for songs, save a few. The trio's tough grind for bringing a varied platter, no matter how little scope the narratives offered, yielded four songs. Sukhwinder Singh's 'Shool Si Chubhe Hai' was poignantly used as a background score in an emotionally charged situation, where Sameer's lyrics contributed more meaningfully to the narrative than the music. The funky electric guitar solo in the interlude sounds stunningly different. Maybe the picturization of the song, with Manoj Bajpayee undergoing rigorous army training, helped Ehsaan demonstrate a flash of his brilliance that took a fuller shape in similar situations in *Lakshya* and then in *Bhaag Milkha Bhaag*.

But the song that gave SEL their first super hit was the one quite unlikely to have come from them. Item numbers were much in vogue and so was the voice of Sapna Awasthi. She would be belting out raunchy and sultry folk songs that exacted high pitched singing in Ila Arun mode. After her phenomenal success singing 'Chaiyya Chaiyya', the unique timbre of her throaty voice was used by SEL in 'Main Aayi Hoon UP Bihar Loot Ne'. Harmonium, banjo and dholak arrangement and the peppy, desi, dance-induced rhythm brought an earthy rawness to the song.

The song became so popular back then that, as Loy recounted later, 'They had to stop the film in the theatre because people would be throwing money at the screen.' Shankar said that the film's male lead, Manoj Bajpayee, had predicted this mania even before the song got released. Despite the phenomenal success of the song, SEL never came up with anything similar to this item number that became synonymous with Shilpa Shetty's killer *thumkas*.

A Warbler in the Woods

While taking baby steps towards fame and success as a music composer, Shankar continued working for other music composers as well. In Shankar's discography, there are obviously some songs that raise eyebrows and make one wonder why Shankar sang those songs. But that is the grind that every aspiring and successful singer has to go through. Besides laying the groundwork as the music composer for Hindi films, Shankar kept on accepting whatever offers came his way as a singer.

Nana Patekar romping with Tabu in the most bizarre steps, wearing dark shades, looks so unusual and surprising as Shankar screams out 'Pagal Hua Hua Hua' (*Kohram*). Shankar was chosen by the National Award winning singer Bhupen Hazarika to render a hard-core classical number 'Deepak Raga' for M.F. Husain's ode to womanhood *Gaja Gamini*. The *pakhawaj*-based song sounds more like a classical tarana than a normal Hindi film song. For their version of 'Vande Mataram' for the film *Maa Tujhe Salaam*, Sajid–Wajid used Shankar's voice. Jatin–Lalit came up with another impressive soundtrack for *Raju Chacha*.

While all the sonorous and romantic songs went to the popular singers of the time, Shankar was chosen to be the voice of the elderly Rishi Kapoor for the song 'Ek Sher Tha Ek Sherni'. There was a stock theme in the Hindi films of the time, where one or two songs would be lip-synced by street singers. The lyrics would be aphoristic with a bit of devotional angle and the singers would invariably sing in a high pitch. So, while the popular singers would bag the songs picturized on the lead actors, Shankar would be given songs on these fringe characters. Songs like 'Bant Raha Tha Jab Khuda' (*Bade Dilwala*), 'Pyar Ho Na Jaaye' (*Bichhoo*) and 'Jo Ishq Ka Matlab' (*Tera Jadoo Chal Gayaa*) were meant only for such song sequences.

Sometimes, Shankar's alaap was used in the most incongruous and atrocious songs like 'Har Dam Dam Bedam' (*Prem Aggan*) and sometimes he was given some more words apart from the alaaps and sargams that would be limited to one-liners (like just a three lettered expression 'Kahe Rahi Hai' in *Duplicate*, 'Raghupati Raghav Raja Ram' in *Kuch Kuch Hota Hai* or 'Mujhse Shaadi Karoge' in *Dulhan Hum Le Jayenge*. In *Biwi No. 1*, Shankar was given just one song among eight numbers, and he was paired with Hema Sardesai. This song went on to become one of the major hits of the year—'Ishq Sona Hai'. The song went well with the street-smart Salman Khan riding high on the success of the romcom movies of the 1990s. Anu Malik was a rage with these peppy, mindless songs, often with asinine lyrics. David Dhawan comedies were the perfect place for such foot-tapping beats.

Notwithstanding the music composers' predilection for falling back on Shankar to bring added texture to their compositions, more often than not the songs could not hit the charts. But in *Hum Dil De Chuke Sanam*, Ismail Darbar used Shankar's vocals to great effect. The high-energy singing brought a great appeal to the folksy tune of 'Manmohini' which sounded apt in the background when the beauteous Aishwarya Rai enters the screen. In the 'Love Theme' for the same film, Shankar let the expanse of his vocal jugglery go all out, effortlessly travelling in all octaves. In a 2-minute theme music, Shankar brought in all diverse elements of his skill. In the superhit 'Albela Sajan', Shankar is a perfect foil for the classical maestro Ustad Sultan Khan. Shankar sang in a pitch several scales higher than the other two singers, and amply demonstrated his skill for which he was the invariable choice among the music composers of the time.

But A.R. Rahman's treatment always had a distinct stamp. The song 'Ghanan Ghanan' from *Lagaan* had multiple singers, as the song was picturized on different members of a community waiting feverishly for rain. Shankar's voice was used in parts that needed a higher pitch but it had a near similar presence as that of Sukhwinder, Shaan and Udit Narayan. A.R. Rahman exploited Shankar's entire range of singing in a high-energy, folksy song called 'Rukhi Sukhi Roti' from *Nayak: The Real Hero*. Shankar wandered in every *sruti* of the sargam and moved from one octave to another effortlessly. This has always been Shankar's trademark in all his years.

∽

A.R. Rahman brought Shankar close to the heart of the South. Shankar always believed that Rahman's contribution to Hindi film music notwithstanding, his achievements in Tamil music are immense. Shankar had had the opportunity to sing small parts in the dubbed Hindi movie *Gentleman* with Rahman earlier in 1994. He still had to wait for three more years till he got to croon a full-fledged song for a Tamil movie. The song was 'Netru No No' from the film *VIP* (1997), and the music director was a person who always supported Shankar and recognized his immense talent. It was none other than Ranjit Barot. The song was a regular foot-tapping number with high energy to match the dancing steps of the supremely talented Prabhu Deva. Slowly and steadily, Shankar's voice caught the attention of other music directors including the legend Ilaiyaraaja himself.

Under Ilaiyaraaja's baton, he got a chance to show his versatility with the folk-based song 'Thai Thaga Thai' from *Anthahpuram*. Ilaiyaraaja, who was a master at using folk beats along with classical and contemporary music, used a hauntingly rhythmic beat and Shankar's rendition built a trance-like feel. But according to Shankar, the song that made him a household name in every nook and corner of Tamil Nadu was 'Varaha Nadikkarai Oram' from the film *Sangamam* under the music direction of A.R. Rahman. The love song with a folksy beat had a classic touch and became one of the biggest hits of the year. Apart from Ilaiyaraaja and Rahman, Deva—one of the most talented music directors in the 1990s—also gave Shankar major opportunities to sing his compositions.

But Shankar was given the most memorable songs that explored his versatility and range to the fullest by Rahman. While 'Varaha Nadikkarai Oram' marked his first major hit, he followed it up with the playful and unabashed singing of 'Uppu Karuvadu' for *Mudhalvan*; the rhythmic 'September Madham' for *Alai Payuthey*; the soulful 'Thaniye Thannanthaniye' for *Rhythm*; and the super stylish rendition of the title song of *Thenali*. 'Thaniye Thannanthaniye' became extremely popular and Shankar's appearance in the song—wearing dark glasses and a French beard with a full-on swag—was unforgettable.

The scintillating combination of Rahman and Shankar culminated in one of the finest compositions of Rahman, 'Enna Solla Pogirai' from the Rajiv Menon film *Kandukondain Kandukondain*. The haunting romantic number with an unusual rhythm had a striking use of Naveen Kumar's flute and the symphony of violin interludes. The fascinating picturization of the song amid the barren deserts and the pyramids of Giza was enhanced by Shankar's evocative singing. This was the song that fetched him his first National Award for Best Playback Singer in 2000. Shankar mentioned an interesting anecdote of recording the song in Rahman's studio in Chennai. Rahman is famous for recording at night. As usual, the recording for 'Enna Solla Pogirai' started at 11.00 p.m. The recording of two more songs, 'Varaha Nadikkarai Oram' and 'Thaniye Thananthaniye', continued till 8.00 a.m., with an hour's break between the last two songs. Shankar had a flight from Chennai to Mumbai at 9.30 a.m. and he rushed to the airport after the recording of the third song.

☙

The start of the new millennium saw the rise of Shankar as a popular choice of many music directors like S.A. Rajkumar,

Vidyasagar and Ramani Bharadwaj. Shankar got an opportunity to sing the foot-tapping number 'Thalattum Katre Vaa' (*Poovellam Un Vaasam*) which was picturized in a very similar way to Kishore Kumar's iconic 'Mere Sapnon Ki Rani'. Vidyasagar brilliantly used the rhythm of the moving train and Ajith Kumar lip-synced to Shankar's romantic voice from an open Jeep parallel to the train with Jyothika Saravanan at the window. He also worked with young talents like Devi Sri Prasad and Yuvan Shankar Raja.

His first song in the Kannada film industry was 'Dennanna Dennanna' (*Janumadatha*). Shankar's first song with the noted music composer Hamsalekha was 'Om Mahaprana Deepam' from the film *Sri Manjunatha*. He not only worked with eminent and established music composers like Gurukiran and V. Ravichandran but also sang for new young talents like V. Harikrishna and Arjun Janya. For the film *Hatavadi*, V. Ravichandran wrote and composed a socially relevant song 'Yaaru Yaaru' that speaks deeply about life, its lessons, society and the environment. He chose Shankar to sing this song which became an anthem.

Shankar's debut in Malayalam film music was with 'Pakkaala Paadan Vaa' from the film *Dreams*. He went on to work with many old music composers like Ouseppachan, Mohan Sithara and S. Balakrishnan, and new talents like M. Jayachandran, Alex Paul and Deepak Dev. Another noteworthy thing is that Shankar worked with some music composers who are famous instrumentalists as well. Vishnu Vijay is a prolific flautist; Stephen Devassy is an extremely talented pianist and keyboardist; and Suresh Peters is a professional drummer.

∽

As the popularity of SEL increased with every passing year, Shankar sang much less for others and more for SEL compositions. By then, the paradigm shift of the sound of Hindi film music was complete. If A.R. Rahman was ubiquitous and unanimously held as the pioneer of new-age music, SEL was a close second.

Saturday Night in Bombay

Shankar was always restless to dabble in various disciplines of music-making. He would keep on exploring avenues to do something new. The commercial viability of any project notwithstanding, he would make music, as that is the source of his joy. So, besides singing for advertising jingles or in mainstream Hindi films, there would be something like *Breathless*. Despite tasting gradual success in composing Hindi movie scores, he would go back to his earlier days of doing remakes for his friends Ehsaan, Loy and Farhad Wadia, and recorded the fresh interpretation of Kishore Kumar–R.D. Burman classics in Instant Karma projects.

The jazz fusion shows of SILK would happen at home and abroad. The fusion gigs intrigued him more, as here he could apply all his musical knowledge in its most diverse forms. He could not deny the unmatched popularity and reach of Bollywood film music, but when he blended Hindustani classical and Carnatic music in a much different format from Louiz Banks' jazz harmonies he would find it intellectually challenging and stimulating. And very often, the three friends—Shankar, Ehsaan and Loy—would meet in Purple Haze, order their favourite food and start breaking into impromptu jamming. These jam sessions would go on for hours and many new tunes would come out. Music was their way of living and nurturing their friendship.

Once, Shankar was at Studio Gallactica to work on a project by Taufiq called *Rhydhun (Nothing but Voice)*—an album dedicated to their father Ustad Alla Rakha Qureshi. In one of the songs in

Rhydhun, Taufiq experimented with voice percussion and tapped the universal language of rhythm. There were the effects of bass guitar to lead guitar, drumsticks hitting the cymbal to shehnai, and all were done with Taufiq and Shankar's mouth percussion. Shankar shared his experience, saying:

> He called me to sing this number which was not planned at all. When I came to the studio, I thought that Taufiq must have some sort of melody lines, something composed, and at least something elementary must be ready. But all I could hear was that the click track was going and he said now 'let us clear the song together'. I was wondering how we could do this. I saw no instruments also. Though I had no idea how we would do it, I was intrigued. We started with a pad-like sound. It sounds exactly like that of a synthesizer, a drone, or pads, but actually it was our voice. The high-pitched shehnai sound was my voice. We produced the bell sound also with our voices. Later the entire rhythm track was created by mouth.

In another number from *Rhydhun*, titled 'The Other Rhythm', along with Taufiq and Shankar, Zakir too joined in. He recited *konakkol* and played several percussion instruments. Taufiq experimented with an unusual Brazilian instrument called berimbau and also with Japanese tyco drums. The music video for the song was done by the Bollywood filmmaker Kunal Kohli. Kunal was making an ad film those days, where Taufiq played the percussion and Shankar lent his voice. So, in a way, these two were like the team in demand for their unique quality—one for percussion and the other for vocals.

When the *Rhydhun* project was going on, one day, Taufiq dropped a proposal of joining Shakti, the most iconic and prestigious Indo jazz outfit of all time, to Shankar. Ever since he sang in fusion bands like Divya, Surya and then SILK, he had dreamt of being a part of Shakti but Taufiq's proposal took Shankar by surprise. With his induction in Shakti, an extremely significant chapter was added to his musical journey and things seemed to be falling into place like a jigsaw puzzle.

လ

When Zakir came in for a couple of compositions for *Rhydhun*, the bandmates of Shakti got together after a hiatus of nearly two decades. They were having a UK tour and John McLaughlin and Zakir Hussain—the two founders of the band—had to reform the original Shakti that also had Vikku Vinayakram (the ghatam player) and L. Shankar (the violinist extraordinaire) at the time of the band's inception. Following the death of his father, Vikku had to take care of his music school in Madras and L. Shankar almost took a self-exile. Zakir and John invited Pt Hariprasad Chaurasia as a guest artist for their concerts. The first album with this reconstituted outfit, under the banner of Universal, was a result of a live recording of that tour.

The newly formed Shakti was renamed 'Remember Shakti' as a homage to the original band. After the release of the album named after their band, they got the offer to continue their musical tours all over the world. The reunion of the bandmates gave John and Zakir immense satisfaction, as after 20 years they would get an opportunity to unfold magic on stage with their unique repertoire of fusion music. But with time, they had to evolve with newer interpretations of their old classics. They also wanted some new compositions with newer ideas. Unfortunately, Hariprasad Chaurasia could not continue visiting with the band because of his preoccupation with other concerts. The baton of Vikku Vinayakram was handed down to the next generation of musicians. V. Selvaganesh, Vikku's son and hugely talented kanjira player, was roped in. The mandolin sensation U. Srinivas was inducted as well when he caught John's attention at a concert where he was performing with Vikku. At the same time, John was thinking of having one voice in the band. That was just before the winter concerts of Shakti in India and John expressed his desire to Zakir.

Coming to India for the recording and successive release of *Rhydhun*, Zakir shared the idea with Taufiq. He was even toying with the idea of including guest artists like a sitar player, a flautist or a Carnatic violinist if there was no vocalist to meet up to their standards. Without a second thought, Taufiq dropped Shankar's name to Zakir. But Zakir was not very sure how Shankar would fit the bill. He asked for a sample of Shankar's vocal pieces which he could send to John.

The day Taufiq dropped the proposal to Shankar in Gallactica, Shankar couldn't believe it. The moment he understood that a sample of his singing was to be sent to 'The' John McLaughlin, he immediately stopped the recording. He asked the assistant in the studio to put on any loop or rhythm. A sruti came to his mind. Within 15 minutes, he recorded it in Todi Raga decorated with alaaps and sargams in Carnatic style. For many days, there was no response from John or Zakir. A few months after, when Shankar had almost forgotten about it, he received a call. John was at the other end. John had decided to contact Shankar immediately after hearing the first 30 seconds of the CD.

John McLaughlin remembers the impact of Shankar's voice. He said:

> I got a call from Zakir and he told me that he had met Shankar and expressed my desire to have a vocalist join Shakti. A few days later I received a CD from Shankar which had him singing various classical pieces and improvisations. The moment I heard him, I immediately felt that his was the voice I was looking for. I called him to tell him how impressed I am with his singing.

The next destination of the band was Mumbai. The rehearsal was on the next day after their arrival and the show titled *Saturday Night in Bombay* was scheduled a day after. But even on the day of the rehearsal, Shankar did not know a single piece from Shakti. That is when, to quote Shankar himself, 'a sweetheart of a man' U. Srinivas connected with him. Shankar went for the rehearsals at Taj Lands End, Bandra. U. Srinivas taught Shankar his own composition of a Tyagraja kriti 'Giriraj Sudha' which Shankar had never heard before. This was the morning of the show day. He heard the composition, practised it and the same evening he performed it with the group as though he had been a part of the band for a long time. The show was a stupendous success. Shakti made a unanimous decision to include Shankar in their ensuing US tour. Meeting John McLaughlin was the experience of a lifetime for Shankar. He spoke very fondly of this, saying:

> This is what it is about great people. In a minute they make you feel at home. I did not feel out of place even for a minute because they were so welcoming. John had not come in the first day. When I met him for the first time, he had a fractured foot. Suddenly, Miles Davis and all the great names started coming to my mind and I was getting nervous. In just a second, he came and so lovingly hugged me praising my voice, speaking so kindly that in a minute I felt so comfortable.

∽

Zakir remembered that the performance of Remember Shakti in several Western cities left the audience 'floating on the aisles'. The band had a strong momentum with a deeper understanding of each other. The soundscape, made with the fusion of North and South Indian rhythms, the frenetic interaction of strings between U. Srinivas and John McLaughlin, and the interweaving of Shankar's sedate vocals was truly unique. Shankar incorporated Hindustani light classical and thumri with the harmonic progression of John McLaughlin's guitar. Shankar introduced kritis with the lyrics, bringing in free improvisation of voice like alaap and flowing melodic sequences. A new dimension was added. He carried the same energy that Shakti had always put out, but it opened greater avenues for the band to evolve in different directions. When one heard the instinctive sound of L. Shankar, John McLaughlin, Zakir Hussain and Vikku Vinayakram expanding into the more diverse sounds of Remember Shakti, it truly showed that this was a band on the path of further evolution. U. Srinivas' untimely death in 2014 gave a sad blow to the band.

More than the collaborative endeavours that these musicians had, each of them treasures each other's company. Individually, they had foreign tours in different parts of the globe. But given a chance, they would rush in to have some hours of music and fun together. Salim Merchant spoke of an incident that shows how music is a binding force for all musicians. Salim said:

> Outside India, I once met Shankar in New York City. It was so crazy. I was in New York holidaying with my family. Shankar was around in Boston or somewhere. He flew to New York because Zakir bhai decided to come for John McLaughlin's concert at the Blue Note [The famous Jazz Club in New York]. So, Karsh Kale, Zakir bhai and Shankar all went to Blue Note to watch John McLaughlin play live. We met in NYC, had a beautiful time together, had dinner at Blue Note and heard some great music by John.

∽

The albums of Remember Shakti were the result of the recordings of their concerts from time to time. Under Universal Music, three Live albums were released: *Remember Shakti* (1999), *The Believer* (2000) and *Saturday Night in Bombay* (2001). The first studio album of the band, *Is That So*, came out in 2020. The album was produced after a creative collaboration of six years between John McLaughlin, Shankar and Zakir. About the album, John said, 'The concept of East and West meeting in a new way encouraging the listener to abandon not only all preconceived notions of how a composition should be sung, but also how it should be logically structured. This can be a liberating experience.' Zakir said that he felt lucky to be included in this project.

John remembers the making of the album with great fondness. He said:

> The recording of *Is That So* is a dream come true for me. I am a guitarist as you know, and yet I am a great admirer of the human voice which manifested itself in Shankar being invited into Shakti in the year 2000 which had been, until that point, a very instrumental band. This dream was in my mind and heart even before that time. However, when Shankar joined Shakti, the sound of his voice was so inspiring I decided to ask him to experiment with me. The basic idea in the dream was to take a recording of Shankar singing an alaap of any raga, or a traditional bhajan or just simply a spontaneous improvisation of which he is a master. In the end, we used all these forms in *Is That So.*

Soon after the release of the album, Covid-19 stalled the world. Thanks to technological advancement, the three connected online and enthralled the audience worldwide with their virtual performance of 'Sakhi', one of the most popular compositions of the album. The album earned rave reviews from the critics. Ian Patterson, a jazz impresario dedicated to the promotion of jazz and creative music wrote in his column,

> Though the three musicians combine beautifully, it is Mahadevan who is undoubtedly the star of the show. The Mumbai born singer seduces with his alternatively powerful and caressing lines. The songs' unifying themes of spiritual— and earthly—devotion and love, lend themselves to heartfelt interpretation, but Mahadevan's ability to take a phrase from tender confessional to soaring release in a heartbeat is captivating. His undulating embellishments, notably at

the end of stunning sustained notes, find their echo in McLaughlin's own improvisations.[2]

჻

During one of the Shakti's shows in Rang Bhavan, a young boy among the thousands was dazed. He knew the other stalwarts like Zakir Hussain and John McLaughlin but wasn't aware of Shankar. So, when the announcer announced Shankar's name with all the extended introductions, he was curious. When the young singer came on stage and started singing, the boy felt overwhelmed. In the boy's own words, '[Shankar] blew the socks off me with his incredible vocal prowess.' Years after, while remembering that evening, he said that the memory of that concert is indelible just because of the performance of Shankar. The new entrant in the long list of admirers that day was Farhan Akhtar. The 'Breathless' music video happened soon after and that marked the beginning of a cherishing relationship.

[2]Patterson, Ian, 'John McLaughlin Shankar Mahadevan Zakir Hussain: Is That So?', *AllAboutJazz*, 3 February 2020, https://tinyurl.com/dywc27es. Accessed on 6 December 2023.

Mission Kashmir

Soon after Shankar's *Breathless* was released, Vidhu Vinod Chopra was on the lookout for a music director for his new film, *Mission Kashmir*. Vidhu had spoken with Sandeep Chowta, Vishal Bhardwaj, Anu Malik and Jatin–Lalit but he was yet to finalize any of them. Harish Daya of HMV put in a word about SEL to him and when they were called in, all three of them were excited but scared. Vinod Chopra Films was a very big banner and Vidhu was the best as far as the Indian filmmakers were concerned.

When they met Vidhu, he handed them the lyrics of the song 'Dhuan Dhuan' and asked them to come up with some ideas about how to develop the lyrics into a song. When SEL presented the tune, Vidhu was amazed beyond words. He got the interpretation that he was looking for. After the entire script was developed, they were called for song recording. 'We were just fooling around with some ideas and simply trying them out. We came up with four melodies that day,' Ehsaan recalled. The director okay-ed all their songs. Bagging a major film with a big production company, with one of the topmost directors, gave a huge boost to their careers. The album turned out to be their first mega-hit.

∽

In 'Dhuan Dhuan' we find Shankar's commentary-like singing of Rahat Indori's hard-hitting lyrics. The song sounds like a prayer, and also a painful acceptance of the aftermath of a bloodbath. The lull after the explosion in the houseboat, set against the placid landscape of Dal Lake with the creaking sound of embers smouldering, reflects the chilling narrative of the distraught people of the Valley. The ambient sounds, along with Shankar's vocals, makes the song sinister and sums up the sordid tale of the distressed Valley. SEL composed the sound that seemed to come out of Kashmir itself.

Kashmir had become one of the most sought-after locales for cinematographers, ever since the monochrome days gave way to coloured films in the 1960s. But unlike many of its predecessors, the music of *Mission Kashmir* was not just an appendage to the film but an integral part of the narrative. SEL brought in local flavour in the songs with a typical Kashmiri style of singing and an arrangement based on Kashmiri folk songs.

'Bumbro' comes straight from the repertoire of Kashmiri folk songs. The script called for a wedding sequence and this was supposed to be a mood song to be played in the background. Vidhu wanted a very innocent voice and newcomer Sunidhi Chauhan's husky voice just suited the bill. The way the song turned out inspired Vidhu to think on different lines and he decided to mount it on a huge canvas with its picturization. 'Bumbro' was the first song Sunidhi sang for SEL.

Sunidhi remembers that experience of meeting SEL with great fondness. She said:

> The first time I met SEL, it was magical. I had gone with my mom to make them listen to my voice. They were already recording a song where some other singer was coming to sing the song. When they heard me for the first time, they liked it very much and VVC and all of them made me sing that song instead. That's how it all started. They were as lovely as they are today. It didn't feel like I was meeting them for the very first time. Shankar himself being a singer made me feel so comfortable. In fact, from then till now whenever I have recorded with them there is no strain, no

pressure or anything close to 'recording' a song. It's always a very easy vibe. They let you be, they let you sing the way you want to sing. It's magical and amazing. I have had the fortune to sing so many different styles with them.

'Rind Posh Maal' continues with the same feel as 'Bumbro'. It is based on a 200-hundred-year-old Kashmiri folk tune. The first line of that song means 'girls are making garlands as they are celebrating the colours of spring'. Shankar outpours his infectious vitality in his singing, and the peppy beats made the song an automatic entry in the playlist for Independence Day or other functions. The use of matka and the gentle strings of a Turkish instrument bring the sublime vibes of Kashmir in 'Socho ke Jheelon Ka Shahar'. Taufiq spoke about the challenge while recording the splashing sound, as in those days sample sounds were not available. He said:

> At the studio, everyone was so surprised when I called for a bucket half filled with water and a plastic sheet. We used the actual sound by splashing the water in the bucket with our hands and recorded it by holding the mike near to it. (sic) The mic used to get wet and they used to cover it with the plastic sheet.

Mission Kashmir was the first film where SEL was credited as the background score composer. They gave their best to bring in the intensity of this script-driven film. Vidhu was bowled over watching them writing the background scores. It is striking to note how in a melodramatic situation, 'Dhuan Dhuan' is played and then following the sequence of a kid's death in terror strike, a soothing piece of cradle song is juxtaposed. Shankar's trademark alaap blending along with the chords on the keyboard is used in the background to create an atmosphere of tension and claustrophobia. The background score reminds one of the famous background scores of riot-stricken Bombay where A.R. Rahman used Shankar's voice to bring the drama needed in the sequence. Vidhu was so pleased with the background score and the songs that he wanted to use them again in *Munna Bhai MBBS* as well. Unfortunately, SEL couldn't accept that proposal, as they didn't have the available dates.

∽

Within six months of the release of *Mission Kashmir*, there came a film by a debutante director that changed the very course of Hindi film music. But the man had already made his presence felt in the contemporary music video circuit, after directing the eponymous music video of 'Breathless'. The association between Farhan Akhtar and Shankar was growing. While doing the music video for 'Breathless', Farhan had mentioned to Shankar that he was working on an idea for a film. Farhan first had A.R. Rahman in mind for the music, but Rahman was preoccupied with other films. After Rahman, SEL were the ones to have the same sensibility. When Farhan finally put the script together and met SEL, he, in his own words, 'felt that it was just meant to be'.

While Rahman gave the cinephiles a classic named *Lagaan*, the same year SEL produced *Dil Chahta Hai*. The film's soundtrack was striking enough to make a mark that separates two eras— Hindi film music before and after *Dil Chahta Hai*. Hindi film music got rechristened with this album. Music for the new millenium was ushered in by SEL.

Five

Hum hain naye, andaaz kyoon ho purana...

⁓❦⁓

Dil Chahta Hai

Dil Chahta Hai went on to be one of the most defining movies in the history of Hindi film and music industry. For the rookie music-composer trio, the film became the most significant landmark in their career, since it played a crucial role in SEL making a mark in the industry. The very making of the film speaks of a fresh cinematic experience for the urban movie-goers of the time.

The film stunned the audience from the very onset. An unusually poised and hep title credit card fades in and out with a subtle keyboard backup. It is not loud or extremely filmy. It doesn't conform to the so-called Bollywood fare. It is rather sedate, yet it immediately excites the viewer's imagination. An intelligent blend of silence and a soft background on the keys runs for a few minutes before the narrative goes into flashback mode.

The soundscape metamorphoses accordingly. The effects coming from the low-frequency oscillation hits a quick crescendo. A techno beat starts panning from one channel to another, synchronizing with the dazzling psychedelic rays rotating in breezy circles on the screen. The audience in the cinema hall immediately gets a rare adrenaline rush. Within seconds, the rhythm gets louder, the audience screams out with spontaneous expressions of excitement. And finally, when the three young men burst into the scene dancing to the tunes of 'Koi Kahe Kehta Rahe', the audience goes crazy. It was a completely new phenomenon.

The scene preceding 'Koi Kahe Kehta Rahe' invariably gave the audience a feeling of déjà vu. Aamir Khan and his friends were shown to be graduating from their college. Standing at the threshold of youth, with an innocent smile on their lips and twinkling dreams in their eyes, one of the boys sings out his dream for the future. This dream is nothing but castles in the air and taking things in stride. Udit Narayan sang 'Papa Kehte Hain Bada Naam Karega' in *Qayamat Se Qayamat Tak* with Aamir on the screen. Twelve years down the line, in *Dil Chahta Hai*, the scene shifts to Aamir graduating from college again. On a similar note, grabbing hold of the microphone, Aamir gives a similar farewell speech that speaks of a glorified uncertainty and the need to take the future as it comes. The setting changes from the college campus to a night club and instead of the lilt of guitar and trumpet, there comes the new age electronic dance music. Majrooh Sultanpuri's poetry for *Qayamat Se Qayamat Tak* contains a wishful juvenile thought: '*Mera to Sapna Hai ek Chehra/ Dekhe Jo Usko Jhumein Bahaar*'. In *Dil Chahta Hai*, Javed Akhtar's lyrics carry a verve, a cool confidence and an assertion of the carefree attitude of three young men: '*Gaayenge hum apne dilon ka taraana* (We will sing the tune of our heart).'

The song stunned the listeners. The voices of KK, Shaan and Shankar came one after the other with thumping assertions. The strong body language of the three buddies and the aggressive singing of Javed Akhtar's lines declared the advent of the new age. If 'Papa Kehte Hain' became a common song for the college union back in the 1990s, 'Koi Kahe' became the anthem of an entire generation in the 2000s. This is how SEL became the voice of the youth. The techno trance music enticed the minds of the youngsters, who felt a tremendous urge to break free and express themselves animatedly.

Initially, SEL weren't satisfied with the song and kept changing it before settling on one final version. Farhan spread the word that in the song 'Koi Kahe', Saif Ali Khan had sung his part when it was actually sung by Shaan. He was initially supposed to sing Akshaye Khanna's part, but later the director found that

Shaan's voice fits better with Saif. Shaan considered the film to be a landmark in his career, as the film's soundtrack broke his jinx of having only sung for movies that did not perform well at the box office.

∽

While speaking of the recording of the songs, Farhan recalled a break he had taken and gone to his business partner Ritesh's farmhouse in Lonavala. Shankar–Ehsaan–Loy went along and together they planned to compose the tunes of the films while staying there for a week or so. Though the plan was for a longer stay, they finished composing the tunes in just four days. They spent time chatting and discussing food, and amid everything, they would often retire into their rooms and start writing or playing the tune. It was a pleasure trip with a gang of like-minded people. They were in such a fun mood that even before the tune took final shape, all of them started cheering one another and moved on to the next song. Interestingly, all the tunes were composed in that light-hearted and cheerful way.

The composition process for the songs had started a few days earlier, when all three of them were busy with Instant Karma, the first fusion band of India. Together with their friend Farhad Wadia, they used to work in Power Productions (Farhad's studio). Farhan would sometimes drop by with his plans, and Shankar would compose the basic tunes. It was a very small room where musicians used to get cramped with their instruments. Yet, they would jovially compose tunes. These tunes would get recorded in an audio cassette but quite naturally, Farhan didn't realize the immense recall value those tunes would have later. They were looking for a tune to be used for the title track. But what SEL composed sounded conversational to Farhan, and he decided to use the tune for the romance theme for Aamir and Preity.

In Lonavala, when they got together to finally compose tunes for the film, Farhan played it to Javed who was to write lyrics having that conversational flair. The plan to write a title song went a-begging till they went to sleep that night. The next morning, Farhan woke up much later than the two early birds, Shankar and Javed. He was greeted by them with a large grin on their faces. Farhan understood that the two restless souls had finally hit upon the idea for the title song and must have finished it. However, they played a different tune altogether and that became the tune of the romantic number 'Jaane Kyon'.

The bass line of the earlier tune, composed for that romantic situation, kept haunting Shankar. He placed the words of the title in that tune and found the syllables were fitting to a T on those three notes on the bass. Thus, the tune meant for the romantic song became the title song. Farhan recollected, 'It was just amazing. That was magic and there is just no other word for it.'

The picturization of three cheerful lads in fancy shades, riding a convertible Merc, racing with the train and playing pranks with one another, gels so well with the playful voice of Shankar. Shankar wanted the song to be lip-synced by at least one of the actors. This idea was dismissed by Farhan and instead, he brilliantly captured the three of them driving on the highway with a freewheeling spirit as the hook line played in the background. It does cast a terrific spell. What makes the song stand out is the use of the rock guitar. In the brilliant second interlude, Ehsaan plays a differently patterned solo, heard only in the songs of rock bands. The song became an all-time ode to road trips.

'Dil Chahta Hai', the title song, established SEL as a brand of vocal harmony. One of the main reasons for those beautiful harmonies was the vocal arrangement that SEL did with Clinton Cerejo. Their way of using the chorus to refine and embellish the texture of a song lends an exceptional and distinctive edge to the SEL repository. They had a group of five singers. While some of them sang in a melody, other voices were layered on top of that. These elements are complex but haunting and hitherto unknown in film songs. The musical bridges, in between the antaras of the songs, get a different texture with stacks of vocal harmony.

Shankar–Ehsaan–Loy used some of the most talented voices, inspired by the happenings in the Western musical scene. They thrived in the jingle-making industry, where producers were into experimental stuff. Shankar–Ehsaan–Loy's prolonged stint in the jingle-making industry got them acquainted with many who became a part of their music production in Bollywood films as well.

Ehsaan and Loy called up one such singer, Caralisa Monteiro, whom they knew very closely from their jingle-making days. She got an interesting brief when SEL were recording 'Jaane Kyon'. Shankar–Ehsaan–Loy didn't even play the melody for her and just explained what was expected of her. When Loy gave her the brief, he wanted a spontaneous response. The result was a great vocal motif interspersed in the main lyrics of the song, which brings a global feel to the song. The lyrics may sound like 'abracadabra', but the vocal harmony brings in a unique texture to the soundscape of the song. This technique of not using any words in vocal singing is called 'glossolalia', where the singers utter words or speech-like sounds that fit in phonetically to the background. Caralisa had created a language of her own. When she finished singing, Loy gave an appreciative laugh, as that was exactly what they were looking for. That brief part lifted the song and made it global.

The popular duo, Udit Narayan and Alka Yagnik, are potentially the most prominent link between the sound of the '90s and that of the 2000s. In 'Jaane Kyon', Aamir Khan had suggested SEL to use Udit's voice for him. While the song made a new age sound with an Australian instrument called didgeridoo, which had not been heard before in Hindi films, the interlude incorporated a strange and striking African chorus. Javed Akhtar's predilection for using anaphora, consecutive sentences starting with the same words, came in handy to bring in the flavour of an old, Hindi conversational song.

'Woh Ladki Hai Kahan' took shape from a Celtic tune that

the trio and Farhan were listening to in the in-car stereo while going to Lonavala. There have been instances where modern-day films paid tribute to yesteryear filmmaking through a song sequence. This song surely tops the list in that category. The picturization of two lovers munching popcorn in a cinema hall and imagining themselves in the days of black-and-white films, along with the music, is a sheer delight to watch. The music had to be retro in its appeal to take one back to that groove where heroines would be gaping at the moon, singing and dancing on the shining cloudlets, with their satin sarees shimmering in the backlight. The song spans over a long time: from club music in monochrome, to the imitation of the Titanic pose while standing at the edge of a cliff. The innovation comes in when instead of going desi in its instrumentation, SEL source elements from Scottish folksy tunes.

In the song, a guitar solo leads the way in old bluegrass mode. Then a lot of acoustic music comes in for small but significant passages, with a bagpiper phrase coming in the background where the dancers flutter their arms like birds flapping their wings. The rhythmic guitar riff keeps moving while fiddle, flute, piano and offbeat clapping wait to come in. The song sounds like old-fashioned Welsh country music. However, it also brings out the authentic high-energy, party atmosphere where along with Saif Ali Khan and Sonali Kulkarni other young lovers in the movie hall also had the pleasure of replicating the antics of their celluloid icons.

Shaan spoke of his experiences of singing the long, stretched notes in the antaras. With autotune, cutting and pasting yet to be in vogue, Shaan exerted his potential to the fullest and did justice to the stretched notes of the song. His voice wasn't in the best shape then, and he was a bit stressed to bring it out. Zoya and Sagarika, sisters of Farhan and Shaan respectively, were close friends and Farhan got to listen to Shaan's songs through that connection. The music of *Dil Chahta Hai*, as Shaan said, 'broke the "shackles" of Indi-pop music and transited into a newly defined film music'.

In the song 'Kaisi Hai Yeh Rut', the use of chorus comes into play big time. Though it is much less pronounced compared to the other songs, different layers of the chorus give a unique texture that complement the dreamy vision that the lyrics churn out. If the use of bass and multiple drum pick-ups with crisp cymbal sounds and keys make it urban, Naveen Kumar's flute solo throughout the melody keeps it earthy. Shankar–Ehsaan–Loy's signature tune comes in the chord patterns that get shifted from the *mukhra* to the antaras. It immediately places one's mind on a magic carpet that keeps floating further into fantasy, with the enveloping ambient guitar tunes. Shankar–Ehsaan–Loy used a wooden percussion instrument which sounded almost like the falling rain. This is a South American instrument called the rain stick. It was being used for the first time in a Hindi film song. It consists of a long piece of wood with beads and as one turns it, the beads go from one side to the other side creating the sound of rain. There is no Indian instrument used in this song, except for Naveen Kumar's *bansuri* which brings in elements of psychedelic trance music.

Naveen Kumar's bansuri dominates 'Tanhayee' and takes it to a whole new level, bringing out the archetypal sad-song feel present in Hindi film songs. Sonu Nigam pours his energy to bring out the pangs of a lovelorn heart. The yearning of a lover, the emptiness of lost love and a trepidation for lovelessness in the protagonist's life demanded soulful singing, and Sonu delivered the best with his immense talent. Shankar–Ehsaan–Loy's instrumentation and arrangement bring out that sense of emptiness on a whole other level. The assertive bursts of the bass guitar riff itself are pretty unusual for a sad song where a jilted lover complains of betrayal. As the song is not lip-synced, it helps the composers go wild with experimentation, with the big sound of American movies and the strings of Western classical feel. What stands out is a unique rhythm pattern that runs throughout the song. Later, Taufiq said that working with SEL in *Dil Chahta Hai* made him discover the rhythm arranger in him. The time and freedom he got working for SEL helped him explore more of his skills. He shared his experience of working on one of the best songs whose rhythm he arranged, saying:

> SEL have always maintained the pack up time at 9.00 p.m. Very rarely do they go beyond that. They called me for the rhythm of the song 'Tanhayee'. Since I had some previous commitments, I said I would be there by 8.30 or so. Shankar gave me the song to develop the rhythm and left for the day. The moment I heard the song, the Muharram processions near the Mahim Dargah flashed in front of my eyes, where the mourners beat their chests in sorrow. There is a hauntingly sad but powerful drum beat played during this procession. This was so relatable to the song where the hero is mourning. I accordingly arranged the rhythm pattern and recorded it till one in the night and came back. The next day the trio were hugely impressed by the pattern. With so much freedom they give, one can come out with the best.

Shankar–Ehsaan–Loy added a few things to the song like banging of the thali in between, a sound of the bead shaker and made it sound like what it is now.

There is a funny story attached to 'Tanhayee'. There is a percussive sound coming just before the music part of 'Tanhayee'. When Farhan was working on the cuts for the film, instead of its designated frame, that sound got synced with the scene where Preity Zinta is pushing the trolley in the airport while coming back to Mumbai. Though it was unintentionally done, they decided to keep it as the background music.

Dil Chahta Hai became the anthem of the youth not just because of the sassy presence of three vivacious youths and their paramours, but also because of the background music pieces of the film. The colourful beach volleyball scene, skimpily clad people basking in the sun on white sands and the rock guitar strum come alive with a chorus going 'oo la la' in the background. Each character, with their idiosyncrasies and attitudes, was given different background scores. When the three boys were shown to be holidaying—wearing cool shades, flashing brilliant outfits and moving with an infectious insouciance—the electronic dance music and the background vocals with dummy words perfectly bring out that camaraderie and fun element. When Sid discovers his love interest in a lady much older than him, the music changes and becomes sedate and poised. A beautiful string and piano groove and a delicate tune in English flute bring out the sensitive part of the narrative. Aamir listens to Dire Straits in his testing moments. He gets a groove on drums when he lands in Australia. Saif gets a jazzy background for the hep class he belongs to.

∽

If the music of *Mission Kashmir* earned SEL a place in the industry, *Dil Chahta Hai* took their music all over the world. That was the year when other musical superhits like *Lagaan*, *Gadar*, *Kabhi Khushi Kabhie Gham* and *Tum Bin* also released. *Dil Chahta Ha* stood out among them due to its freshness and long-lasting appeal. Shankar says that he has no clue why the album is popular even now. Perhaps, their collective unawareness of what was going on in the music landscape of the day brought out the most unusual sound.

Shankar–Ehsaan–Loy's fearlessness of approach was the key to giving out something well and truly path-breaking, as there was no insecurity among them to stay in the rat race. They just ventured into the arena with no baggage or expectations. As Loy said, 'It was as if three kids were being handed over paintbrushes and colours and they did whatever they wanted on a canvas.' Ehsaan recounted, 'This album gave us a new face. People knew who we were. It launched us into the thick of industry. Having composed the music ourselves, we have never been able to live up to that level.' That year, at the Filmfare Awards, Ehsaan and Loy received the R.D. Burman award for new and upcoming talent in music. Shankar wasn't present that evening. That is when the spotlight fell on them for the first time. It was almost as if they were declaring their presence through the lyrics of their own song: '*Hum hai naye, andaaz kyun ho purana.*'

Dil Chahta Hai marks the beginning of the time when the movie-watching experience underwent a huge paradigm shift, charting an evolution from the coins-throwing, hip-shaking loud audience of the single-screen cinema halls to the posh and upscale movie-viewing experience of the multiplex. The music of the film was rejected by a couple of music banners because they felt that the songs of the film sounded like 'non-film Indi-pop' music. History has repeatedly proved that anything new has faced an instinctive rejection, but only the dreamers dare to stay resilient. It was owing to these rejections that even after such phenomenal success, SEL had no work for nine months. But this album sowed the seeds of a unique sonic experience, giving respite to an audience that was seeking a break from the existing pattern of music in Hindi films. It generated an expectation in the sects of listeners looking for a neo-urban soundscape. The hangover of the soundtrack of *Dil Chahta Hai* stayed for years and the films that came later carried the trail.

∽

When *Dil Chahta Hai* happened, a little girl went to theatre with her mother. She still remembers the craze of the crowd and how people were going mad. They were getting up from their seats and dancing. The girl was not exposed to this kind of craze for her father and his friends. She also attended a party for the first time in her life. It was celebrating the success of the film at Taj, Lands End, Bandra. Everything appeared surreal to Loy's daughter, Alyssa Mendonsa.

Another kid was just coming into the world when *Dil Chahta Hai* released. Years later, people discovered a junior Shankar Mahadevan in him. On 19 January 2001, Shankar and Sangeeta became the proud parents of their second child, Shivam Mahadevan.

Armaan to *Kuch Naa Kaho*

For the trio, it was not a cakewalk to jump onto the bandwagon of music direction for Hindi films owing to several reasons. Shankar, with a predominant background in Indian classical music, had teamed up with two very unconventional people who were not even remotely connected to Hindi film music (and they didn't have a desire to be a part of it either). Ehsaan was a premiere blues guitarist of the time. The dreamy ambience of a smoky, snug nook—where some like-minded guitarists jammed with only a handful of people in the audience—intrigued him more than the pompous sets of Hindi films. For him, Hindi film music was an avenue that he had coincidentally trod upon. Loy, being a Western music teacher and a steadfast follower of jazz music, was not aware of the sound of contemporary Hindi film music at all.

So, when Shankar, Ehsaan and Loy became SEL and started composing songs for Hindi films, none of them were sure of their survival. This was mainly because each one had a predilection of his own and they had distinct personalities. But this ignorance about the formula of contemporary film music turned out to work in their favour. They did not have to match with anyone and they did not have any role models to follow. Each of them carried their own sensibilities, and the three of them with their unique likings and tastes for music merged into one team. With the dissipation of their individual musical credo, they formed a separate identity and totality in itself.

But Hindi films were still largely in the single-theatre domain and the sound of SEL was yet to cut a mark in the collective psyche of the masses. Jatin–Lalit were the most sought-after music-director duo before the two brothers decided to part ways. When SEL made their debut, Jatin–Lalit had scored music for five out of 10 musically successful blockbuster movies like *Kuch Kuch Hota Hai*, *Pyaar To Hona Hi Tha*, *Pyaar Kiya To Darna Kya*, *Ghulam* and *Jab Pyaar Kisise Hota Hai*.

Anu Malik was the busiest music director of the day, and he gave the biggest hits of that time. In the year when *Mission Kashmir* was released, Anu had four big hits under his belt: *Refugee*, *Josh*, *Har Dil Jo Pyar Karega* and *Fiza*. Rahman's outings in Bollywood produced inevitable winners like *Dil Se*, *Taal*, *Lagaan*, *Saathiya* and *Swades*. They came in tandem and bagged consecutive jackpots. Rahman's songs created an impenetrable fortress that was impossible for anyone to invade in terms of popularity.

For SEL, after *Dil Chahta Hai*, the next super hit came with *Kal Ho Naa Ho*. In between, almost two years passed without any significant box-office contribution from the trio. Before *Dil Chahta Hai*, they had nothing to prove and no pressure to carry forth any benchmark. All they had to do was deliver to the best of their abilities, without really thinking about keeping pace with the contemporary trend. *Dil Chahta Hai* turned the tide significantly. With its distinctive sound and the craze it generated among the youth, it raised the bar of expectation from the trio.

The films that they worked on immediately after this could not match up to this level, but that lull period proved to be the time to hone their skills and gradually prepare a separate niche for a brand-new breed of listeners. Shankar–Ehsaan–Loy stayed loyal to their audience, delivering the style that these fans, mainly fed with the rock and pop music, were looking for.

In 2002, Hansal Mehta came up with two back-to-back releases: *Chhal*, an action flick; and a trendy potboiler comedy, *Yeh Kya Ho Raha Hai*. Unlike the former, where music didn't have much to contribute, the comedy with a bunch of incognito actors had a good scope for music. After churning out an album with predominantly youthful vibes in *Dil Chahta Hai*, SEL got another one along the same lines with *Yeh Kya Ho Raha Hai*. There is one song called 'Kuch Hum Bhi Pagal Hai', where SEL tried to bring an all-girls version of the 'Koi Kahe' song with electronic dance music and lounge music feel.

Between *Dil Chahta Hai* and *Kal Ho Naa Ho* SEL composed music for five films. Out of these, two of them—*Armaan* and *Kuch Naa Kaho*—can feature among their best works of all time, even though those films didn't do well.

∽

In 2003, SEL got two films, one was *Armaan* directed by Honey Irani, and the other one was *Kuch Naa Kaho* from the eponymous Sippy camp.

Armaan has some great melodies that merge the feel of the 1990s, while also having some elements of new age music. The leading actors lip-syncing the songs were still much in vogue and the film offered scope for them to take a leave from the linear narrative and romance in an idyllic setting. And where situations were scripted for mushy romantic songs, SEL excelled. Two songs from the film 'Mere Zindagi Mein Aaye Ho' and 'Jaane Yeh Kya Ho Gaya' abound in the melody of old Hindi films. While in the former, Niladri Kumar's brilliant sitar passages and Sonu–Sunidhi's wonderful singing make it sound sublime, in the latter, the use of Loy's delicate piano lines and saxophone create a sophisticated groove and make it a modern-day song. In 'Jaane Yeh Kya Ho Gaya', Shankar's voice travels from the lowest to the highest notes, and Alka Yagnik sounds like a perfect counterpart to him.

'Mere Dil Ka Tumse Hai Kehna' is another situation-induced song where Preity Zinta, in an unusual femme fatale avatar, seduces Anil Kapoor in 'Raat Akeli Hai'-mode. Shankar–Ehsaan–Loy make use of the sonorous voice of Chitra to give a different edge to this song, and the legendary South Indian singer sang it to perfection. There is a very subtle and restrained use of tabla pickup in the song that never goes berserk. Unlike the other two songs, the indoor feel of the song is sustained with a restrained tabla rhythm. About this song, Sunidhi said, 'I don't think I have loved Chitra ji as much in her low tone maybe because we never heard her sing like this. The way they made her sing this song, the kind of scale they chose for her it was so beautiful. That's the magic of SEL and their journey has been great. They have delivered every emotion.'

These songs follow the glorious tradition of Hindi film songs, as they create a separate space for easy listening. The script might have often failed to keep pace but the songs give the audience a charming respite. The film has a brilliant background score that uses the sounds of saxophone and flute, with the instruments corresponding to the distinctive traits of the two leading characters played by Anil Kapoor and Amitabh Bachchan. The violin player, Shriram, was one of the best in the industry, and the saxophone player was Kevin Hamburg from New Zealand. He was performing at the Grand Maratha and that's where SEL had heard him for the first time. They wanted to create the 'Kenny G' kind of ambience and found that in Kevin.

As *Armaan* was Honey Irani's debut film, and *Nayee Padosan* was Tharunkumar's debut, two movies of two debutant directors were released back-to-back. Shankar spoke of one song 'Dil Mein Dhadkano Mein' from *Nayee Padosan* which might not have caught the audience's fancy, but the phrasing of the tune stayed in Shankar's mind. Some years later, Shankar made use of it in another song that became superhit. It was 'Bol Na Halke Halke' from *Jhoom Barabar Jhoom*.[3]

Pointing out the differences between the two masters, Rahman and Shankar, Mahalakshmi Iyer, who sang tons of songs for both of them, said:

---

[3]Information courtesy: Kalpana Swamy and the magazine *Nostalgiaana*

I can say there is a similarity between Rahman Sir and Shankar. Both of them are extremely spontaneous and extremely open-minded, and both of them are extremely giving composers. But the difference I would say is that Shankar is a terrific singer, so he would come up with certain interesting contributions to the song. Rahman Sir would push you to try something more but maybe not vocalize it, Shankar would be able to sing what he had in mind. For example, I have sung the song 'Mera Man' for the film *Nayee Padosan*. When I was recording the song, it was a three-antara song, after some time my imagination reached a saturation level. I went into a mental block and at that time a composer like Shankar was like a mental relief to me because, after every antara, he suggested ways to sing it differently. It was very unusual and it suddenly opened my imagination.

∽

Rohan Sippy, son of Ramesh Sippy, made a somewhat weepy debut with *Kuch Naa Kaho* but the film has some wonderful songs. When Rohan Sippy approached SEL, the fun element in the script attracted them to agree to it. There was a shared enthusiasm and love for jazz between the director and SEL, especially Loy. They had, initially, even thought of bringing in some jazz in the songs, but the typical filmy situations didn't allow them to do so. But the songs did have some long trumpet scores played by one of Rohan's friends. Shankar–Ehsaan–Loy made the most of the romantic situations of the narrative and came up with one ace after another.

'Kuch Naa Kaho', the title song, came out of various patterns of whistling that happened one day in SEL's jamming sessions. The whistling pieces were originally a bit longer, and the song itself was slightly more extended than the final version. It was Javed Akhtar's suggestion to avoid the repetition of lines and keep the structure brief and taut. The song sounds as soothing as any melodious number of the time, with two of the most loved and popular voices of the time—Sadhana Sargam and Shaan—lending their voices to the song. The song leaves a lingering trail with the whistling done by Shankar himself. That was the first example of Shankar's whistling in any SEL song. Whistling became a unique tool in the SEL's kitty that continued through the years. The lounge music feel that started with 'Koi Kahe' is seen here again in 'Tumhe Aaj Maine Jo Dekha'. This song has an electronic qawwali kind of sound which wasn't common in those days, and SEL executed it perfectly. The infectious vitality with which Shankar sang the tune makes the song a sure winner.

In the mid-1990s, Sooraj Barjatya pioneered a trend of Hindi films having a grand-scale family drama with opulence, glamour and razzmatazz. Films championing the virtues of the traditional joint-family system and fun surrounding grand Indian weddings came in large numbers. This became a favourite trope in Indian filmmaking. In *Kuch Naa Kaho*, 'Baat Meri Suniye Toh Zara' is one such situational song that adds to the colour and glitz of Indian wedding ceremonies. The Indianness of the song is brought out with the traditional instruments like dholak, tabla, bamboo flute and *ghungroo*. SEL and Javed Akhtar strike a great camaraderie where metres keep increasing in successive lines in antaras. The unusually asymmetric antaras, with winding lines, make it a highly interesting listen. The conversational singing and the lyrical expressions of dialogues, is reminiscent of the cult hit *Hum Aapke Hain Koun* and some other Rajshri Productions films. Mahalakshmi shared the story of how the song took shape:

The song 'Baat Meri Suniye Toh Zara' has shades of 'Breathless', as during that period due to the popularity of that song all the producers were insisting on a 'Breathless' kind of song. And the beauty of the trio is that they won't repeat the same type of composition unless, of course, it falls into that theory. The director said that they wanted it like a *sawaal jawaab*, like a *nok jhonk* [teasing] that happens at weddings. So, Shankar just sat and started humming the first part of the antara and Javed Saab wrote to that and then the whole song was written like a question-answer mode. Javed Saab was writing and Shankar would sing in tune immediately after that. Then Javed Saab would write something and Shankar would say one word extra. Javed Saab would either drop the word or would tell Shankar to compose an extra note there. So, the whole song is not equal in the words or notes. Since you can't have back-to-back verses, they were filled by all those chorus portions like a tarana.

'Achchi Lagti Ho' is a quintessential traditional dream sequence with the familiar vocals of two popular singers of the 1990s: Udit Narayan and Kavita Krishnamurti. This song only reiterates the grand old tradition of popular Indian films, where the romancing of star-crossed lovers in sylvan surroundings was a common trope. One fine evening, SEL were occupied with some jingle-making when Rohan Sippy came into the studio. They broke out into a spontaneous, playful and impromptu jamming session where several patterns of music came along. Shankar improvised on those patterns and it gradually took the form of a song, like a jigsaw puzzle slowly falling into place.

In the late 1990s and early 2000s, the songs of separation had a *sufi* kind of feel, where singers would sing in a high-pitched vocal pouring out the pangs of pain that the lovelorn soul felt. Richa Sharma was one such talent who shot to fame after A.R. Rahman's music in *Taal*. Shankar–Ehsaan–Loy tapped into her potential in the years to come. In 'Kehti Hai Yeh Hawa', Richa Sharma's voice lent that earthy rawness and Shankar brought himself to match the husky timber of her voice with a higher-pitched reprisal of the 'Kuch Naa Kaho' tune.

∽

At this juncture, the process of filmmaking was going through a fast and imperceptible transition. Quite discerningly, a new sound arrived with a new breed of music composers. The films were also coming of age, appealing more to reason than being merely an escape route to something fanciful and larger than life. With single screens decidedly giving way to plush multiplexes, the profile of the audience was changing noticeably from rural to semi-urban and urban. More importantly, with more opportunities to reach bigger business orbits, Hindi films became flagbearers of Indian culture worldwide.

The music of the Hindi film industry was not just a regionally or nationally constricted entity, but had become a global presence. Musical acculturation reached newer heights. Shankar–Ehsaan–Loy became the prime moving force at this transitional juncture, and the person who contributed significantly to this emerging and evolving trend of Hindi films was Karan Johar. The music contract for the next film from Dharma Productions was offered to the trio. They took this opportunity and gave their best shot with an impressive mix of a soundtrack. *Kal Ho Naa Ho*, a big banner film, was an album that had versatility written all over it.

Kal Ho Naa Ho

A trend of larger-than-life love stories in Bollywood was set off when Aditya Chopra's *Dilwale Dulhania Le Jayenge* and Karan Johar's *Kuch Kuch Hota Hai* created waves. Shah Rukh Khan used to get the most popular character names, Raj or Rahul, as a lover boy counterpart to the angry young man, Vijay, played by Amitabh Bachchan. Unlike the mythical rebel, packing a punch and delivering melodramatic lines at the vanquished villains, Raj would open up his arms with an impish smile winning the hearts of the damsels across generations. While Vijay had with him the dialogues penned by maestros like Salim and Javed, lover boy Raj or Rahul had the lover's romantic words woven into songs.

Films set in overseas locations, before those days, were fewer in number and were essentially restricted to the occasional dream sequences when the lovers would take refuge in idyllic escapes to foreign landscapes. But films belonging to Yash Raj Films and Dharma Productions gave Bollywood a global presence, in the sense that almost the entire movie would happen overseas. By the time *Kabhi Khushi Kabhie Gham* was all set to release, Karan witnessed the furore over *Dil Chahta Hai*. Karan was highly impressed by the debutant director's ace and realized that the language of filmmaking, the art of film production and virtually all aspects connected to that craft, were undergoing a transition. He feared the inevitable failure and was almost on the verge of a mental breakdown.[4]

---

[4]Johar, Karan, and Poonam Saxena, *An Unsuitable Boy*, Penguin Random House India, 2018.

Kabhi Khushi Kabhie Gham kept following the earlier footprints and became another mega blockbuster. However, once the hysteria of success was over and Dharma Productions thought of bringing out their next love story, Karan thought of switching to a new mould. The look, feel, texture, aims and objectives remained aligned with the signature Dharma Productions films. But they got a completely new makeover in terms of music and soundscape. Most significantly, he relinquished the director's chair to another debutant Nikkhil Advani. There was no hero named Raj or Rahul dancing amid the sun-kissed mustard fields. Rather, here came a mellowed Aman, gentle and calm in his countenance, spreading an air of positivity and coming to terms with the fleeting and ephemeral joys and sorrows of life. The all-encompassing flute and piano notes later permeated every corner of the theatre before the sublime 'Har Ghadi Badal Rahi Hai' started. Shah Rukh opens his arms again and this time to own up to life with all its uncertainty and unpredictability. *Kal Ho Naa Ho* declared the arrival of a new age film sound, a leap into the sound of a new millennium.

∽

When Nikkhil and Karan came to SEL, Nikkhil was looking for that 1990s Jatin–Lalit kind of sound with dholak and all other Indian instruments. Karan did not agree with Nikkhil and was very interested in the new sound that SEL wanted to bring in. Parts of *Kuch Kuch Hota Hai* was set in Mauritius and Scotland, while *Kabhi Khushi Kabhie Gham* had parts in London and Egypt. For *Kal Ho Naa Ho,* the setting is Toronto and New York. The music of the film is expansive, providing an international vibe to the film. The title music blends the sounds of an international philharmonic orchestra with bhangra beats to bring the desi flavour to the diasporic audience. So, SEL brought a twist to what Nikkhil had wanted. The dholaks were played but with a difference. Aman brings with him a high-sounding ambient sound, in sync with the larger-than-life image of the protagonist. This background score comes in a loop every single time the script needed Shah Rukh to deliver axiomatic lines.

'Maine Jise Abhi Abhi' has a nearly similar guitar riff to Roy Orbison's classic 'Oh, Pretty Woman', on which this desi bhangra cum hip hop song is based, in parts of the interlude music and the title. Karan took prior admission to use them in his song to avoid any legal suit like they had to face for using the tune of American band The Weather Girls' song 'It's Raining Men' in their last film. For the scene of Shah Rukh seeing Preity for the first time, SEL had another song ready and they had recorded it as well. Then the idea of using 'Pretty Woman' came up and they felt that the reworking of the tune would do better. Javed had some initial reservations about using the Western song, but got around to liking it when he heard the SEL version. Films aiming to woo the diasporic audience accommodated the scope of bringing in elements of Indian folk tunes in their context. Picturized on a local Punjabi sect settled in the US, the song simultaneously carried a Punjabi folk tune with an American upbeat style.

The song that was initially recorded for Shah Rukh's and Preity's first meeting was not approved by Nikkhil Advani, and the trio decided to use it in another film that got released within a year. In Sajid Khan's directional debut *Heyy Baby*, Shankar sang this super melodious solo with Loy's back-up vocals and layers of vocal harmony in the song 'Jaane Bhi De'. However, the most unfortunate part was that the song was brutally chopped off the film. The film has another melodious number in its place, 'Meri Duniya Tu Hi Re', an all-guys song where Sonu, Shaan and Shankar sing in tandem. The song sounds like a stylish urban soft rock song. The tacky rhythm and catchy hook line; a very jazzy and bluesy interlude on guitar and keyboard; and more significantly the use of vocal harmony have SEL written all over it.

After 'Maine Jise Abhi Abhi', SEL effortlessly transited into a chirpy, buoyant party song with 'It's the Time to Disco'. The song sounds pretty cool with the very stylistically processed vocals of

'Rabba Rabba' famed Vasundhara Das. Layers of synth sound and backup vocals make it hep, but the SEL mark of exclusivity comes in their innovative blending of tabla in an out-and-out Western framework.

'Kuch To Hua Hai' is the song for which every SEL lover would flock to the theatre. The use of urbane, metrosexual synth sounds make the song international in its feel. The vibrant and freewheeling choreography, complementing the rhythm of the song, and the playfulness of Saif Ali Khan and Preity Zinta make it a modern-day variant of the ever-popular romantic duo Rishi Kapoor and Neetu Singh in the 1970s. Javed Akhtar also seemed to be growing younger with every new lyric he penned for SEL. Shaan brilliantly carries the onus of sustaining the youthfulness of a new generation on his shoulders. Alka Yagnik poured in an added dose of sweet and savoury texture to the song and SEL's instrumentation did the rest.

'Maahi Ve' is yet another party song one expects to see in a typical Dharma Production film. The liveliness of bhangra comes in handy to bring the dancing groove. However, in this song, it also becomes the stuff of uber-cool, discotheque, dance-floor music, when the traditional beats of dholak and dhol merges with cymbal and bass drums and a jazzy saxophone. The song has every element to fall in the category of another desi song for Indian weddings, but the layers of back-up vocals smear the tune in such a way that it breaks the confines of the familiar desi mould.

Film songs that go beyond their identity of just being part of a film, create a separate identity for themselves. Songs like 'Kuchh To Log Kahenge', 'Zindagi Ke Safar Mein', 'Zindagi Kaise Hai Paheli' and even Gulzar's odes to life, went beyond the movie context and got a life of their own. The title song of *Kal Ho Naa Ho* also earned the status of a cult classic and won a place in this category of songs. The simplicity of the tunes and candour of the lyrics are what make these songs so popular. Javed Akhtar, known for writing his verses with the choicest figures of speech, came out with the quintessential reality-of-life song in the most simple language. Chiselled lines of truth came out sans any decorative language:

Har ghadi badal rahi hai roop zindagi
Chhaon hai kabhi kabhi hai dhup zindagi

Life's changing every moment
Sometimes life is shade, and at other sunshine

For Sonu Nigam, singing this song was a moment of epiphany. He sang it twice in five months. The first time, Nikkhil instructed Sonu on how to sing. The next time, Sonu wished to sing it the way he wanted. He took only 10 minutes to record the song. In that sudden moment of truth, the lines, as he said, 'brought in me a feeling of relief, a renaissance in my heart'. He continued, 'I did not want to get bogged down by the industry and grow into a frustrated old man whose life revolved around the next car he wanted to buy. This song came to me when I was going through a significant change. Thanks to this I had begun to appreciate life and respect myself as a person. That is when I learnt how precious life is.'[5]

Sonu was called by Karan when he was shooting for the film *Love in Nepal*. Karan assured him that they would wait for him till his return. Shankar recorded the demo track himself and normally they would have proceeded with that. On the night of the Filmfare Awards, Sonu said, 'I believe every piece of art has its destiny. I was meant to sing the biggest song in the history of Indian film music. Going by what Karan told me to do, I can only say "Thank God" that the most loved song of all time came to me.'[6]

---

[5]Bhattacharya, Roshmila, 'This Week That Year: Shah Rukh Khan, Sonu Nigam's Ode to Life in Kal Ho Naa Ho', *Mumbai Mirror*, 1 December 2018, https://tinyurl.com/r2utcmm9. Accessed on 24 November 2023.
[6]Ibid.

The piano piece that precedes the song has rightfully earned its place in the Bollywood hall of fame. The story behind Loy creating the melody of the prelude, while having breakfast in Pune's German Bakery, also deserves its own hall of fame. Shankar has the prodigious talent of composing tunes out of thin air. When Loy got the tune in his mind they rushed inside the hotel. Loy played the tune he conceived on his piano, and Shankar immediately composed the tune of the mukhra. Ehsaan picked up his guitar and wrote the notes of the lines that came after—'*Chahe jo tumhe pure dilse...*'

As a guitarist nurtured in Western music and blues, Ehsaan couldn't sing with inflexion. Shankar continued it and carried the tune further into the second antara. Shankar reversed the first antara and composed the lines, '*Palkon ke leke saaye...*' The song was created not just for the philosophical musings of the terminally-ill protagonist, but also served as the message in a bottle for generations to come.

Sonu said in his thanksgiving speech at an award function, 'I know that the day I die this is the song that will play on radio and TV. This is the song of Karan, Nikkhil, Shankar, Ehsaan, Loy, Javed and Shah Rukh. They will be remembered with this song. It is the biggest song of our lives.'[7] The reprisal of the song in the film's dramatic moments is a typical Dharma Production fare. Richa Sharma's rich and earthy vocal merging with *shehnai* of *bidai* and bamboo flute is used to bring in the sadness and poignance of the situation, where the bride is all set to leave her maiden household.

One of the best renditions of the title song comes from Shankar's live shows. Thousands of listeners, who are screaming for the peppy numbers are always stunned to silence each time Shankar sings 'Kal Ho Naa Ho'. The highest pitch that Naveen plays on his flute sits effortlessly in Shankar's voice, as he

---

[7]Ibid.

vocalizes the interlude music leaving the audience in awe.

Shankar used his own voice in the background music of the film too. One of the most evocative scenes, where Shankar's vocals were blended with Loy's piano, was when a contemplative Preity—brooding on the transient life of Aman—walks up the promenade while dry leaves are flying. The foreboding in the mise en scène is accentuated by the heartbeat sound that comes in the refrain.

The background music switches to quirky when Saif, the happy-go-lucky guy, is invited for dinner, which leads to confusion, as they go to wrong people's homes. Using funny vocals like '*galat ghar*' when they go into the wrong house and Instant Karma's 'Baahon Me Chale Aao' in Mahalakshmi's voice when Saif is with Lillete Dubey bring the comic elements into the essentially feel-good film.

Kal Ho Naa Ho gave SEL their first National Award. Ehsaan retrospects that *Kal Ho Naa Ho* was a good amalgamation of songs they are capable of making (modern and contemporary) with the kind of songs Dharma Productions wanted. Because of their association with directors and producers, they knew exactly what sort of sound they are more acquainted with or have a liking for. Accordingly, they have always been the directors' music composers.

Kal Ho Naa Ho was their highest-grossing album till it was walloped by Dharma Productions' next venture that got Karan Johar his director's throne back—*Kabhi Alvida Naa Kehna*. There were many critics speaking against *Kal Ho Naa Ho*. Though Ehsaan often blew the top listening to unfair verdicts from the music critics of the time, in retrospect, the harsh and unfair statements of a few critics might be tickling their funniest bones now.

∽

In their continued quest to explore newer domains and untested styles and techniques in music, SEL became any debutant director's favourite. They earned the confidence of newcomers coming into the scene with novel aspirations. Samir Karnik followed the line of Farhan Akhtar, Honey Irani, Nikkhil Advani, Tharunkumar and Rohan Sippy by bringing SEL as the music composers for his debut film. When Samir, the director of *Kyun! Ho Gaya Na* met SEL with the script, the trio found it interesting because Samir's approach towards the same stock theme was different. The glitzy looks of the sets; the hit pair of Vivek Oberoi and Aishwarya Rai; and the presence of an amusing and vivacious character, essayed with great aplomb by Amitabh Bachchan, do make it vibrant in parts. However, ultimately the songs and dance sequences were only sporadic in their presence. They look more like colourful music videos and the beautiful songs couldn't reach the larger audience because of the film's box-office failure, save the Udit Narayan–Sadhana Sargam duet 'Aao Na'.

Shankar–Ehsaan–Loy composed a song with a striking melody, having a feel-good vibe. The song was there to stay, completely independent of the film's trajectory. 'Pyar Mein Sau Uljhanein' has a retro feel of the 1960s, with a bit of unusual SEL instrumentation. Piano accordion, violin ensemble and the traditional use of chorus following the main singer's verses make it sound like an old Kishore Kumar classic 'Hum The Who Thi'. Mahalakshmi sounds exceedingly sonorous as SEL bring elements of Western classical music with wonderful use of strings. Thanks to the old school of filmmaking, the long interlude offered them scope to recreate the ambience of the Broadway musicals of the bygone era.

'Baat Samjha Karo' was the first song SEL composed for Amitabh Bachchan. Shankar has one solo, 'Dheere Dheere', used in a stock situation of the hero sulking after being betrayed in love. Though the picturization is a little too tardy for anyone to watch through, the effect of the song is refreshing to hear. The songs of this movie make one wonder how great songs often get lost when they are used in films that do not become box-office hits.

In between the blockbusters, mediocre films kept coming in. Even though the films they worked for didn't often have the content to win a larger audience, SEL's quest in redefining themselves didn't cease. The indifference shown by the music labels towards promoting such lesser-heard numbers, once the films failed, led the songs to fall through the cracks. But thankfully, that didn't happen when *Lakshya* met with an unexpected failure at the box office.

Lakshya

Three years after the phenomenal success of *Dil Chahta Hai*, Farhan Akhtar, Ritesh Sidhwani, Javed Akhtar and SEL geared up again to produce another film with even greater hype. The film couldn't gain popularity, despite having the vibrant looks of another slick Excel Entertainment movie. If the success of *Dil Chahta Hai* and the super hit pair of Hrithik Roshan and Preity Zinta in *Koi Mil Gaya* were instrumental in generating excitement for *Lakshya*, the songs were also one of the prime reasons for its pre-release hype. Shankar–Ehsaan–Loy had by that time garnered a listeners' base and had a sizeable fan following. Their continuous strive to do something untested and unheard of kept the anticipation of the audience alive with every new release.

The film starts with the trumpet piece, whose sound invariably reminds one of the marching army bands or the sound heard in Hollywood war movies. It sets up the ambience of exuding the highly charged nationalistic feel of war films. The trumpet, played by a South Indian musician named Thomas, with the backdrop of the arid valley of Ladakh, fascinated the filmmaker duo so much that it became the Excel Entertainment theme music. This is similar to what Dharma Productions did with the title music of *Kuch Kuch Hota Hai* after its success.

Shankar–Ehsaan–Loy said that they composed 'Main Aisa Kyon Hoon' keeping the incredibly gifted dancer Hrithik in mind. The promo of Hrithik dancing on a kooky interlude music of 'Main Aisa Kyon Hoon' created sheer hysteria. When the tune was played to Prabhu Deva, the choreographer of the song, he was so intrigued by it that he instinctively felt like doing something new. The casual funky groove of the tune was trendy, futuristic, avant-garde and daring. The audience gets to listen to a highly stylized sound design, as Shaan's voice seems to get split and the dual voices of one singer overlap with the other. All of them decided to try out the sound on the spot. It wasn't conceived beforehand and while producing the song, ideas were all in a flow. Shankar–Ehsaan–Loy rewrote their signature build-up of crescendo leading to a catchy and peppy vocal motif as they had done with the title song of *Dil Chahta Hai.* Listeners wait for that bridge where backup vocals croon 'Oh we ee aa owe ee oh/ Oh we ee aa owe owe owe owe'.

The tune evolved out of a guitar jamming that Ehsaan and Farhan had in the studio. The casual strumming led to Farhan bringing the idea of inserting elements of hip-hop. However, the tune came in apropos with the character that Farhan had conceived. The languid pace that comes from the guitar riffs churns an image of a laidback Hrithik Roshan. The riff further evolved into a chilling background score for Farhan's *Don,* a few years down the line.

Even 'Agar Main Kahoon', the Udit–Alka duet, also comes from a guitar riff. Javed Akhtar again goes into the 'Pyar Mein Sau Uljhanein'- and 'Jaane Kyon'- mode and takes a light-hearted jibe at the paradox of falling in love. In this song, for the first time in any SEL composition, the guitar is paired with the blues harmonica, played by Kalyan Baruah. It creates a groove and resonates inside one's mind.

During this time, there was a decisive shift in the trend as far as the background scores of most contemporary films were concerned. The songs or parts of it were now used in the background and carried the ethos of the film. So, the concept of relating any particular voice with any star was getting further outdated. The background score being the effective cinematic ploy to carry forward the action was becoming important. Shankar's bold and energetic singing in 'Haan Yehi Rasta Hain Tera' thus became the most compelling voice of a war cry. With *Dus*, SEL had made it clear that for the contemporary song with a patriotic feel, the trio as the composers and Shankar as the vocalist are the best bet for the producers. As mentioned earlier, Anu Malik used Shankar's voice in a lesser-heard 'Hindustan Hindustan' in J.P. Dutta's classic, *Border*. In that song, Shankar injected his verve and gusto that brought goosebumps when blended with Kulbhushan Kharbanda's recitation on patriotism. Before *Lakshya*, Anand Raj Anand used Shankar's voice in a motivational song 'Zindagi Ek Daud Hai' for the movie, *Ehsaas: The Feeling*.

For *Lakshya*, Farhan didn't just want to make a war film. Based on Kargil's war story, he wanted to portray the inner struggle of a man aiming to excel against all odds. War is just a metaphorical representation of this inner strife. Thus, the soundtrack is not like that of other war movies where the songs often project melodrama and theatrics. Here, Javed Akhtar's lines uphold not just the soldiers' marching on the battlefront, but it shows them finding inspiration from within. The restrained and controlled instrumentation in the song renders this realistic essence to the film.

∽

Lakshya was a decisive point in the trio's career. Ehsaan's guitar peppered the entire narrative of the film, turning it from a mere war film to the likes of a modern-day sports film. The funky rock guitar riff that comes in loop in the climactic war scenes formed the base tune of the title music for *Rock On*. Farhan mentioned that the background score of *Lakshya* was one of the best, according to him. He continued:

> *Lakshya* was a mammoth film to score, there was just so much going on in the movie, from the war scenes to this personal intimate story with his dad, to the conflict with the

girl, there is so much going on. It was not an easy film to
score. And to me, that is the most memorable one in terms
of all the scores that we have done. So far [as] the sense
of background music is concerned, I don't think anybody
can do it like them.

These background scores continued to leave a strong impression
and they reached newer heights in musical and sports genres
of Excel Entertainment's later productions, *Rock On* and *Bhaag
Milkha Bhaag*.

Lakshya was one film which did not do well when it was
released, but now, after so many years, it is received well on
film channels and streaming mediums. With time, it has now
become a cult film. It also motivated a lot of people to join the
army. Loy said, 'I have seen many people getting very emotional
when they hear the theme. I know a couple of people who did
join the army just by hearing the theme and seeing the film.'
When *Lakshya* could not earn the tag of a 'hit' film score, Ehsaan
philosophized, 'So what is a hit and what is a flop! Music has
many places, it holds many places. It cannot only be for dancing
and entertainment. It doesn't make one frivolous after a point.'
Loy further said, 'Of course, we all like to feel good and happy
about it but there are times when somebody is recovering from
some health issues and emotional issues and needs a place. You
might not have a friend beside you when you need it, and at
that time music is your friend. This is the role that music plays
and that's how we see music.' Maybe this grit and mentality is
the reason for Shankar coming and working together for so long
with Ehsaan and Loy.

၄၃

Besides the big banner films, offbeat directors of low-budget
but creatively rich films also started approaching SEL. Besides
having different approaches to music, all three of them are very

down-to-earth and ever-smiling. It made it easy for new directors to approach them without any inhibitions. Revathy, Shankar's compatriot from Palakkad, was the director of the film *Phir Milenge* which addresses the social stigma surrounding AIDS. On the day of the recording, she was in a hurry, as she was flying back to Cochin the same evening. She called up Shankar and conveyed the urgency to him. Though Shankar was not ready with the tune, from the moment he received her call, a tune started taking shape in his mind. By the time Revathy entered the studio, the song 'Jeene Ke Ishaare' was ready for her. The commercial failure of the film deprives the expectant viewers of the chance to watch it on-screen. When songs like these are composed for a low-budget film with a niche target audience in mind, the shelf life gets even further minimized.

Shankar–Ehsaan–Loy was always conscious of not getting straitjacketed within any typecast. They constantly and consciously went on changing their sound, and in *Bunty Aur Babli* it took a marked departure from what they had been doing. With the success of this film, the audience base expanded and SEL reached the theatres of rural India from the plush multiplexes of the urban space. The ethnic sounds and desi beats, that the small-town audience of Northern India is more familiar with, made a return.

Bunty Aur Babli recounts the tale of a small-town couple who con everyone, and go on a roller-coaster ride through the unknown roads of smaller towns and cities until they land in Mumbai. The soundscape adapts to the narrative accordingly. The couple's adventures, their devil-may-care attitude, their invincible winning ways and their vulnerabilities carry an earthy charm. This charm would have been lost in the digitized electronica. Thus, SEL's instrumentation made a marked shift in the movie. Their expertise and felicity in this film was at par with the elites of the yesteryears.

Six

Bada bada koyale se naam falak pe likhna hain...

❧

Bunty Aur Babli

When Ketan Mehta was making the film *Oh Darling Yeh Hai India*, Shankar sang all the songs under Ranjit Barot. Shaad Ali was assisting Ketan but when Shaad came on board Shankar had already finished recording. Shaad met Shankar for the first time in the premiere of his directorial debut *Saathiya* and they started vibing with each other almost instantly. Shaad promised that he would work with Shankar in his next film. When Yash Chopra and Aditya Chopra picked Shaad for their new film *Bunty Aur Babli*, Shaad wanted to honour the commitment he had made to Shankar. That marked the beginning of a rich and endearing relationship between the two.

Writing music with folksy inflexion was not SEL's forte till then, barring the exception of one track for the movie *Shool*. Reviewers described the score as 'over the top, uninhibited, rustic and teasing spices' and thoroughly infused with the flavour of Indian folk.[8]

In *Bunty Aur Babli*, the folk style of the compositions is expanded to create the specific dialect of the part of rural India shown in the movie. The song 'Dhadak Dhadak' has this diction of Hindi-speaking rural folks. The rhythm of the train and the use of Indian percussion sounds—like that of the dholak, violin and bamboo flute—are blended to give the song a certain dynamism as well as an earthy feeling. It goes in sync with the narrative that depicts two people from second-tier cities trying to inch their way

[8]Verma, Sukanya, 'Bunty Aur Babli's Music Rocks!', *rediff.com*, 18 April 2005, https://tinyurl.com/4p4wka5n. Accessed on 6 December 2023.

to Mumbai to fulfil their ambitions. The instrumentation relies more on the heavy orchestral music of the past. The character of SEL's chorus changes here. The layers of backup vocals give way to the conventional chorus of the Hindi songs of good old days in their rhythmic 'dhinak dhin dhin dhin ta' trail.

One thing that takes the song to a different level is Gulzar's timeless lyrics. The images and metaphors that the maestro conceives, speak of his sheer poetic brilliance. Phrases like 'oye Ramchandra re' remind one of the common parlances used in Uttar Pradesh (UP). Particularly noteworthy is the way he has fused poetic images with the dialect. If the onomatopoeic 'dhadak dhadak' instantly bring in the rollicking rhythm essentially needed for a road movie, Gulzar's famous association with the moon and the lunar imagery make these earthy tones equally poetic. Shankar-Ehsaan-Loy show their mastery in the crossline of each stanza where Gulzar's lyrics reach the heights of imagery. The gradual addition and subtraction of layers from the main track helps one focus on the poetry of the line. The gradual progression of the lines make one introspect about people's dreams and aspirations. Adding to it, Sunidhi's lines are even more melodious: '*Chand Se Hokar Sadak Jati Hain/ Usi Pe Aage Jakar Apna Makaan Hoga* (The street that passes by the moon/ There, a little way ahead, would be my house).'

The lyrics keep the humour alive while also retaining the poetic appeal. The brilliant blending of English words with refined Urdu reflects the juxtaposition of magic and reality. Of course, the array of colours, peppy rhythms and vibrant pastiche of fast-moving locales, take one's mind away from the intricacies of SELs' instrumentation here. One needs to listen carefully to the song, barring the visuals, to go on a journey with the two people whose story the song embodies.

In the title song of *Bunty Aur Babli*, the bhangra beats with dholak keep the rural mood alive. But unlike any other bhangra, this has a sustained rhythm with a dholak that underlines the inherent dynamism of a road movie. As a title song, it carries the theme of the movie, and the progression of sound speaks of fast-moving vignettes of life as the characters journey towards their dreams. The antaras sound melodious as Sukhwinder and Jaspinder bring in the essential raw and earthy texture with their singing. Shankar–Ehsaan–Loy imaginatively bring a bridge between two antaras, something like a *sanchari* of an old film song, where the melody takes a detour before coming back to the rollicking rhythm of the mukhra.

Gulzar gives his poetic best for the title song and amusingly depicts the funny ways and means of this conning couple. From a melange of sound coming from multiple singers, suddenly Shankar picks up the melody, sustaining and savouring the beauty of the images that lie underneath these lines. This stroke of genius comes both from the lyricist and the composers, where a sudden withdrawal of percussive beats diverts one's attention from rhythm to melody, and the lyrics help build the poetic shades of the characters.

'Chup Chup Ke' is one of SEL's best romantic songs of all time. It is not in many songs of theirs that one comes across such a stunning and breezy violin ensemble. The progression on the violin creates tension and takes the imagination to idyllic heights. The flute weaves patterns in and out of piano chords making it an aural feast. Niladri Kumar's sitar and Naveen Kumar's flute duets in the interlude seems to have come straight from the stage of the classical fusion concerts. The crescendo builds up with the piano run in the antara, and then a sudden fade out with a brisk flute passage makes it dramatic. With the scintillating trans-Himalayan backdrop, this gradual crescendo–diminuendo of tempo suddenly opens up an ethereal dreamland. Gulzar's words paint images in the sky.

According to Mahalakshmi, this duet is one of the most beautiful songs she has sung. She marvelled at the way the minor notes of antara got shifted to major notes of the mukhra. When

Niladri walked into the studio to record 'Chup Chup Ke' and asked Shankar what was to be done, Shankar replied, 'What am I supposed to tell you what to play, you just go and play.' Niladri played for 45 minutes. It was just like a jam session. Shankar recorded everything and then selected parts of it to write the second interlude of the song. So, in the second music, there are various portions of the 45-minute piece that Niladri had played, but it sounds so seamless.

Shankar–Ehsaan–Loy got to write a 'Salaam-E-Ishq Meri Jaan' (a cult song from the film *Muqaddar Ka Sikandar*) type of song when they composed 'Kajrare'. Like the iconic *mujra*, this modern-day song earned cult status. The song starts with a couplet, where Alisha Chinai pours her oomph, and then Amitabh Bachchan, while reciting the *dholak bol*, sets up the boisterous mood of this number.

If Aishwarya Rai spreads grace all over, the screen sizzles with the towering presence of Amitabh. This falls in the modern genre of item songs, as the situation doesn't have any inseparable presence in the script. But, the poetic brilliance of Gulzar makes it an unconventional mujra that doesn't fall in the claptrap of bawdy sensuality.

The story behind the iconic song is equally interesting. After the recording of the music for *Bunty Aur Babli* was completed, one day Shaad was travelling with Shankar in his car. During that car ride, Shaad told Shankar that it was a very rare and extremely valuable coincidence that both Big B and Junior B were together in his film. He said that it would be a treat if they could bring them together in a song at some point in the film. This film was a tribute to the 1970s and 1980s cinema that they grew up on. Speaking about the composition of the song, Shaad recalled:

> Shankar told me that he had a hook of a tune but other than that he had not done anything. And he started singing

the phrase 'kajrare, kajrare'. He sang only this much and I immediately said this tune is mine. Amit ji has such a good sense of music, and the song was going to be pictured on him. So, we thought let's make him hear it. As decided, he came for the music sitting, heard the tune very carefully and after a long pause said, 'It looks as if it is starting halfway, do something else.' We were all trying to think of ideas when he came up with the brilliant suggestion of adding the bol '*dhin dhinak dhin*'. I told Amit ji to sing the song but he immediately said that since Shankar had sung it so well no one else but he would sing. He added, 'In fact even for my next film too Shankar will sing for me.'

The beginning of 'Kajrare' was a bit lengthy with quite a few hook lines. It was edited out and it gave birth to another beautiful song a few years later. That song was also a chartbuster. It was 'Tere Naina' from the film *My Name Is Khan*.

The phrase 'kajrare' was written by Shankar himself. He remembers very fondly, 'The line "*kajrare kajrare tere kale kale naina* (Your kohl-lined black eyes)" just struck me and I was very casually using it to write the tune.' Gulzar recalled, '"Kajra re" is Shankar's phrase. I had used "kajrare" in a song with Daler Mehndi. I said to Shankar that I will give you an equivalent good word. Then Shaad looked at Shankar and he looked at me in turn and said, "You write a new song, but this 'kajrare' I started humming when I was taking a bath and forming a tune." I joked that if you did it while taking a bath it is obvious that it must be cleaned of all the dirt so I think I'll keep it.' Gulzar just brought a minor change. Instead of '*kale kale naina*' Gulzar wrote '*kare kare naina*' to make it sound more rustic. Gulzar says that besides being a phenomenal singer, Shankar is a thinker too. He is always spontaneous in putting dummy words to remember the tune. Shankar is so rich with words that he used to help Gulzar with interesting words when he used to get stuck on something.

'Kajrare' was inspired, as Shankar himself said later, 'by *sankirtan*, where devotional verses sung in the praise of the Lord are repeated'. Shankar received a call from Pt Jasraj the day after the song was released. Shankar was apprehending that Pandit ji would now go after him and chide him for this 'item number'. But to Shankar's biggest delight, Pt Jasraj said, 'All day the tune of "Kajrare" has been going on in my head! I simply can't get out of it.' To this day, Shankar considers it as one of the best compliments he has ever received.

With this song, Alisha Chinai came back from a sabbatical and churned out a winner. Her recollections on the making of the song are quite interesting:

> Before 'Kajrare' they had never worked with me as a playback singer. This was 2005 when Ehsaan called up and I was in my Alibaug house. I had at that time gone into my limbo kind of, I kept taking these periodic breaks and long sabbaticals. 'Made in India' had become phenomenally big and I was in that whole space, doing shows and I was not too focussed on playback singing and all. Ehsaan told me to come back to Mumbai, and I said not today maybe some other day. But he insisted I be there in three hours and told me that this song is great, an item number and so on. So, I got into the car and went to Purple Haze. He started singing and I thought he was randomly singing some qawwali and I said this is fine but I need to listen to my song. And he said, 'This is your song, Alisha.' And I was like, 'A qawwali? This is not my style.' They said, 'Forget your style, you got to break the mould and do something that is not Alisha's style. This is a take on modern qawwali and just sing it in your style or *ada*.' I sang and it turned out to be quite amazing and they wanted to put more of it, I think. That's when they wrote the alaap, right there. Gulzar Saab penned the lyrics then and there. The magic of that gave me and

everyone goosebumps. This is a very unpredictable style for me so there was a surprise element with a new twist. Shankar knows how to exploit the lower and higher pitch of my voice. He does it so beautifully and it just became a winner. It's a Bollywood anthem.

As we all know, the song became an overnight sensation.

Speaking about Alisha lending her voice to the song, Shaad said:

Taking Alisha Chinai was Loy's idea. When he came up with the name, Shankar's eyes immediately lit up as all of us loved her voice. We were not 100 per cent sure how it would happen but I said that since the idea has a surprise element to it, it will work. Nobody would imagine Alisha singing such a song and she had not heard it for a long time too. As the song was not of her genre at all, she found it very difficult initially. But she also didn't let go and was very persistent. But when Shankar composes, he puts a very good singer to the test. I had seen the best of the best go through a grind because that's the way Shankar's compositions are. The top singers try to figure out what is in the tune because while you are hearing it in Shankar's voice one feels that anybody can sing it. The moment you actually sing it you realize the level of difficulty. Shankar is such a seamless singer himself, but a brilliant teacher as well and at the same time he comes with no baggage of ego.

Along with recording the song, SEL have some lovely memories with Amitabh as well who made them very comfortable. They always exchanged pleasantries whenever they met. They were also invited to his sixty-first birthday celebration. The music of *Kal Ho Naa Ho* had just come out at that time. They were so overwhelmed when he told them so appreciatively that he just loved it. His handwritten letters as a token of appreciation are more than an award for any artist and they were lucky to get them on more than one occasion. He did it again when the music of *Lakshya* was released. When they were doing the music for *Bunty Aur Babli*, initially he was not very happy with 'Kajrare'. He felt it was not good enough to match the stature and hype, as it was a special sequence where for the first time he and his son were coming together. But Aditya Chopra convinced him to not worry and to trust them. It was hardly surprising that this scintillating number became the biggest song of the decade, and continues to win hearts even now.

Ehsaan spoke of an interesting anecdote of the songs of the film. He said:

> We did market research on the songs. We played songs for a target audience, as to which was our best song or worst song. The best song for them was 'Chup Chup Ke' and the worst song was 'Kajrare' right at the bottom. And Adi kind of wondered, 'How's this!' Then when the song came out, it just went haywire, literally. I was out of town for four days. The song was released on Friday, I came back on Tuesday and I heard a wedding band at the airport playing 'Kajrare'. And it was like O My God! We then knew it was a big hit.

ᔕ

In the same year, 2005, Shankar won the Filmfare Award for the best male playback singer for the song 'Chandrullo Unde' of the Telegu film, *Nuvvostanante Nenoddantana* under the baton of Devi Sri Prasad.

With three musical blockbusters—*Dil Chahta Hai, Kal Ho Naa Ho* and *Bunty Aur Babli*—under their belt, SEL were touching the zenith of excellence. Expectations mounted on. All the big banner films were coming to them. Both for the class and the mass, the songs of SEL kept crossing milestones.

Kabhi Alvida Naa Kehna

After *Kal Ho Naa Ho*, Karan Johar took back the director's chair once more with *Kabhi Alvida Naa Kehna*. The passing away of Yash Johar bequeathed the mantle of Dharma Productions entirely to Karan. For the first time, Karan became a producer, director and writer all rolled into one. The tried and tested combination of Javed Akhtar and SEL was an inevitable choice. Staying true to the grandeur of a Karan Johar movie, SEL came out with a magnificent and opulent soundscape. The intensely personal approach towards the liaison-armouries of two married individuals, and the largeness of the film's premise, might have gone against the ambitious project of navigating the sensitive topic. The film earned polarized verdicts, but the songs of the film became blockbuster hits from their very release.

The team was in Taj Village in Goa when they were composing music for *Kabhi Alvida Naa Kehna*. But the supposed 'workation' to compose music for the film turned out to be yet another cheery vacation. They whiled away the time laughing and having fun. Ehsaan recollected with a smile, 'When you go away from the city, suddenly the pace slows down. For us, Goa has always been a place to detox, just going and lying down in the sun. No work and nothing to think about. The pulse automatically came down the moment we landed at the airport and immediately went into the relaxed zone.' The *Dil Chahta Hai* vibes had caught them yet again.

For Karan's movies, from the promotional stuff to the posters the films would invariably come with an anticipation of something bigger than the normal fares. The soundtrack by SEL for Dharma Productions played a large role in bringing modern-day Indian Bollywood music to the international doorstep. The extensive and overarching sound, commonly associated with Hollywood productions, started to be heard even in Indian films. Karan had always attached a lot of importance to the soundtrack of his films and wanted the music of his directorial comeback to be extremely impressive.

In the opening sequence, the blend of piano, English lyrics and an Indian wedding song instantly struck a chord with the diasporic audience. The mellow visuals of dry leaves flying off the ground, matched with the sound of a large orchestra, help prepare one for a cinematic extravaganza. The voices of two of the most popular singers—Sonu Nigam and Alka Yagnik—make 'Tumhi Dekho Na' a retro-style Hindi love song. The song was developed on a riff from the interlude music of the title song.

The title song with all its high emotional quotient, sounds a bit weepy. The *thapki* of the dholak has the feel of a heavy heart struggling to beat sorrow. But the trance version of the title song, with Western techno arrangement, is strikingly dissimilar. The unfamiliar trance sound in a Hindi movie shows that SEL were now truly becoming a global phenomenon, and were not just the flagbearer of the Bollywood movie industry. Shankar–Ehsaan–Loy's talent also comes out in 'Where's the Party Tonight?'—a disco song with a certainty of finding a place in the dance hits or playlists of party hoppers.

The song 'Mitwa' blurred the boundary between a film song and a classical fusion number. The filmy situations often take away the music composer's freedom to write songs. But here, one complemented the other. The guitar pick-up; the prolonged straight notes of the song that follow the guitar; and the camera rapidly panning 360 degrees on the iconic Shah Rukh Khan

standing with open arms, left a lasting impression in the mind
of the audience. This and the one where Shah Rukh was running
on the promenade with street lamps lining the way, created iconic
frames for Bollywood romances of the new millennium. The tune
was inducive to bringing in the images of romance that later, Vidya
Balan wanted to play it on the sets of her film *Kismat Konnection*
to bring alive her romantic scenes with Shahid Kapoor.

Shankar's trademark sargam in the interludes; the prominence
of the sarod that Shankar himself played and used so masterfully;
and the delicate use of the tabla make the song classical. But the use
of English lyrics and the guitar riffs make it sound Westernized in
parts, complementing the foreign locales where the song was shot.
Caralisa's one-liner of 'love will find the way' was composed and
sang in a typically hushed style, bringing in the groovy Western
element in the essentially Indianized song. While recording the
song, Shankar told Caralisa to sing the way she felt was right.
The confidence shown by him made her comfortable to deliver
her best. Caralisa's distinctive style of singing was used by SEL
in so many songs in which they wanted to create a groove that
typically goes with Westernized tunes. In a song from *Dil Jo Bhi
Kahey*, the theme music with Caralisa's vocals gave one the feel
of a Broadway musical. In another background vocal of a beach
sequence, Caralisa sang French lyrics in sotto voce, making it
sound even groovier.

Shankar's confidence in his singers has always charmed the
people who record for him. Farhan said, 'Shankar is a packet of
energy. Shankar walks into the room as if a heart has walked in.
He has such a positivity around him.' It is that infectious energy
that brings the best out of everyone. Caralisa was done recording
'Mitwa' after two or three takes. He was pushing Caralisa to give
her best, and once he was satisfied with the output, he shouted,
'Finished Cara. Done. Get out.' Caralisa smilingly said, 'He used to
make me sing and when you got what you wanted it was like get
out of this place. It was done.' Caralisa also got the credit in the

song where she sang just a few words. Caralisa said, 'The credit to an artist has been a very hierarchical thing in this industry. But these three are of the same belief that it is impossible without teamwork. Without the artists' involvement, how can the song be a success? And they do give credit to all the artists.'

The song's high impact was also owing to the talented Pakistani singer Shafqat Amanat Ali, son of noted classical vocalist Ustad Amanat Ali Khan. Ehsaan had heard him singing 'Aankhon Ke Saagar' in his band Fuzön's superhit album *Saagar*, and suggested his name to Shankar. Shankar too had heard his songs in his car when a radio channel was playing it and had loved Shafqat's voice texture. Shankar–Ehsaan–Loy deliberately kept 'Mitwa' in the same key as that of 'Aankhon Ke Saagar'. Shafqat came in, sang and literally won his way into Bollywood. With his usual tongue-in-cheek humour, Ehsaan said, 'Fuzön band broke up because of us. After "Mitwa" his whole career changed.' Indeed, post 'Mitwa', Shafqat made a song march in Bollywood film music. His unique singing style with his mastery of classical music gave him a new identity. Hindi films got a fresh new voice as well. And Shankar got the fodder of adding one more ace up his sleeve to enthral thousands in his concerts.

At the 'Aman ki Asha' concert, held on 13 February 2011, Shankar and Shafqat enthralled the audience with their *jugalbandis*. Both have immense respect and fondness for each other. Shafqat holds Shankar in high regard and says that he is a very cool and chilled-out person despite being supremely talented. He says that SEL gave him the freedom to contribute to the very enriching song. The camaraderie between the two is extremely infectious and the live concerts are a treat for the fans from both sides of the border.

∽

As filmmaking is a collaborative art, there have always been some instances of partnership where any music composer shared creative vibes with particular directors and producers. After the 'Breathless' music video, *Dil Chahta Hai* and *Lakshya*, Farhan Akhtar and the movies of Excel Entertainment had SEL as the automatic choice of music composers for any of their ventures. This led to many fruitful endeavours and the next one that came from their camp was for Farhan's *Don*.

Don, Salaam-E-Ishq and Beyond

When Farhan Akhtar decided to give a refurbished look to one of the classics of all time, he knew that there would be an inevitable and painstaking comparison with the old iconic film which had etched itself in the psyche of the Hindi moviegoers. For any middle-aged Hindi movie lover, there would be an inevitable hangover of the Amitabh classic but for the younger audience—armed with the taste they had picked up from MTV and Coke Studio, accustomed to the pyro techniques of modern-day Hollywood flicks and jazzy electronic sounds—there was no falling back on the narrative structure and technicalities of old Hindi films. Farhan gave a glitzy and avant-garde look to the old film to woo the young audience. So, for them, *Don: The Chase Begins Again* is actually a tale of a new chase and not one that follows any beaten trail. This freshness of approach towards something tried and tested needed a filmmaker with a vision, an aim to experiment and take the craft of modern-day filmmaking forward. Farhan did a stupendous job of taking a leaf from the 1970s classic and reshaping it with a newer style, suited to the modern-day taste.

After making a sensational debut in *Dil Chahta Hai* and dealing with a tough theme in *Lakshya*, with not much of a commercial success, Farhan zeroed in on this audacious remake. Apart from using the modern diction of filmmaking, the off-beat camera movement and the use of muted colours, Farhan brought in a different electro feel with SEL's music. The soundtrack of *Don* finds SEL's experimentation at its very best. They served a fare that could not be branded as an insouciant shrug towards the towering presence of the fortress created by Kalyanji–Anandji, Kishore Kumar and Asha Bhosle. They created a soundtrack that catered to the taste of generation next. The theme music of this new film was sourced from the original Kalyanji–Anandji background score but was robed with a modern contemporary twang that borrowed heavily from electronically synthesized music.

This remake would have bordered on blasphemy if the director and the music composers hadn't kept the original song that gave the film its identity. The modern version of 'Main Hoon Don' is classy and sophisticated. A song-and-dance situation in a villain's den has been a popular trope ever since the inception of Hindi films and film music. But Farhan made this contemporary version with a lot of thought and played with the use of camera, lighting and even the colour of the sequence. Everything has a style in its making.

Shankar–Ehsaan–Loy's music is an integral part of the entire process. The song almost issued out of the *Don* theme, or rather the *Don* theme grew into a full-bodied song through this. There is a cool confidence in Shaan's voice, and an element of tension with the sustained electronically-programmed beats. The gradual progression towards the hook line; the phrases with keyboards; and the brilliant camera movement with close-ups of the characters, in the backdrop of large-sounding organ music, make it feel sinister. It has the charm of a background score of a Hollywood flick, with its unpredictability and non-linear approach. The techno sound vibes well even with today's audience, and simultaneously the song keeps alive the memories of the Kishore Kumar classic.

'Yeh Mera Dil' was another iconic Asha Bhosle number that outlived the popularity of the film itself. The situation being similar to 'Main Hoon Don', SEL didn't fool around with the main melody of this song but gave it an electronic twist with programmed beats and great sound design while using Sunidhi's deep hushed voice.

There was always a scare of receiving brickbats while recreating this evergreen Asha Bhosle number. Shankar-Ehsaan-Loy took up the challenge and gave it their best shot. The prelude being the same, and Kareena Kapoor enticing Shah Rukh the way a cat-eyed Helen had done with Amitabh, brought back the memories of the original. The pace of the song is as infectious as the one before. The verve in Sunidhi's singing takes one back to the disco era of Nazia Hassan or the American singer Donna Summer. But the techno sound and the rhythm program bring a club feel to it. It keeps the nostalgic value intact, while bringing glitz into it. Sunidhi recollects:

> I can never forget the recording of 'Ye Mera Dil'. I was very sceptical as a singer because this song was sung by Asha ji and people were already so very crazy about the original. I was worried about how would I do justice to such a song. But I think it was Shankar's clear vision. He wanted me to sing it not generally how I do on stage. He told me to go a little huskier and a little sultry and I think that worked. But I was very worried because when you think of Helen ji and if I don't sing in that particular way then how would I do justice to the song? But I knew when I heard the track as to why he was saying all this to me. The track was completely different from the original. The approach was different; it was very new age with new sounds. The groove was very different and that helped me sing in a softer and sultry voice and it then sounded good.

When the song started making waves after its release, Shankar got a call from Dubai. A lady, in a voice filled with affection and mock anger scolded him, saying, 'I am very angry with you. Why did you give my song to Sunidhi? This is *my* song and I should have sung it.' Both Shankar and the greatest diva of all time, Asha Bhosle, broke out in laughter.

Shankar-Ehsaan-Loy stayed truest to the original tune of

'Khaike Pan Banaraswala' and made Udit bring in that rustic flavour as a departure from the film's predominantly urban tone. Shankar–Ehsaan–Loy introduced a new stanza at the beginning and made Shah Rukh Khan croon a few lines. Ehsaan's explanation can throw light on what was going on in their mind during the recording of this Kishore Kumar classic. He said:

> We were very scared about this song. If we had to change it, it would have been very difficult to compose a new song that would stand up to that. So, when we started recording it, we thought to make it a little different by putting a rap part in between, so that gives it a slightly contemporary feel to the song.

'Mourya Re' is one of the two original numbers in the film. The song was picturized on a situation that was a quintessential part of Hindi films—the Ganesh idol immersion scenes in Mumbai. The song follows this tradition with the added zing that came from the SEL camp. The banjo, dhol tasha and nagada beats sustain the ethnic elements common to the songs popular during these festivities where people dance with gay abandon, in a unique style called Ganapati dance. Shankar was quite invariably the best bet to sing the song, as the multifaceted singer possesses a strong proclivity towards singing devotional and high-energy numbers.

The other original number that SEL composed turned out to be one of the best-ever compositions from them. Alisha Chinai made another gorgeous comeback after the sensational 'Kajrare'. Mahalakshmi proved to be SEL's most trusted voice in all sorts of musical experiments that they had, and Sonu injected a fresh lease of life in 'Aaj Ki Raat'. Javed Akhtar, the ultimate link binding the eras of the past and the present, penned the lines and weaved images of growing mystery.

The song is placed in the film's narrative in the climactic moment, before the action reaches its end. The gradual tension towards the hook line increases the suspense. The electro beats keep a sustained tempo, and an upbeat lounge ambience brings a shimmering effect to the entire soundscape. With a unique sound processing, the voices seem to be in the background as music takes centre stage. Farhan said, 'In "Aaj ki Raat" what we wanted people to groove to was that very '60s-'70s disco feel; that classic groove. That was something that had to go into your inside. You have to get possessed by it. So, that is why it is processed like that.'

Shankar–Ehsaan–Loy were a little apprehensive about the outcome of the song but it turned out to be the main hit of the film. In the film as well, the song happens during an action-heavy time when in the middle of the song a lot of crucial plot devices are unfolding. That is why there is an extended musical piece in the song. Farhan did not want to cut the music or the song, as he wanted to show that scene and come back to the song. Throughout the music piece, one can see what is happening— something similar to the films of the past like *Yaadon Ke Baaraat* or *Arjun*. This was a quintessential 1970s song, with a modern feel to it.

Don was released at a time when people of the millennia took it to be a film for their generation. If a remake had been done within a decade of its original release, it would have called for immense criticism. But a gap of more than three decades helped this new-age *Don* get an identity of its own. As a gangster film, Farhan made *Don* very contemporary. Shankar–Ehsaan–Loy took another step ahead in producing an album based on electro music. This further got enhanced in thrillers like *Johhny Gaddaar* and the sequel of *Don*.

∽

Shankar–Ehsaan–Loy completed the first 10 years of their musical journey in style. The triumvirate who got into mainstream Bollywood movies as passing wayfarers—to sneak and peek before retreating to their pastures of music—became discerning figures and the pioneers of new-age sound in Hindi movies. They sauntered with a cavalier attitude of setting their own terms, marking it with an affable nonchalance to the conventional fares. Within a decade, it was no surprise that their coterie of admirers grew. The music of *Don* was released with great fanfare and so was their next release *Salaam-E-Ishq*.

The critics who found the music of *Dil Chahta Hai* to be nothing more than a frothy Indi-pop album started writing paeans of praise for the innovative and experimental approach of the trio. *Salaam-E-Ishq* was much touted at its release with a stylish poster, the very title reminding one of a ditty that remains enmeshed in one's sensibilities with an enviable ensemble of cast. The film eventually turned out to be a drag in its interminable length of almost four hours. But the album only goes on to show the versatility of the trio.

∽

Producers Mukesh Talreja and Sunil Manchanda produced three movies with Salman Khan as the lead and Himesh Reshammiya as their music director. In their fourth outing, they had Nikkhil Advani as their director and, after the resounding success of *Kal Ho Naa Ho*, it was quite natural that Nikkhil asked the producers to rope in SEL. With Salman being the hero of their fourth consecutive film, *Salaam-E-Ishq*, dedicated to the memory of Late Mukul Anand, was the first major Salman film that SEL worked on. Shankar–Ehsaan–Loy composed seven diverse songs that carried their winning streak despite the film failing miserably.

In apropos to the theme of having multiple love stories tying into one, SEL composed an assortment of varied tunes. It has Adnan Sami's 'Dil Kya Kare', a lilting number having an outlandish feel of an urban vagabond's life of culling pleasures. In the song, an innocuous, nearly missable tinkling sound suddenly evolves into a fascinating progression of tune from nowhere. It also has a Shaan–Nihira Joshi duet, 'Mera Dil', which can easily be touted as one of the most mellifluous SEL romantic song. There was a qawwali 'Saiyyan Re' and a bhangra 'Tenu Leke'. But SEL brought a twist to the conventional genre with controlled use of percussions and an infusion of stylish beats and piano lending it a lounge qawwali feel. And then, there was also the soulful 'Ya Rabba' from Kailash Kher.

Nihira was another find who was asked to sing a little part of the 'Dhadak Dhadak' song from *Bunty Aur Babli*. Shankar knew her from his jingle-making days and had mentored her. When Shankar used to work for a pithy cameo, singing songs with the towering presence of the big names of playback, he loved to see his name on the inlays of the cassettes. Now Nihira was, to her biggest delight, accredited for the smallest part that she sang.

Salaam-E-Ishq had the promise of an unusual theme, but the script somewhat faltered while dealing with the complicated web of plots. But T-series is said to have minted a good amount of money for this album and the blockbuster *Taare Zameen Par*. With *Salaam-E-Ishq*, SEL came out with an album that could eventually make a presence of its own, undeterred by the film's fate.

Shankar's Parents: R. Narayan and Seetha Narayan

Shankar's father

Shankar Mahadevan as a kid

Shankar in his teens

Shankar with his friends at a picnic (*left to right*: Rajesh, Shankar, Manoj, Umesh)

Shankar on a horse ride at Matheran

Shankar sharing a late night, fun moment with friends after having pav bhaji and juice in Central Mumbai

Shankar with his veena

Shankar in one of many competitions where winning first prize was a cakewalk for him

Shankar and Sangeeta in the early days of their relationship

Shankar and Sangeeta on their marriage day

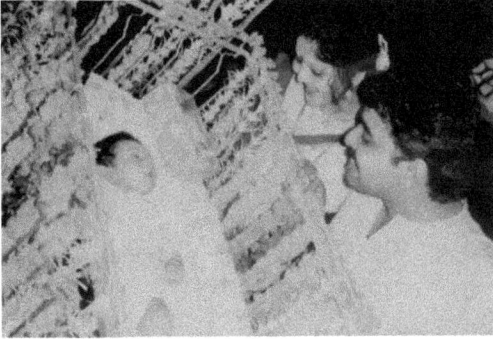

Birth of Siddharth

Shankar and Siddharth spending quality time together

Shankar with the kids in the family including young
Siddharth and Shivam

Shankar–Ehsaan–Loy

Sangeeta with the amazing trio

Shankar–Ehsaan–Loy with Karan Johar

Shankar, Ghulam Ali and other musicians in the sets of a reality show

On the stage of 'My Country, My Music' with his fellow singers

Zakir Hussain, Louiz Banks, Shankar, Sanjay Divecha

Performing at a Remember Shakti concert (*left to right*: John McLaughlin, V. Selvaganesh, Shankar, U. Srinivas, Zakir Hussain)

Shankar with the teachers of Shankar Mahadevan Academy

Shankar with Zakir Hussain

Shankar with Javed Akhtar

Shankar with Gulzar

Shankar with Shivam in a concert

Shankar receiving an honorary doctorate from Birmingham City University in England

Shankar receiving the prestigious Padma Shri award

Shankar, Sangeeta, Siddharth, Shivam and Shankar's mother, Seetha Narayan

Shankar, Sivamani, Karl Peters and Louiz Banks (*sitting at front*)

Shankar–Ehsaan–Loy at a concert

The close-knit, happy family of the Mahadevans

Shankar at his old school

Shankar in *Katyar Kaljat Ghusali*

Shankar–Ehsaan–Loy with Farhan Akhtar

Shankar and The Originals at the fiftieth birthday celebration of Mohan Vijayan. He was the first Original to celebrate this milestone. (*left to right*: Umesh, Mohan, Shankar, Rajesh, Manoj, Suresh, Sudarshan and Sangeeta)

The Happy Family: Shankar, Sangeeta, Siddharth and Shivam

Shankar with The Originals

On the fiftieth anniversary world tour of Shakti (*left to right*: V. Selvaganesh, Zakir Hussain, Shankar, Ganesh Rajagopalan, John McLaughlin)

Shankar and Sangeeta at the Ganesh Puja at their home

Jhoom Barabar Jhoom

Shankar–Ehsaan–Loy had two back-to-back releases in mid-2007 which were strikingly dissimilar to each other. *Jhoom Barabar Jhoom* was a love story and *Johnny Gaddaar* was a slick crime thriller. But both the movies took their cavalier streak to new heights. The brilliance of the music composers, riding high on the crest of supreme confidence, comes across loud and clear in the wantonness of both these movies. *Jhoom Barabar Jhoom* marked an upward curve in the career graph of the two-film old Shaad Ali, who wanted to bring in modern jargon in conventional love stories. If *Saathiya* is an urban love story and *Bunty Aur Babli* is the tale of a small-town couple, *Jhoom Barabar Jhoom* shifts gear to a surreal love story. Despite being a contemporary slice-of-life movie, it borders on exaggerated and hyperbolic expressions of love, overtly dramatic situations and a series of improbable probabilities of a fantasy film. Thus, the language of the same old love story got an avant-garde twist in this one.

Shaad reiterated the story of how once he went to the railway station to receive someone. While waiting, he visualized an idea of what would happen if he met a stranger who had come there with the same purpose. The story of *Jhoom Barabar Jhoom* was built around that hypothetical situation. The film needed a background score that would sync with the theatrical plot. Shankar–Ehsaan–Loy came on board again with their out-of-the-box ways of framing a soundscape.

The narrative is frequented by the title song all throughout the movie, and every time the song is heard, it appears to be a lyrical extension of the series of events that follow. The tune evolves and adopts itself to various situations, actions and characters at different points in time, going in sync with the narrative flow. Instead of penning different songs or remixing the root version, SEL brought in subtle changes to the root tune with a shift in tempo and instrumentation. Gulzar's lyrics carry forth the action, lending more evolved dimensions to the characters and events.

As the image of a phantasmal Amitabh Bachchan in sartorial flamboyance springs up in the scene, with Shankar singing out a Punjabi bhangra, the aura seems to emanate a charm much reminiscent of 'Kajrare'. The woodwind sound has a zippy feel that instantly hooks the listeners. The brilliance in the verse, the dialect that renders it a typically North Indian regional flavour and the cheekiness with which it was written help create a mystical mood.

While Shankar's emotive rendering blends sufi notes with the bhangra beats, the guitar riffs bring a spirit of rock. The experience turns out to be carnival-esque when the rhythm matches with Amitabh's infectious histrionics.

The version changes pace when the two couples, Abhishek–Lara and Bobby–Preity meet in a dance competition. The bhangra beats break into a lounge EDM rhythm. The tempo becomes faster, with the young, dynamic characters sizzling and dancing in colourful sets. Multiple singers bring a party-like feel to the tune. And finally, when Amitabh, the highway troubadour, appears with his double-neck guitar—the same one that Shaad had gifted Ehsaan—flashes his boisterously impish smile and jigs against the backdrop of bursting laser rays, it simply leaves the viewers breathless in admiration.

Amitabh's character, wearing a mosaic of carpet-like costumes, was based on the troubadours one comes across in Europe. Shaad said that it was a very difficult costume to put together and dance in as well. Shaad made him a *sutradhaar* who connects the stories of different characters from the past and present. After the success of *Bunty Aur Babli*, it was quite likely to be used as the reference point for new songs. But on the contrary, Shaad wanted to create a new variant. Later, Yash Chopra told Shaad that this was India's proper musical film that had a story and music like a Broadway show.

Shankar–Ehsaan–Loy left their mark in the film's best number, so to speak, where the lovers are transported into the dream world by the sheer melody of 'Bol Na Halke Halke'. It strikingly stands apart from other songs. The dream-sequence intermission gave them a chance to go traditional with the sound of *matka* and strings. The melodious sarangi, played by Dilshad Khan, was heard after decades in a Hindi film song. The *sufiana* of Rahat Fateh Ali Khan and the sweet voice of Mahalakshmi made it a song that listeners fell back on long after the film fizzed out. Mahalakshmi threw light on the process of composing the melody of this song, saying:

I have never heard them say 'let's do something'. It has always fallen into place. I realized how they bridge the gap because one is a blues specialist, one is an Indian classical specialist and one is a Western classical specialist. But how they brought together those three styles and merged them without overpowering anyone! For example, 'Bol Na Halke Halke' is co-composed half by Shankar and half by Ehsaan. I remember Ehsaan humming the 'Bol Na Halke Halke' tune very early and then Shankar brought in the other part. So, most of the compositions would be like that, one line Ehsaan would sing, Shankar would add the next line or vice versa.

Shaad, the man who started his career with A R Rahman and then remained steadfast either with him or SEL, pointed out how the trio worked. He said:

SEL are like any other creative force, with their highs and lows, good and bad, but at the end of the day, the consistent thing about them is their integrity and their purity. Their

honesty is unquestionable and incomparable with anybody
I have seen or heard of in our contemporary time. They
will never try and push even a palm of a song that you are
unhappy with. It comes from an advertising background
experience that you are used to very easily, so-called
'bouncing of a track', or rejection of a track. But it is very
difficult to say no to a Shankar tune.

Fellow musicians and directors attributed the carefree atmosphere
of SEL's studio to them giving their best and being content in
the creative process. There is a 'band boys' kind of vibe they
carry everywhere. The propensity to include everyone in their
creative process never allows any unease to grow between any two
professionals. Vishal Dadlani who sang 'Kiss of Love', admitted
that despite being a contemporary of his, Shankar was also a
'kind of mentor'. Vishal knew him from the 'Dance Masti' days,
when Shankar used to sing Kishore Kumar numbers. They had
that sort of relationship where they could hang out in each other's
sessions. Vishal said that Shankar has always been someone who
is very encouraging, and is always open to using new sounds. He
is inventive in every context. Vishal had no qualms playing all
the Vishal–Shekhar compositions to them and Shankar would be
calling him to sing any SEL song where he felt that Vishal would
do justice. Two films under the Yash Raj banner were happening
simultaneously, *Jhoom Barabar Jhoom* and *Ta Ra Rum Pum*, where
Vishal–Shekhar were composing the music. Vishal recalled:

> There was great excitement in Yashraj studio regarding the
> music of JBJ [*Jhoom Barabar Jhoom*]. We were working in
> adjacent rooms and used to have lunch together regularly.
> We used to sit together, chat and talk about all the bizarre
> things that happened in the film business. When I went
> to sing 'Kiss of Love' they were all very kind to me, as
> they always are. That is actually the song that gave me an
> understanding of how different we are. There is so much to

learn from interacting with other musicians. Every time I have interacted with Shankar I have always learnt something without question. There are few people I have seen through whom music flows. I don't think I can ever imagine Shankar being stuck for an idea. Music is there and he is the channel for it.

Vishal–Shekhar's and SEL's studios were in very close proximity and they used to visit each other very often. There was mutual appreciation and admiration, where each sourced inspiration from the other. This solidarity led them to sing in one another's camp as well. Shankar started singing more for these next-generation music composers. Songs like 'Desi Girl' from *Dostana* happened that way, when just a sudden flash of imagination led to the composition of the song. Shankar was called in and the song was done in a jiffy. Shekhar on the other hand, was called in to sing 'Yeh Zindagi Bhi' for *Luck By Chance*, where the song was recorded within 20 minutes. Both the songs were extremely popular.

Johnny Gaddaar

The trio kept pushing their limits with astonishing consistency. With 10 years of experience and quite a few musical blockbusters in their repository, SEL were riding on the waves of confidence like a slap-happy fencer blowing his épée in gay abandon. When SEL met Sriram Raghavan—the man who redefined neo-noir Bollywood movies with his stylized filmmaking—it sparked up a scintillating reciprocity of ideas. The thriller, *Johnny Gaddaar*, came straight from the director's obsession with the caper movies of Vijay Anand, James Hadley Chase's novels and French noir films. At the same time, it also had a Quentin Tarantino swank that simply stunned the audience with its tautness in narrative. It needed a soundtrack to bolster the mood and elegance of the film. Shankar–Ehsaan–Loy carried out the task with an unpronounced swagger. The flamboyance is felt in every note they composed. The scores they wrote carried the theme with elan and infallible precision.

The audience was frustrated to find no full-length song in the film. Especially when they had heard the songs on other online platforms, they were expecting them to be picturized as well. But the director didn't compromise the relentless pace of the thriller with any song interpolation. Songs were used in bits as the background score of the movie. Sriram Raghavan sourced from old Bollywood stuff, the movies of Vijay Anand and as a stylish tribute to the late maestro titled the film *Johnny Gaddaar*. He wanted the 1970s music scene to be recreated on the modern canvas. Hence, came the luxurious use of trumpet, whose blasts invariably recall R.D. Burman's iconic 'Duniya Mein Logon Ko'. This is an incredible pastiche of music, which at once has a retro feel and a never-heard-before recklessness.

He used strains of *Bandini's* cult Lata Mangeshkar song 'Mora Gora Ang Laile', casted Dharmendra at its backdrop to trigger the vintage value of the character and feel of an aura of a bygone era. Dharmendra even utters a Sergio Leone-esque dialogue, 'It's not the age but the mileage that counts.' Shankar–Ehsaan–Loy left their indelible mark when they blended the retro feel with a new age sound. In order to break new ground, they kept only one familiar voice and that was Shankar's. This brings a new timbre, an unheard feel, and sustains the surprise element much in sync with the thriller's narrative.

Shankar–Ehsaan–Loy used the rapper Hard Kaur for the first time in 'Move Your Body'. In this song, one gets a strong dose of electro bhangra and hip-hop beats. But this techno sound comes blended with a voice that sings 'doob ja mere pyar mein', which has a texture of early 1950s Bollywood black-and-white movies. The bass groove and the eclectic electric guitar riffs jolt anyone whose ears are used to the common songs of the time. This is iconoclasm at its best. Anusha Mani's way of singing has the déjà vu feel of *Don's* 'Aaj Ki Raat'. The techno beats captivate the mind to take a sneak peek at the underbelly of one's psyche. The music has a visual appeal that evokes a sense of foreboding and premonition, as expected in a thriller. The gung-ho attitude of the singers, the wildness of the sound and the unbridled energy that sizzles out of the track only speak of the rebel's insanely unconventional approach.

Even with all of this, it is in the title song that SEL seem to have excelled. They constantly keep setting up new benchmarks, which they take up as a challenge to surpass with elegance. It is a pity that this particular song remained constrained only to snippets in the film. But the title song is the truest example of the global reach of a Bollywood flick, and the music of a thriller that beats any international project hands down. There is a distinct retro strain but the electro feel with the dangling, languid guitar loop give it a psychedelic trance feel at its best. The guitar gives it a sinister edge. Even with its frenetic pace, its trump lies in its languid long notes, the contrasting singing style of a shrieking Suraj Jagan and a near whisper of Akriti Kakar. The antaras hit the mind straight, releasing a gust of adrenaline with hard drumming. The sensuous undertones of the aphoristic lyrics, placed in a hard rock psychedelic soundscape only goes to prove SEL's disdainful brushing aside of anything tried and tested.

∽

The dearth of a neo-noir movie in Hindi didn't allow SEL to replicate this sound, till a similar situation came up in one of the latest movies of 2022, *Dhaakad*. Or even if thrillers came, they were conscious to keep the sound of *Johnny Gaddaar* exclusive. However, *Dhaakad* with the premise of a thriller might be an intolerable drag with an excess of mindless violence. But the Nikhita Gandhi–Shankar Mahadevan duet, 'Namonishan' is a great recall of the songs of *Johnny Gaddaar*.

Seven

Tu dhoop hai chhan se bikhar...

Taare Zameen Par

Once, when asked about SEL's sound and its distinctive features, Ehsaan remonstrated that there was no such thing as 'SEL sound' because it kept on changing as per the demands and objectives of the films. They consciously kept themselves malleable. Notwithstanding this conscious effort to search for newer sounds and more innovative idioms of musical expressions, there was an unmistakable identity that the trio left in most of their compositions. There was a style, sophistication and aesthetics of sound that was quite discerningly theirs.

When Aamir Khan launched his own movie house, Aamir Khan Productions, and made a directorial debut with *Taare Zameen Par*, one expected that it would not be the usual run-of-the-mill fare but something different and fascinating. As expected, the music falls in line with Aamir's out-of-the-box ideas. The entire soundscape doesn't have a resemblance to any pattern or style of music SEL had written in their first 10 years, and neither is it similar to the work they did later. The film marks a transition in their career where they paused and produced one of the most introspective and thoughtful music of their career. The film tries to explore an untested domain of the problems of a dyslexic kid. It boldly renounces the normal pattern of storytelling in Hindi films, as Aamir makes his entry in the second half.

Shankar–Ehsaan–Loy were the obvious choice because of their non-conformity with any pattern that existed before. But for a single song, where Aamir peps up the sagging morale of a norms-afflicted bunch of school kids with an energetic 'Bum

Bum Bole', all songs are used as background scores. But unlike the modern-day movies, where only a strain of the background score is heard, here songs are used in full because songs form the lyrical expressions of the narrative.

The title song of *Taare Zameen Par* finds Shankar singing at his emotive best. Prasoon's earnest lyrics and Shankar's voice at the backdrop of a flurry of special kids rejoicing in an atmosphere of abandon and gaiety, make it an intensely personal experience. The honesty with which Shankar outpours his heartfelt feelings and prays that the little stars don't crash from the sky to the ground—'*Kho na jaye yeh, taare zameen par*'—tugs the most delicate emotions that lie within everyone's heart. Prasoon's use of metaphors sound as simple as the innocence of kids, but the thoughts expressing the pristine feelings of children touch the soul when they are garbed with the tune.

Shankar has never sounded as soulful as he does in the title song. As sunshine lights up everything that lies in the dark, here the melody lights up the lyrics and the sentiments they carry. This song was added to the quiver of songs that Shankar performs in every concert. In some concerts, the presence of a band of beautiful kids crooning along with the maestro creates a profound atmosphere rarely experienced on stage shows.

'Jame Raho' is based on peppy rhythm and Vishal brought out the realistic as well as the funny undertones of the lyrics with his energetic singing. The song is used as a background to capture the world of the central character. The rap and reggae style of singing make it a lyrical commentary on the child protagonist Ishaan's daily life, infested with the cruel demands of his routine-bound existence. Thus, the song is not just a musical break from the continuity of the narrative, but an interesting look inside the mind of the protagonist. While narrating his experience of singing the song, Vishal only reiterated what every other singer has also pointed out—the preceptor in Shankar and how he draws the best out of anybody who comes and sings for them. Vishal said,

'Jame Raho' is a very special song for me. Before the recording when Shankar effortlessly sings to demonstrate, everything sounds so easy. But when a singer goes on to record, he realizes that even if it is effortless for Shankar, it is not half effortless for him. The way Shankar would make you sing when you are at the mic, he makes you feel that you are the greatest singer on earth. Like there is no one better, bigger than you at that moment. This [is] an art because the singer can deliver with inventiveness when you have an atmosphere of confidence, when you feel like everyone is on your side. You are not fighting a battle, you don't have to win against anyone but we are all together. That is Shankar's uncanny ability. So, in the song 'Jame Raho' there is a breakdown where I am singing exactly like Shankar and I do sound like him. Imagine what a good teacher he is that without effort, he has never said that to me in words but, somehow, he has communicated that and it is so audible.

'Kholo Kholo' is a cinematic experience by itself, as the visuals that supplement the song present a separate film within the film. Even if one hears the song without the visuals, the audio itself churns up images that have the capacity to recreate a film-scape within the mind. This has been an example of SEL's minimalism working at its best. Of course, it has the strength of the lyrics from Prasoon Joshi. However, the musical arrangements of the lyrics effectively bring out the profound sensitivity of the expressions. The song is a poetic representation of the opening of a mind. The progression of the tune is parallel to this gradual proliferation of a kid's imagination.

This is a journey into the deepest core of the kid's mind, where an intangible yearning lies dormant. It is based on a brilliant progression with rhythm guitar. Ehsaan's guitar and Raman Mahadevan's whisperings stealthily take us into the inner world of a child. The guitar riff continues to the next level, where the lyrics become even more symbolic. Prasoon goes Gulzar-esque to bring out Ishaan's world. The metaphors stream through the melody:

Tujhmein agar pyaas hai
Baarish ka ghar bhi paas hai

If there's thirst in you
The house of rain too is close by

Here, a bassline is added and the pattern of the riff changes. Quite imperceptibly, the horizon broadens. The melody guides one to a more open space where the imagination journeys through and inundates the sky. The guitar carries one to that space.

This is how a teacher envisions his child to be. This is how he wishes for the flowering of a child's soul. The climactic rise of sound, where the crescendo comes with layers of electric guitar seamlessly blending with Loy's keyboard, encompasses the universe of Ishaan's imagination. The chimes from multiple guitars create ripples in the brain, as it further opens. With the soundscape of guitar, keys and drums, the mood gets uplifted. An extremely delicate visual landscape, distilled with the most subtle nuances of the mind, opens up. The film version of the song has an extended use of Loy's keys. It matches with the picturization of brilliant images of colours merging to give shape to a concrete picture.

The kid's flight of fantasy reaches idyllic heights. The music here is cathartic. The layering of sound fixates the listener to a state of blissful stillness. Like many SEL films, even in *Taare Zameen Par,* songs and soundtracks of the film are extensions of one another. There is a piece of rhythm guitar backup, when Ishaan is slowly picking up his lessons. The guitar brings in an element of optimism. The same can be said of an imaginative background piano piece, when Aamir motivates the kids by speaking of the geniuses of the world who were also dyslexic. As Ishaan's confidence grows, the piano piece rises to a crescendo. Ishaan is seen standing in front of the vast expanse of the mountain almost in meditative stillness and it transpires something epiphanic within the boy. The wordless sequence with the background music brings in a stunning effect that stays with the audience for a long time.

'Maa' has been one of the most iconic songs that has had a huge impact on people across the globe. The basic simplicity of the song, along with the heart-wrenching emotions that the words and Shankar's vocals carry, strike the most emotional chord for any listener. The pangs of separation that a child undergoes while being separated from his mother is relatable for everyone. Playback singing is a technical process, where music comes from the instruments and is synthesized in a machine. It is then matched with the visuals on-screen and lyrically expresses the conversations of the characters. However, some songs go beyond the periphery. The honesty in Shankar's voice, the simplicity in the tune and the lyrics, free of any pretentious metaphorical ornamentation, create an aesthetic one rarely comes across in film songs of recent times.

Shankar was always game for taking the risk of going into unknown territories. When he did the song 'Maa' it was with one guitar. Shankar recalled:

> Many people thought you should dub it in a child's voice because it is a child's emotion. How can an adult male be singing for a child's emotions? We gave it a thought should we dub in a child's voice? (sic) Then we just let it remain an adult's voice. We feel that a child's voice always appeals. Somehow subconsciously people feel that it is a children's song. Whereas with an adult male singing, it becomes a universal emotion. And that is what it did. The whole country cried.

A few years later, in 2014, Shankar sang another melodious paean to motherhood in a film, *Manjunath,* based on the true story of Manjunath Shanmugam—a graduate from Indian Institute of

Management, Lucknow, who was killed in Lakhimpur (UP) for his stand against corruption. The song, 'Amma', was composed by the famous Delhi-based Indian rock band Parikrama featuring Sonam Sherpa, Nitin Malik and Subir Malik. The song has a rock ballad vibe.

Surprisingly, when Shankar sang 'Maa', it was only as a scratch for some other singer to come and record. But as it happened many a times, the producer or director wanted to keep this scratch once they heard it. Aamir couldn't think of any other singer when he heard Shankar singing 'Maa'. Shankar–Ehsaan–Loy have extremely treasured memories of working with Aamir. The unit went together to Panchgani to compose the background music. They especially loved to listen to the experiences of the good old days of his uncle Nasir Hussain. Aamir chose to release the music of this movie in a small intimate get-together at Shammi Kapoor's house. Aamir was a huge fan and had always admired him. Like the film, there was simplicity in the promotion of the film as well. Ehsaan narrated it with a smile, 'Just the four of us went to launch the music and we sat with Shammi ji. We had tea and biscuits, and were sitting and talking for long. He was talking about his experience and his driving. It was such a beautiful experience of listening to the stories of those old times.'

∽

The year 2007 turned out to be one of the most significant years for SEL. From the swashbuckling *Jhoom Barabar Jhoom* and *Johnny Gaddaar* to the most melodious *Taare Zameen Par*, the year once again showcased their non-conformity, versatility and eclecticism. But the initial reaction of the audience to this album was tepid. However, it slowly took off. Similar things happened with the films released in 2008. While the music of *Rock On* gradually grew in the audience's mind and became one of the biggest hits of their career, the songs of the film *Thoda Pyaar Thoda Magic* couldn't reach where they could have, as the film didn't do well.

Thoda Pyaar Thoda Magic brought SEL back to the Yash Raj banner after *Jhoom Barabar Jhoom*. The production house had come up with the fourth consecutive production with its home-grown lad Kunal Kohli. With the three musical superhits under his belt—*Mujhse Dosti Karoge*, *Hum Tum* and *Fanaa*—*Thoda Pyaar Thoda Magic* created a lot of expectations with SEL coming on board and Prasoon Joshi teaming up with them.

Following the basic premises of a children's movie, Prasoon wrote some refreshing lines that invariably bring a smile to one's face. Shankar–Ehsaan–Loy wrote music exactly in the same fashion that promotes the happy-go-lucky mood of the film. In 'Bulbula', Shankar was at his poetic best when he brilliantly enlivens the mood with his unpretentious and easy singing. There is a fairy-tale like feel in the song which is carried throughout. Often in Walt Disney Productions, moviegoers come across such visuals of a fairy dancing on the clouds flapping her wings. The accompanying music has that faraway feeling that carries kids into that realm of magic and fantasy. Loy's understated piano almost misses one's ear, but it forms the backbone of the score. The trademark SEL harmonies have an infectious mood-uplifting joviality in them. As the film is chiefly a fairy tale, the song 'Pyaar Ke Liye' sets the mood of the film with guitar, piano, use of vocal harmony and Shankar's mellifluous singing.

The next project that SEL got was from their favourite banner of Excel Entertainment, and they produced one of the most defining albums of their career. This was the time for them to keep rocking on.

Rock On

In 2008, when heavyweight films like *Jodhaa Akbar, Sarkar Raj* and *Race* had already proved to be blockbusters; and the much-awaited releases of *Golmaal Returns, Ghajini* and *Rab De Bana Di Jodi* were slowly creating ripples of excitement in the public imagination, the never-tested domain of a true-blue Hindi rock movie was much like sticking up a misnomer's head in the ocean of bigwigs. With no glamour quotient donning the promotional videos or print ads, it didn't promise to start with a bang. But the title of the film framed inside an audio cassette; four boys posing in all-black shades and black T-shirts flashing a weird skeleton or a Che Guevara imprinted on it, or staring at you intensely through the posters; and the highly unusual sound of the songs in the promotional videos intrigued the audience.

There was always an audience who were quite immune to the larger-than-life, unreal saga of love and vaudevillian romcoms and family drama of brave heroes and lissom heroines. They keep waiting at the sidelines for films that won't see heroes mouthing whistle-induced dialogues; songs that meander around the highfalutin imageries of women; or metaphors of love. Rock is the resort of the rebels and nonconformists. And Hindi films and film music hardly offered them any groove to squeal and scream the way it is done in rock concerts.

Quite naturally, when Excel Entertainment thought of producing the movie with no big names and a one-film old director helming the all-important chair, it didn't get more than 400 screens countrywide, while most other films enjoyed double or even triple the number of screens. But the camaraderie of SEL and Excel Entertainment remained steadfast. Unarguably, SEL were the biggest names in the film's banner. Their names were enough to incite the expectations of watching a movie based on rock music. And it worked, with a thump and thud. After the tepid opening, there was such a rapid rise of excitement by the first weekend that the producers hiked Abhishek Kapoor's amount to double of what it was.

And SEL did what they do best: unlearning what they had produced before and scaling newer heights with something untested. Distorted guitar and bass programming of Western rock bands and exotic drum rolls barged in. Sound seemed to emerge, not from the insides of the glass room of the studio but from the amplifiers and speakers—raw and unprocessed. The audience is carried to a different zone. The use of muted colour with the camera catching the ambience of an ill-lit garage; the click of the opening of the guitar box; the mild guitar strum; hi-hats clapping and the drummer shouting the instructions to his band members ('standard 4/4 groove'); the keyboardist adding 'entry chord D-major'; and the natural echo of the vocalist's voice...this is how the garage band barging in a scintillating concert scene took it beyond Bollywood.

The background picks up the mood. There is the trendy groove of a Western musical. Even the humour comes from their common parlance during rehearsal. A musical conversation issues out of nothing. These are good, light-hearted, fun moments that never sound filmy, but are so relatable to the young, rock-crazy folks. There was nothing so-called 'Bollywood' here. Songs came one after another. Guitar and drums kept resonating like peals of thunder. Even silence had a language here, especially when accentuated with a gentle piano or a very mild guitar riff. The rehearsals took place in an ill-lit ramshackle garage. The shots of cables lying around; someone pulling out the wire and plugging into an amplifier; the electric sparks chasing around the room;

and the scenes of the rock concerts triggered sheer adrenaline rush. The soft, rock-styled guitar is heard throughout.

There is a scene with a music van screeching to a halt amid the gargantuan roars of the audience. Four ramblers with their guitars and drumsticks romp onto the stage. An electrifying guitar loop signals the thunderous entry of the band. Crisp drums start rolling frenetically. Aditya, the band's lead vocalist, starts spinning the mike stand like a baton, throws up his body in the air and lands among the insane audience who lap him up while shouting in unbridled rapture. As the guitar sound rises in a crescendo with frenetic drum roll, to the boisterous jibbing and jigging of a frenzied crowd, the music sounds uncontrollably exuberant. From 'Socha Hai' to 'Sinbad The Sailor', music had never been so pulsating for the trio. The voice behind the songs shunned the soft, velvety, familiar ones of the known singers. Farhan's grassy and throaty timbre sounded rebellious as the rockstar sang passionately.

The hard rock-induced guitar riffs in a Hindi mainstream film were a rare phenomenon. But just like the sound of a rock band, it has precise use of bass, drums, keys and guitar with great use of backup vocals. The music of this film threw SEL on their home turf and they were ecstatic. The songs and film sequences were interlaced. Everything appears in real-time. In 'Pichle Saath Dino Mein', the silhouette of Arjun Rampal's long mane matches the psychedelic guitar riffs. Arjun replicated what he saw in the by-lanes of Bandra, where boys sporting long ponytails with guitars dangling on their shoulders, would walk with an air of mystery around them. These are high-energy street shows, where the band members throw the hook line 'na na na na' to the screaming audience and the clapping and screaming audience reach a high crescendo, with thumping guitar riffs that make it exciting.

Present Mili Ek Ghadi, Pyaari Thi Mujhe Badi
Meri Jeb Ka Ek Packet, Meri Denim Ki Jacket

A lovely watch that I got as a gift
A small packet in my pocket and my denim jacket

Javed Akhtar's lyrics drew flak when the song was released. For a moment, it may read pedestrian and sacrilegious when a man who had penned some of the most poetic lines in the history of Hindi film songs could write something like this. But this only shows the malleability of the wordsmith. The man who could pen metaphors of the highest order, could also bring out lyrics that could resonate with the sentiments of the young crowd that had grown up watching American cinema and listening to Western music. Javed says that these songs are not stock situational songs. That is why he could make use of the chance to write anything because those would be sung by the rock stars on the stage. The words are real, urban and contemporary with images reverberating the normal life of the youth.

The rock band sound went to the extreme with Suraj Jagan belching out the venomous 'Zehreelay' with explosive hurling of words in a high-octane number. The sound that SEL brought out belonged to the hard rock domain, aeons away from the traditional fare of staple Hindi film songs. Ehsaan said in an interview that the guitar that he played didn't belong to his style.[9] It was acid rock and the bluesman that Ehsaan is, brought out a sound almost by chance which he himself could never replicate later. Suraj, a Mumbai-based rock singer, sang for them for the first time. Farhan had suggested his name to them, and they had also heard of him. He was the lead singer of his band Ajay-Chakravyuh. Suraj Jagan's words on the song-making highlight how organically the songs were written and recorded. He said:

'Zehreelay' was an experience which I never had before.
In the studio, everyone was there. All the musicians were

---

[9]'Ehsaan Noorani || on the Inspiration behind "Rock On" | the MJ Show', YouTube, https://tinyurl.com/3ch7e5dh. Accessed on 6 December 2023.

there. The drum kit was set up in the vocal booth and
Ehsaan and Loy were in two corners. I reached there and
asked Shankar where the song was. He said with a smile, we
have to make a song and gave me the mic. Ehsaan started
playing the guitar part and I said just keep playing that.
I would sing over this and I sang whatever came to my
mind at that time. The whole vocal line and the melody of
it were there. That was my own thing. They have given me
credit also on the CD for composing that song. That was
an amazing experience because it doesn't happen like that.
In the first take itself, Shankar was fully excited. Then we
did one more take and that was it. The whole structure of
the song was ready. Javed Saab had to write the lyrics. Then
after two weeks I went and did the final recording.

Javed Akhtar understood what the concept of heavy metal was when
he wrote about all these dark and grim things. And the idea was to
make it sound venomous. Incidentally, that was the first example of
death metal in Hindi songs. Soon after, there were more popular
songs, like the Ram Sampath composition 'Bhaag DK Bose' of *Delhi
Belly*, that fall in this genre. Then after from A.R. Rahman's *Rockstar*
to the music composer Amit Trivedi's songs in *Udaan*, Bollywood
soon got flooded with songs based on rock music.

The recording, as Suraj said, was something contemporary
Bollywood music wasn't familiar with. Since the story of the
film revolves around the music of a band, there had to be a live
music feel to it. *Rock On* was the first film where they recorded
with the whole band. Just like the recording style of yesteryears,
all the musicians were together. There was no retake kind of
thing. The musicians had to play the entire song. Only Farhan
could retake it, as he was in the control room singing all the
time. The band was completely live, with everyone playing in
real-time. Abhay Rumde, the sound engineer who won the IIFA
award for this film, said,

I remember the first day when Shankar said that we would record *Rock On* at Purple Haze and I was allowed to record that whole album. That was such a learning experience because recording-wise I had recorded everything but a whole band of musicians together at one time. That was my first experience. Since it was the story of a band, they wanted that kind of energy in the songs. Hence this idea of a live band was adopted. When all the musicians are in the same room, the energies are connected with who's playing what at that time. So, the number of musicians on-screen was exactly what was there in the studio. Farhan used to sing as well. 'Sinbad The Sailor' was done like a live band with all the musicians in the studio.

'Tum Ho Toh' is a soft rock ballad with minimalist instrumentation. There were no flourishing guitar riffs and exuberant drumming. Shankar–Ehsaan–Loy brought out the innate emotion of a lover serenading his beloved. The groove is created with gentle strokes in cymbal, and wonderful back-up vocals. Farhan worked hardest to do justice to the intricacies of this song. He was taken back to playing guitar and singing Western songs in his college days. While doing the histrionics matching the rendering of a rock song (like bending his voice and distorting 'roya' to a convoluted 'royeea'), he felt at ease, but holding the notes of 'Tum Ho Toh' and the gradual climaxing of notes in a falsetto needed skill. Abhishek wanted the lead singer of the band to sing in his own voice. The grainy and husky texture of his vocals was harnessed to a great effect, both in the faster numbers and in this particular song with suggestive pauses. But recording for a song was never in Farhan's thought. He said:

> There is a difference in just sitting with your own guitar which you are used to, playing something and singing. When you get in front of the mic with those headphones and you can hear every little croak and crack, it's very unnerving and

then you have Shankar standing on the other side who is like this god of vocals. So, one gets extremely nervous. The entire confidence I had that I could sing flew out of the window, completely gone. Sitting and playing with friends is different but this is going to go on an album. At the end of the day, it is a film. The music has to work and it has to sound good. So, I was extremely nervous. So, I would go into the room and tell Shankar that I wanted to put out the lights. I didn't want anyone to see because I would be doing some hand movement, dancing and doing something or the other and I was going to feel very foolish. Shankar said to me, 'Pal, you do whatever you want to do, nobody is going to disturb you.' He asked everyone in the studio to leave. So only Abhay, Shankar and I were there. And I would be in the dark room. Even Shankar could not see me. He could only hear me and I was singing away and then slowly one song happened and one light was put on. Little by little some confidence I gained. But if it wasn't for him being there, it wouldn't be possible. It would have taken longer, it would have sounded different. It would have been something else, but what it is, was only because of him—his being there, his patience, his breathing confidence into me. He said to me, 'Just go for it, don't think about who is listening, just sing from the heart.' So I just opened up. I don't think there could be a better teacher than him.

'Yeh Tumhari Meri Baatein' is a brilliant antidote to the hard rock elements of other songs in the movie. This soft-rock ballad is introspective, more of a monologue that pictures the psyche of the lady. Dominique Cerejo's subtle ways of singing have elegance and sophistication written all over it. The composition only shows the variety that SEL can bring even within the framework of rock music. The same can be said of the excellent epilogue-like sequence where Caralisa croons 'Phir Dekhiye'. It has a cathartic feeling after the extreme excitement that the hard rock sound had generated from a 21-minute-long final sequence of a fiery rock concert. Caralisa said:

> For 'Phir dekhiye' they didn't give me what exactly the song was. I went behind the mic and started singing. But I was so nervous because it was technically my first full solo song. I knew that the Hindi film industry for some weird reason gets very personal sometimes, they don't want you to experiment also, they want you to stick to one kind of style and you have to be from the Indian classical background, knowing that *harkatein* or then it is not a song. So, when I went to the studio I had those inhibitions. Shankar never said even once to do it in this way or that way. He went along with my style and my soul, and he just directed it beautifully. Just by that faith that they put in me, it became such a beautiful melody.

Farhan shed light on the style of the epilogue in Excel Entertainment movies, and said:

> Honestly, it started from the thought that when the film gets over, people get up and leave. We wanted people to stay and see who else has worked on the film. Now what can make you stay? If I just play some random music, nobody is going to stay. So, if I give you a song or I give you something that will keep you there. So, that's how it really kind of started.

〰

Shankar–Ehsaan–Loy surely had the last laugh when the film saw great success. It was brutally and disparagingly stubbed by the critics at its release. In retrospect, the music of *Rock On* is hailed as a pioneer in the genre of rock music in Hindi films.

The film ends with a heart-tugging appeal: 'Don't download

the music. Buy CD.' That was the time when the dynamics of the audio industry were undergoing a distinctive shift. It was gloomy when the medium of original audio CDs was supplanted by downloaded music. But it signalled a momentous change that was inevitable and soon to happen.

In 2012, Shankar, along with a host of singers like Sunidhi Chauhan, Sonu Nigam, Mohit Chauhan, Shaan, Kailash Kher and Zanai Bhosle sang 'Salaami Ho Jaye'. It is an anti-piracy song, which salutes the creative fraternity and gives them their due respect. It is composed by Shamir Tandon.

Luck by Chance

Three friends—Shankar, Ehsaan and Loy—with their individual destinations, crossed ways and discovered that notwithstanding their differences, they did not mind taking the journey together. Each of them made detours into different terrains, but when they happened to meet they couldn't help but marvel at the infinite surprises that awaited them.

While portraying the journey of a wannabe actor in the Hindi film industry, *Luck by Chance* takes an inside glance at the way things function in Bollywood. While referring to the perennial debate of luck vis-à-vis talent to find a leeway in the film industry, Saurabh Shukla's character says that the key to success lies totally in taking the right action at the right moment instead of being carried away by the celluloid glitz that peddles dreams. This somehow applied to the trio as well. Shankar–Ehsaan–Loy remained pretty engrossed in their individual pursuits, but never restrained from responding to newer opportunities whenever the call came. Film music was like a chic convertible rolling out on a highway, with the three of them taking turns on the driver's seat.

Them coming together instantly created a spark—an instinctive, epiphanic momentum that turned the journey into a thrilling roller-coaster ride. The magical chemistry of the trio almost alchemized everything that they touched. An era elapsed and quite deservingly, they won the award for completing 10 years of making music together. So, when the light dims in the multiplex, the mild thump in the bass drum gradually amplifies and the title card of *Luck by Chance* rolls out, Shekhar Ravjiani sings the song that resonates with SEL's journey:

Yeh zindagi bhi kya kya humko dekhlati hai
Sapno ki dhundli raah mein

What all does this life show us
In the hazy path of dreams?

The song 'Yeh Aaj Kya Ho Gaya' portrays the feelings of a girl in love, a situation that happens a zillion times on celluloid. But for such situations, SEL composed tunes that would have an elfin charm. So, songs like 'Pyaar Ke Liye' from *Thoda Pyaar Thoda Magic*; 'Tere Naina' from *Chandni Chowk to China*; 'Aaj Kal Zindagi' from *Wake Up Sid,* and quite a few more, would churn up a dreamy landscape that may not be intrinsically associated with the narrative of the film. They might not have the peppiness of an instant box-office hit, but they would linger in one's mind. The tunes, when heard later on, might not have whipped up images of the actors of the respective songs, but instead created a space in the listeners' hearts with its subtle and intrinsically personal approach.

'Baawre' was Mame Khan's first-ever studio recording. The Rajasthani folk singer, with whom Shankar worked in many of his fusion projects, was asked to join the trio for *Luck by Chance.* Shankar had first seen him singing at Ila Arun's daughter's wedding and had been fascinated. When Shankar called him via Ila Arun, Mame thought it must be for a performance. So, he came to the studio wearing his entire costume—the turban, the colourful Rajasthani dress and everything. Shankar said that he was very surprised to find out that they had called him just to record a song. The innocence of the man came alive in his singing.

Mahalakshmi speaks of a story of recording when she was doing 'Pyaar ki Dastaan' from *Luck by Chance*: 'When I started singing my part with the word *"isiliye"* Shankar was telling Javed Saab that instead of *"isiliye"* the word *"isliye"* sounded better. They had a lot of arguments over this. Javed Saab was very specific in using that word. Ultimately Shankar compromised and the word *"isiliye"* was used.'

Another song, 'Sapno Se Bhare Naina' starts with a *doha* and it plays in the background, with youngsters besotted with the film world queuing up to get one chance for that dream role. Shankar sang it in a thumri style with a lot of modern orchestration. Zoya spoke of the recording of 'Sapno Se Bhare Naina', saying, 'They did that song in just 20 minutes. Shankar sang the Raga Bhairavi in the track given by Ehsaan. And we had the song. It was over by the lunch break.'

Shankar's 'O Rahi Re' plays in the background when the end credits roll. It carries the trail of the film. It bears the stamp of the epilogue style of Excel Entertainment, where songs have an axiomatic purpose as well. Here, Javed Akhtar pens a meditative verse that symbolically sums up the motif of the film. 'O Rahi Re' is an ode to the traveller of life. Life, as an endless flow of moments, is also summed up in 'Phir Bhi Yeh Zindagi' in the end sequence of *Dil Dhadakne Do* and even *Zindagi Na Milegi Dobara* ends with some quintessential reflections on life.

The association of Javed Akhtar and SEL bore the results of some of the finest lyrics wedded to the music. Speaking on their endearing rapport, Shabana Azmi, the lady who has been a silent witness to their creative process, said with a smile:

> When Javed and Shankar work together, the vibrations are very good. They compose things in such an easy way that I always tell Javed that if people come to know how little work you all put into making a song, they will stop paying you the huge prices. So, you better keep the mystique and don't let people know how quickly you all make the song. It's just wonderful.

ॐ

In a touching end sequence of the film, the prospering actor, Farhan Akhtar, is seen chucking out a get-together with his childhood friends for the golden opportunity of meeting the superstar Shah Rukh Khan (a cameo where he played himself) at a glitzy glamorous film party. One of the prime examples of a struggler becoming a superstar, Shah Rukh Khan is shown advising the newly successful actor, 'Stardom is a cocktail of fame, power and money. It is an insane addiction. But one thing I understood early, don't forget that your childhood friends knew you when you were nothing. Because they are the ones who speak the truth every time.'

This echoes the values that Shankar always carries with him. Notwithstanding the pinnacle of success he reached, he remained the good old Jaadya who was always at his elemental best when he returned to The Originals, once the glimmer of the film party went down.

Wake Up Sid

*D*il Chahta Hai is noted to have opened the floodgates of youth-oriented movies. The chutzpah that *Dil Chahta Hai* exhibited, caught the attention of a large section of the audience, encouraging filmmakers to take an active interest in making youth-oriented movies. That is how *Lakshya, Rock On, Wake Up Sid* and *Zindagi Na Milegi Dobara* happened. Shankar–Ehsaan–Loy's music had a vibe that instantly struck a chord with the youth. Shankar–Ehsaan–Loy, being a unit of three individuals, could effectively reciprocate to the collective vibes of a friend group through their music. Their distinctively individual aesthetics of music symbiotically enriched the soundscape that carried the verve of urban youthfulness in style.

Wake Up Sid had the charm of a breezy, youthful film that came from a 19-year-old debutant director Ayan Mukerji. Following the basic premise of a bildungsroman, it places more importance on the internal monologues of the characters rather than on action. Shankar–Ehsaan–Loy's music was an effective ploy to express the emotions that guided a group of effervescent boys. Songs are used in the extended background, where the director captures some of the most beautiful, flitting moments of friendship, fun and fiesta that the juvenile adolescence makes sense of. Shankar–Ehsaan–Loy could immediately hit the right note with the sententious title. The pace of time is expressed in the persistent 'tick-tick' notes that signal the arrival of a new age. The vitality and the exuberance of youth are reflected in the changing scales at the closure of the song. The shrill 'wake up', and the sudden falling of beats at the end, sounds like a veritable wake-up call that makes one alert. Shankar's voice sounds velvety in 'Aaj Kal Zindagi' when he brings out the emotion latent in the lyrics. A feel-good vibe instantly strikes as he sings, '*Tere liye nayee hain zameen, nai asmaan* (For you the earth and the sky look anew).' The bass–guitar–drums groove, with the signature vocal arrangement, comes handy again when Uday Benegal and Shankar sing a delightful 'Life Is Crazy'.

Clinton Cerejo—the man who has been instrumental in doing the vocal arrangements in many of SEL's numbers—fits in perfectly with the youthful, urban soundscape while singing 'Kya Karoon?'. He was asked just to sing the scratch version, but SEL loved the texture of Clinton's voice and decided to keep it.

Clinton catches the sentiments of college going youths, their moments of unbridled fun and absolute abandon where thoughts of future go for a toss. Every single guitar riff catches the montage of the images of youthfulness. This guitar–drums groove goes on in a loop and vocals make patterns in and out of it. Harmonica passages, after *Lakshya*, sounds refreshing and lends the song a dynamism.

∽

With the likes of Vishal–Shekhar, Pritam and Amit Trivedi coming on the scene, the sound of the youth became the order of the day. The clientele base of the Hindi film music was gradually shifting towards the urban youth who were in their 20s and 30s. There was a lot more to offer and SEL experimentation kept breaking newer ground.

My Name Is Khan and More...

A fter *Kabhi Alvida Naa Kehna*, Karan Johar came up with a movie to woo the critics as well as the critical audience by producing and directing a film that went beyond the peripheries of the candy floss movies for which he was primarily earmarked. The film *My Name is Khan* clicked in both ways. The film earned critical acclaim and was commercially successful as well. With a political subtext under the premise of a mainstream film, the director had to use his soundtrack carefully. He had to dispense off the stock situations of romance. Yet, he couldn't take a complete departure from the tried and tested mode because of the star value and the immense expectations that his movies always carried. So, songs had to be there, but they needed to have a purpose and had to be connected with the narrative.

Unlike Karan Johar's earlier films, here the songs are not lip-synced. The songs also carry forward the action without letting the narrative digress into just another dispensable song sequence. Shafqat's soulful and energetic 'Tere Naina' has a sufi strain to bring spiritual vibes to the relationship between two lovers. The song was used to portray the development of romance, a fondness growing in the hearts of two people.

Shankar–Ehsaan–Loy used the conventional structure of sufi qawwali, where the solo and chorus come in alternate lines, with continuous dholak beats and the hook line coming in a refrain. They tried their hand in this domain that didn't have many examples before this, save 'Ya Rabba' from *Salaam-E-Ishq* and 'Mitwa' from *Kabhi Alvida Naa Kehna*. But in both 'Ya Rabba' and 'Mitwa', SEL took liberties with the form of sufi qawwali. While the Kailash Kher number is more on the softer side, and 'Mitwa' is more of a hybrid of rock and qawwali, 'Tere Naina' is truer to the tradition. As mentioned earlier, Shafqat was the son of Ustad Amanat Ali Khan. Owing to this, he had training in Hindustani classical music from an early age. In 'Tere Naina', the spirituality of sufi singing underscores the honesty of the character Rizwan, whose naiveté has a disarmed charm. In a narrative which gradually becomes a brooding and sombre tale, the music offers relief through two melodious sufi qawwali, 'Tere Naina' and 'Sajda'.

Shankar-Ehsaan-Loy worked with Shafqat one more time, a year later, in a brilliant song 'Kyun Main Jaagoon' in Patiala House. The song had a 'Mitwa'-like feel but structurally it was quite contrary to it. Unlike 'Mitwa', where the progression is from a lower note gradually hitting the top with the hook line, 'Kyun Main Jaagoon' starts on a very high note. Gradually, it comes down to a diminuendo. The song has a similar intensity to that of 'Mitwa' or 'Noor E Khuda', but, as it was placed at the very beginning of the film, the audience failed to empathize with the character so soon.

Coming back to *My Name is Khan*, 'Noor E Khuda' took a distinctive place in the entire oeuvre of SEL's career. The song is used as a background score against Rizwan finding his way in a foreign land. Despite being an equally good song, what 'Kyun Mai Jaagoon' could not achieve, 'Noor E Khuda' could. Placed in the crux of the movie's action, the song, on one hand, offers a relief from the heightened claustrophobic tension, and on the other, it carries the narrative forward. Shankar's deeply evocative cry for the light of God (Noor E Khuda) deepens the strange forlornness of the desert, where Rizwan is wandering after being wounded by a heartless world.

The master stroke comes with the introduction of Adnan Sami, whose voice comes in tandem with that of Shankar. The gradual crescendo towards the hook line, with layers of synths, bears the signature of the composer trio. Two different voices, having two different timbres, being used in the background of a single character brings a very interesting blend of sounds to the song. It brings out the psyche of a man torn and split by the events that unfolded in his life, leaving him in tatters and seeking an elusive divine help. The structure of soloists reaching towards the chorus bridge, where the hook line comes, shows the Western rock and folk elements with which SEL was deeply influenced. But having said that, it is Indianized with the elements of classical tarana that Shreya sings so soulfully, and also the Carnatic violin strains in the *koda* part of the song. Loy said, 'Adnan takes a different spin on the songs. His delivery in itself has got a thing to it. And when Shreya comes in, in between these two powerful voices, the song gets a different feel.'

Images deifying the eyes of the beloved come again in 'Sajda', another sufi qawwali where they made use of the deviant, husky vocals of Richa Sharma. Even if Karan Johar wanted to go beyond the familiar parameters of his films, this song was picturized in a typical Dharma Production, traditional Indian wedding situation. The song enfolds the perky mood of the wedding and gets on with the successive events that follow. Rahat Fateh Ali Khan's transcendental voice adds to the elements of passion and pathos, intrinsically associated with qawwali. But it is significantly toned down, as the romantic elements take the mainstay instead of the unmixed spirituality of a traditional qawwali.

Another song that lay boxed only in the album but couldn't find a place in the film was 'Rang De', a duet of Shankar and Suraj Jagan. The song did not seem to fit in the scheme of things as far as this film was concerned. The Westernized feel of the song stands in marked contrast to the predominantly sufi strain of the film's soundtrack. The drum roll, layers of synth sound and Ehsaan's riffs on top of them are heard more in an Excel Entertainment film, than in a Dharma Production with Karan

Johar as the director. But its absence in the film and the popularity of other tracks pushed this wonderful rock ballad into oblivion.

When Suraj Jagan went to sing 'Rang De', he saw that Shankar was already in the vocal booth. He was singing the song then. Suraj never got to hear him sing live as such because whenever he had gone to record songs, Shankar would do the role of music composer and not a singer. Suraj said that it was a treat for him to hear Shankar. He said, 'For me, it was almost like a private concert happening. That is one I will never forget and the fact that I got to sing with him which never happened before or after.'

∽

Songs like 'Rang De' carry the hallmark of SEL music. Songs based on rock and pop came so easily to them, as they were always strongly associated with bands, individually or collectively. In 2009, they made their debut in Telegu film with *Konchem Ishtam Konchem Kashtam* that had a song 'Egire Egire'. They introduced a similar bass–drums–guitar groove in the Telegu musicscape. They rode on the unprecedented success of *Rock On* and within a year came another film, also based on the rock genre. Titled *London Dreams* and having two of the biggest names—Salman Khan and Ajay Devgn—with glitzy scenes of rock concerts in Wembley Stadium used in the promotional clips, the film came with big expectations. The film had some high energy up-tempo numbers like 'Shola Shola', 'Tapkey Masti' and the curiously titled 'Khanabadosh' where they used various elements like beatboxing, rock and trance music. However, only one song stood apart.

As a great example of fusion—where SEL sourced elements from sufi to rock bhangra, electronic dance music to jazzy passages—the song 'Barson Yaaron' sounds electrifying. From the classically gifted Roopkumar Rathod to diametrically opposite hard-core rock singer Vishal Dadlani; from heavy bass and distorted guitar to tabla *chhapki*; the song is a juxtaposition of contrasts. When 'Barson Yaaron' was recorded, Shankar had sung the scratch and Vishal was to sing it later. Roopkumar Rathod had already recorded his part. Vishal was surprised listening to the scratch sung by Shankar. Vishal said that there are very few classically trained singers who could deliver that rock attitude. He believed what Shankar had done was better than what he had done.

In 2011, Vishal Dadlani teamed with Shankar in a one-of-a-kind rock ballad, 'Reham O Karam' in *We Are Family*. The introspective beginning of the song was composed by Loy, but it suddenly flared up with a great rock hook written by Ehsaan. Placed at a dramatic juncture in the narrative, the song stuns the listeners with its very unusual structure. The solo bridges, where Shankar and Vishal use their voices, softly bring out the nuances of the lyrical expressions; and when they hit the higher notes, Ehsaan's sizzling guitar and backup vocals make it sound like a typical rock song. The guitar wrings out the emotions from three individual characters caught in a conflicting web of emotions, constraints and heartaches.

Way back in 1999, Shankar had collaborated with Vishal in Pentagram when they did a song called 'The Price of Bullets'. The music video was shot by Farhan and Zoya and the lyrics were written by Javed Akhtar. The song speaks about the futility of war and how the capital market resorts to jingoism. Channel V had a show called *Jammin* where Vishal and Shankar went to a beach house in Versova and made a song there. Shankar, according to Vishal, was never limited to what he learnt. Vishal continued and said:

Very often a musician who has so extensively studied becomes only about the form that he has studied. But he is way beyond that. You know an intelligent person can adapt to any style any form and any job and so basically, Shankar has that quality plus his knowledge. I have met many studied musicians, be it musicians of Western classical,

Indian classical or any organized form of musical education. That takes away the ability to adapt. But Shankar has been somehow magnified and the amazing thing is that whether he sings a jazz-inspired line or whether is singing a classical line or any of the millions of wonderful songs that he has sung he always sounds like Shankar Mahadevan.

つ

Since her childhood, Loy's daughter Alyssa was largely influenced by Maria Carey and wanted to sing like her. She wanted to learn but did not know anybody who would be teaching those kinds of vocals in India. Alyssa could not understand the lyrics of the song, and would make up her own dummy words. When she sang 'A Whole New World' from *Aladdin*, Loy was shocked. He immediately called Shankar, told him everything and asked him how he should take this forward. From that time, Shankar encouraged her and guided her in the vocal training. In 2010, 19-year-old Alyssa made an impressive debut in Hindi film music when Excel Entertainment produced *Karthik Calling Karthik*. The film saw SEL experimenting further with newer electronic sound.

Karthik Calling Karthik
and Other Films

Unlike *Johnny Gaddaar* which was a true-blue caper film, *Karthik Calling Karthik* revolves around the schizoid mind of an individual. There is a romantic subtext as well, offering the director to use song sequences of romance. But the film is essentially a thriller, where the inner working of a schizophrenic mind is explored. The use of electronic sound gives the much-needed surreal touch to the narrative. So, in the title song, sung by Suraj Jagan and Caralisa Monteiro, there are elements of trance music. The sound processing brings an effect of hollowness to the song, adding to the eeriness of the thriller. The voice of Caralisa was processed in such a way that it sounded robotic. Her voice was to be used as a supposed voiced call. The electro-trance music in Clinton's stylish 'Hey Ya', the interspersing of English lyrics, the highly processed vocal sound, the layering of guitar strumming and the use of synths give an electronic soundscape feel of a hard rock cafe.

The most brilliant soundtrack of all is the one that became very popular because of the unusual sound and a very catchy rhythm. 'Uff Teri Ada' introduced Loy's daughter, Alyssa. The electronic sound creates a groove for dancing, befitting the setting of a nightclub where the sequence was shot but it was done with élan. Shankar's intonation stands in stark contrast to the electronically processed sound of Alyssa's vocals. Shankar's part stands as a perfect foil to the trendy and more vibrant Alyssa singing for a chirpy girl, while the character that Farhan portrays is that of a common man caught in the web of his complicated mind. In 'Uff Teri Ada', when Shankar sings, the voice sounds as if it is near the mic, but when Alyssa sings it sounds as if the voice is coming from far away. Farhan said, 'If you have seen the movie, the hero is like a complete introvert, so we kept his voice like kind of intimate when he is singing and when Alyssa is singing, she is like this larger-than-life, it has got a larger scale, a lot more breathe to the processing.'

The great energy of the song gets translated on-screen with some very ebullient choreography. But the beauty of the composer, Shankar, is that he always likes to keep the Indian element very strong in his compositions. While creating a melody, Shankar always likes to Indianize by introducing the classical elements in a very subtle way. That is what he did in 'Uff Teri Ada', where, in the Western symphony framework, he infused classical strain very delicately. In 'Mitwa', and also in 'Rang De', he had that little sargam part to fuse classical elements. In the song 'Where's The Party Tonight?' from *Kabhi Alvida Naa Kehna*, there is a section that he sings in pure classical form. 'Tere Naina' from *Chandni Chowk to China* is a pure Indian melody, but it was so beautifully dressed up that it sounds Westernized. Shankar has always juxtaposed an Indian melody in a very hardcore Westernized song. A delicate fusion of classical notes in a Western song stands out as the hallmark of Shankar's style. This gives a distinctive edge to any composition of his.

ᴄ⌀

Johnny Gaddaar, Karthik Calling Karthik and *Don* set a trend of avant-garde music befitting the modern-day caper films. Shankar–Ehsaan–Loy continued with this trend with Vishal Dadlani's 'It's A Game' in the film *Game*. Shankar–Ehsaan–Loy kept delivering some beautiful melodies in movies that sunk with those songs. A super melodious 'Maine Kab Yeh Socha Tha' disappears all too soon amid some more popular releases. A couple of wonderful melodies like 'Kyun Hota Hai Dil Deewana' and 'Kal Nau Baje' from *Short Kut* sank without any trace. A couple of beautiful numbers, that could easily be two of the most mellifluous SEL compositions having that quintessential feel-good vibe, 'Dekho Raste Mein' and 'Kal Tum They Yahan' from *Hum Tum Aur Ghost* went out of public memory too.

In *Don 2*, SEL took off from where they had finished in the first part. The hushed-up vocals of Vishal Dadlani and Anusha Mani form an eerie and sinister ambience. 'Mujhko Pehchaanlo' is not just a song with ubiquitous lyrics but an expression of the motif of the invincibility of the Don. The roller-coaster ride of Don's conquest over his antagonists sounds scintillating in the background. The voice of Usha Uthup has been heard over the years in several thriller movies. When she sings the hook line, it sounds like the perfect teaser of a caper. The instrumentation with drums and piano shows how SEL had mastery over the songs to be used as a backdrop of modern-day thrillers. The song was at first supposed to be sung by any male singer with an assertive voice. After a few rough cuts, SEL were not satisfied and then they got in touch with Usha. Farhan tweeted after the recording, 'Recorded a song with Usha Uthup for Don 2. What a voice and what amazing energy and attitude... a rockstar in a kanjivaram saree!'[10]

∽

After *Karthik Calling Karthik*, quite a few films came and went off without making any significant impact on the audience till the phenomenal *Zindagi Na Milegi Dobara* hit the screen in 2011. But the integrity and honesty of the composer trio was never questioned, as even in their lean phase they gave some extremely melodious songs, albeit sporadically, in those films.

---

[10]@FarOutAkhtar, X (formerly Twitter), 28 September 2011, 1.18 p.m., https://tinyurl.com/yb6cm77c. Accessed on 6 December 2023.

Shankar kept shuttling from Bollywood to South Indian movies and singing songs for movies like *Madampi* or *Viswaroopam*. The zippy and cheerful 'Kalyanakacheri' of *Madampi* got him the Kerala State Film Award for best singer. Shankar–Ehsaan–Loy formed a wonderful relationship with Kamal Haasan and it was not a surprise that after *Aalavandhan*, they were again chosen to compose for his ambitious trilingual magnum opus *Viswaroopam*. In *Viswaroopam*, Shankar used thumri for the first time in Tamil. Shankar–Ehsaan–Loy collaborated with legends like Pt Birju Maharaj and Kamal Haasan in the song 'Unnai Kaanadhu Naan'.

In Telegu cinema, Shankar has sung for most of the composers, from prominent ones like Vandemataram Srinivas, Chakri and Ramana Gogula to the Golden Globe and Oscar award winner M.M. Keeravani. He has also worked with the renowned Carnatic percussionist and kanjira player, his bandmate of Remember Shakti, V. Selvaganesh. Shankar's high-energy 'Kabaddi Kabaddi' song, sung in a similar mould to Sukhwinder Singh's 'Chak De India', infuses infectious inspirational vibes with the players jogging barefoot and practising the sport in humble settings. This song was from a sports-drama *Vennila Kabaddi Kuzhu 2*. Shankar won the Asianet Film Award for 'Best Male Playback' and also the Annual Malayalam Movie Awards (Dubai) for 'Best Male Singer' for the song 'Picha Vacha Naal' from *Puthiya Mugham*. The soft melodious love ballad was the biggest hit in Kerala that summer.

In 2009, a film, *Sikander*—based on the sensitive backdrop of terrorism and its evil clutches on the life of an innocent kid—was released. The film had a beautiful song 'Dhoop Ke Sikke' sung by Anusha Mani and Shankar. Prasoon Joshi is at his poetic best with a very delicate portrayal of a boy whose innocence carries a foreboding of it being nipped in the bud. The combination of rock guitar riffs and drums pick-up, and the highly figurative line of *'barood jab baccha tha/ woh titli pakadta tha'* is like the epoch-making stuff of Bob Dylan and the age-defining songs of the progressive rock bands of the West. But as it happens with many songs, it was partially used only as a strain of background music and partially during the end credits when the audience would be busy leaving the theatre.

Shankar sang one beautiful song 'Dhundli Dhundli' for a Sanjay Leela Bhansali film *Guzaarish* in 2010. Composed by the director himself, the song only showed the versatility of the singer. Amid most of the light-hearted fun songs that he was singing at that time, this meditative number with almost nothing but an organ backup and a very evocative violin solo recreated the tranquility of an evening with his singing. Learning of classical music came in handy in his incredible voice control on each note of this song.

ꝏ

This lull of commercially unsuccessful films didn't last long. Several songs slipped away, as these films did not register in public memory. But as had happened before, SEL bounced back loud and strong when Zoya Akhtar's landmark movie *Zindagi Na Milegi Dobara* hit the screen and almost overnight, it swept the cinegoers by storm.

Eight

Kya hua kyun bhala, dil mazaaron se ho gaye...

Zindagi Na Milegi Dobara

From the humble debut in *Luck by Chance* to *Zindagi Na Milegi Dobara*, a movie of a grandiose scale, it was a huge leap for Zoya Akhtar as a director. It replicated the hysteria and popularity that her brother's debut film had created nearly a decade back. In any list of the 10 best Indian movies made on youth, friendship and road trips, this movie would make it to the top three. But more than the commercial success of the film, *Zindagi Na Milegi Dobara* opened up a new direction for modern-day movies on this theme. When *Dil Chahta Hai* released, multiplex culture was yet to start in a big way. *Dil Chahta Hai* came as a stunner. It became a landmark in the way it built up a brand-new niche for Hindi films. But by the time *Zindagi Na Milegi Dobara* hit the theatres, single-screen cinema halls had already become passé; a mere part of nostalgia. Urban cinegoers accustomed to the upbeat movie experiences, with both Bollywood and Hollywood releases in the cool multiplexes, needed something more discerning to find interest.

The promos of this film recalled the same emotions and excitement that the audience had felt after watching *Dil Chahta Hai*. The stylish looks of the film, the strains of music used in the promos and an attractive ensemble cast built up the expectation. But *Zindagi Na Milegi Dobara* went a step further than its predecessor. From the film's technical details to the plot; from the script to the performances of the actors, not once did the film look unreal. Zoya took minute care, from the first frame till the end credit sequence, and made sure that the film never sought any willing suspension of disbelief from the audience. Script and dialogues notwithstanding, the most effective impact that comes from the technical aspect of the film is music. Songs do not have a separate existence here but, from the very first sequence till the last, songs and musical scores run parallel to the development of the narrative. Every single musical phrase is well thought out, and it acts as a thematic extension of the respective sequences. So, the background music becomes as significant as the songs and surely brings a powerful impact.

The film is essentially a portrayal of a road trip in Spain. It moves through fast-changing visuals. The succession of scenes in different parts of the country, as the three friends take a long-cherished bachelor trip, calls for different background scores befitting the visuals and mood of different places. Acoustic guitar strumming with subtle additions of percussion instruments like castanets, bongos and cajón bring this topical flavour throughout. A scene merges with another using this background score back-up. It adds to the dynamic structure of the film.

The song that comes with the title sequence of the film sets the ball rolling. 'Dil Dhadakne Do' is the perfect song for the road. The guitar riffs, the gradual build-up with base drums and then the processed vocals of Suraj Jagan and an Assamese rockstar Joi Barua, straightaway resonate with the disobedient bohemianism lurking in each heart. The beckoning of *'thodi awargi, thodi madhoshiya'* triggers in the mind an irresistible urge to hit the road and break free. The initial guitar and drumming of the prelude and the thumping of heartbeats come in further scenes as well, whenever they embark on adventurous games. Thus, it connects the basic storyline of how the friends want to make the most of their unfulfilled dreams before one of them gets married.

Besides this main plot, certain other significant subplots are linked with the narrative. Each subplot is identified with signature background pieces. A particular guitar riff, very faintly reminiscent of a single guitar strum in R.D. Burman's epic prelude of 'Pariyon Ka Mela Hain' in *Satte Pe Satta*, tickles the funny bone when the three friends remember their bygone college days and play pranks on strangers. The romance angle of the characters, portrayed by Hrithik Roshan and Katrina Kaif, gets a poetic undertone when it is backed up by lovely guitar strums and soft piano. The sequence where Laila decides to meet Arjun and express her seething feelings of love is built up with long passages of continuous rhythm guitar blended with drums pick up and finally it goes in a crescendo with synth sound.

The entire 2-minute-long sequence comes without any word and finally merges with the mild bossa nova beat of the wonderful 'Khaabon Ke Parinday'. The delightful groove that comes from Alyssa's voice sounds as fresh as honeydew. Mohit Chauhan sounds like a perfect foil to complement Alyssa. The long, wordless musical passage climaxing in this dreamy vocal, match with the visuals of the Spanish countryside and mesmerize the audience. Of all the songs, 'Khaabon Ke Parinday' and 'Senorita' stand out to be two of the best tracks of the album.

Alyssa was in junior college when Shankar asked her to come to the studio one day. To get to the studio that day, she rushed from her college to catch the train from Victoria Terminus. On that day, she was a bit under the weather and was not getting the right energy for the song. Moreover, it was quite intimidating for young Alyssa to record a song straightaway in front of some of the big personalities of the industry. Shankar gave her the song and asked her to come back the next day. Next evening, she went and sang only in the presence of Abhay. Alyssa later said, 'When I listen to "Khaabon Ke Parinday" now, I have zero recollection as to how I sang it the way I sang it. It was such a spiritual process. Sometimes it is almost like you are not doing it, like something else is doing that through you. And after listening to it, the team just loved it so much.'

The similar pattern of prolonged wordless musical pieces climaxing into a song, without any dialogues in between, comes again at the most significant juncture of the film. Moments of absolute silence, almost deafening, and a tangible stillness of space when they fly and celebrate life in its most crystallized form, is juxtaposed with Neel Bhattacharya's flamenco guitar solo. Then after a brief passage of Spanish lyrics in the prelude, sung by the Spanish singer María del Mar Fernández, there is the longest pause that mounts the tension of unpredictability. But when the pause breaks into a magnificent and spontaneous overflow of tunes, it brings forth a fountain of positive energy. 'Senorita' will remain one of the most innovative and popular soundtracks of SEL, as very rarely can a musical piece carry the theme of a film as effectively as it did.

For a seamless merging of the song with the narrative, the actors were asked to lend their own voice instead of getting any playback singers. Farhan was a tested voice and Hrithik also had the experience of singing a song 'Tum Bhi Ho Wahi' for his home production *Kites*. Abhay Deol had no exposure to singing. For the Spanish part, they sent the track to Maria. There were a couple of voices out of which SEL selected the one recorded by Maria. The mixing was done in Purple Haze. The guitar, clapping and the use of chorus bring a slice of the bustling streets of Barcelona along with the song. Abhay, the trusted sound engineer, attributes Zoya's presence also in bringing out the infectious vitality of the song. He said, 'The compositions depend on the director also. When it comes to Zoya, the kind of preferences for the making of songs she gave during ZNMD [*Zindagi Na Milegi Dobara*] was never done before. The kind of energy one gets after Zoya gives a brief is such that there cannot be a mediocre song composed. The song goes to another level.'

During the Navratri celebrations in Mumbai that year, people were found playing *dandiya* and *garba* to 'Senorita'. Upon hearing this, Loy was highly amused. He said, 'This is like the complete reversal of what happens in the movie *Rock On* where the band changes their sound. Here people are adapting themselves to our music. This kind of reverse engineering is definitely good news.'[11]

Zoya's words show how thematic the background score was in the movie and highlighted the trio's brilliance as far as the composition of the background score is concerned. She said: 'I tell SEL the mood I want and then they create something fabulous. I feel there is too much background score in Hindi cinema. In ZNMD I think I went against the usual norms of Hindi cinema.'[12]

The lack of sound adds to the dramatic intensity of the scene in which Farhan's character meets his estranged father for the first time. After this sequence, Loy comes up with a delightful piece of piano, Ehsaan strums his acoustic guitar all too softly and Bianca Mendonca plays a deeply evocative cello. When Farhan recites Javed's poetry, and the camera encompasses a vast purple sky of the dawn through which the first rays of sunshine shoots forth, it creates a calming sensation in the mind. The effect is mesmerizing. The poems that the 'closet poet' recites—with the accompaniment of subtle piano, guitar, cello or violin—highlight the ethos and sentiment of the film.

Shankar sang in almost all tracks as a backup vocalist, and chose to record his own voice in the most low-keyed song of the film. Used as the backdrop of all three characters caught at the crossroads of their lives, the song upholds the meaning of life that appealed to them separately.

Der lagi lekin,
Maine ab hai jeena seekh liya

I might have taken little longer,
But I have finally learnt how to live

The beautiful rock ballad comes at a time when all three are on the path to discover themselves, and what they want out of life.

---

[11]*The Score Magazine*, January 2012.

[12]Kumar, Nirmal, and Preeti Chaturvedi, *Brave New Bollywood: In Conversation with Contemporary Hindi Filmmakers*, SAGE Publications, 2015.

The action is suspended for a brief time before it shoots up for the sensational San Fermin festival in Pamplona and the cathartic realization that comes soon after.

Vishal Dadlani attributes to Shankar all that he could bring into the composition. He recalled:

> In 'Ik Junoon', there is a bit of adlib in the end. It was just like when they were composing the song, they asked me to do something out of the box or spontaneous. My biggest memory is the original scratch of the song that Shankar had sung which I thought should never have been changed. For me, anytime he sang a song, I feel it should be in his voice only and any composers who worked with him will tell you the same thing. It is really good of him, considering he is such an illustrious singer, to have that mind space where he has given songs to so many newcomers, so many new singers and so many established singers. Anything that I have done on an SEL song is from them only. All energy has come from them. When you talk about 'Ik Junoon', the key of the song, the way it was sung, every inflexion of the song all of that came from them. I was just the instrument.

Modesty notwithstanding, Vishal echoed the words spoken by so many other singers at different points in time. 'Ik Junoon' was an ambient lounge or house music. The song carried the verve of a high-energy scene of the Tomatina festival. Shankar plugged a vocoder into the keyboard. Playing chords on it, he produced the robotic 'ooos' and 'aahs'. The entire song happened like that.

The spontaneity of music-making comes when some of the best creative geniuses sit together and compose tunes in a relaxed manner. Abhay spoke of the presence of the hilarious father-son duo, Javed and Farhan, who were instrumental in creating an atmosphere of fun and frenzy. When they were doing the background for the 'diamond biscuits' jingle, Shankar started pulling Farhan's leg about what a 'great' tune he had composed.

So, what was happening on the screen—when Hrithik was making fun of his friend's ability to compose tunes—was happening in the studio as well. Farhan had the segment in his mind while writing the script of the jingle. The vibes that SEL exchange with the Akhtars are the source of all the great work that they produce whenever they come together.

ᄋᅠ

Gradually Shankar's and Loy's children began to walk in the shoes of their illustrious fathers. If Alyssa made her debut as a singer in *Zindagi Na Milegi Dobara*, Siddharth was soon to unleash a storm in *Bhaag Milkha Bhaag*. Ehsaan was sentimental when he remembered the time Siddharth was born. He said, 'These kids have grown in front of us. I have seen Siddharth from the time he was born literally. I have been to his naming ceremony. So, it's wonderful to see them come and record for us.' Loy further elaborated, saying:

> It was a beautiful feeling seeing Siddharth and Alyssa entering the recording studio. Alyssa used to come over during summer breaks and hang around in the studio paying attention to what was happening. Shankar would always give her a microphone and urge her to sing a part. So, she was getting a little comfortable. So, one fine day when she did 'Khaabon Ke Parinday', he didn't tell us. He just called her and said, 'You come later and I want you to sing this song.' Later he dubbed the song and told us, that was it. We didn't have a say in it.

It was around 2010, when Siddharth was soon to take his board examinations, when the offer to write music came to him. It was for the Marathi movie *Swapna Tujhe Ni Majhe* that he and his cousin Soumil Shringarpure debuted as music composers. However, their first composition was not for the film but for Neeta Lulla's show at the Lakmé Fashion Week. Alyssa was also a part of the show. She recalled that memorable event when she was recollecting how Shankar had been a mentor in her life. In three days, Alyssa, Soumil and Siddharth wrote the song together, sang and played it at the studio. It was a matter of extreme pride and pleasure when Shankar, Ehsaan and Loy imperceptibly left a legacy for the next generation of musicians.

Shankar Mahadevan Academy

By 2010, Shankar had completed more than 15 years in the music industry. Glories and laurels came to him from all corners of the globe. Most importantly, the life he braced—chucking the much-haloed pasture of a successful computer professional—turned out to be infinitely more propitious. Music earned him everything he could aspire for and sharing his life with his childhood sweetheart gave him the ultimate satisfaction. He realized that in this world he could never be lonely as long as music was there. Often, at the end of the day, he would retire into a silent corner of his home and share with Sangeeta his dream of spreading the happiness of music to the world. He felt that even if he was successful, his job was not complete until he had spread Indian music to every nook of the world.

Both Sangeeta and Shankar would discuss how setting up an academy might help them fulfil their dream. This academy wouldn't be a traditional music school. The purpose of the school would not be to produce musicians, but to help the learners inculcate music as their soulmate—as the very cornerstone of their psychic development. Shankar saw that the existing system of music education was so constricted that it took away the joy of learning. Music as a career option should not be the motivator. Rather, music should be the source of joy. He feels that this kind of joy is within everyone's capability, provided they are shown the right way. So, to spread the invaluable treasure of Indian music among the young listeners, Shankar thought of setting up a music institution. He found that despite the mushrooming of numerous music schools all over the country, there wasn't any at the level of Berkeley in India.

Shankar started looking for a land grant from the Government of Maharashtra to open an academy of music and expressed this idea in an interview. Sridhar Ranganathan recalls reading this interview while on a flight. He was two years senior to Shankar both in SIES and Ramrao Adik Institute of Technology. He had graduated to become a successful professional and had settled in California as vice president of Yahoo. Soon, he came to stay in India for a couple of years on an official project. For his work, he started visiting schools and found to his dismay that the teaching–learning process was still moving in the same restricted manner. After another disappointing meeting with the school administrative committee, he was returning to California from Mumbai when he came across Shankar's interview. Sridhar felt excited to know about Shankar's dream of a music school and his application for a land grant. Through a common friend, he e-mailed Shankar expressing his idea about cyberspace and an online music school because he knew that a land grant from the government would probably take 10 to 15 years.

They two met and to his greatest delight, Sridhar discovered that Shankar was also toying with a similar idea. Sridhar said, 'Call it divinity, call it serendipity, call it luck by chance or whatever, it just gelled. And he said, "Let's do it. I will put half the money, you put the other half. We will just start."' They had some pilot classes in 2010 and within a year, on Shankar's forty-fourth birthday on 4 March 2011, the academy was launched. 'Shankar Mahadevan Academy' saw the light of day.

The Shankar Mahadevan Academy (SMA) first started only in the US because in India there was no Internet bandwidth in people's homes at that time. Once digital subscriber line technology was introduced here, the academy was launched in India as well. One of the earliest and most popular curriculums of the academy was 'Grow with Music'. In this curriculum, they came up with the idea of converting rhymes to swaras. This coding and decoding of sargams became the signature of SMA. The first problem that SMA faced while creating the curriculum was that the classical music wasn't secular, so to speak. Every song that they took had some references to gods like Rama, Krishna or Govinda. That is why they created a fresh curriculum which was based on the principles of Indian classical music. In Shankar's own words:

> I would like to do one Carnatic concert with absolutely new kritis infused with fresh thoughts and messages. I want to sing of humanity, of friendship, of what is happening to the Earth and the like. And it will be in a language that everyone will understand. It will not talk of gods but go on beyond that. Kritis that will inspire the youth to wake up and do something for the nation.

Besides experimenting with several genres of music, they started new concepts to make learning fun. With the watchword of spreading joy through music, they wanted to reach the children living in poverty. Their aim was also to discover untapped talents that might have been left buried and unnoticed. Besides inspiring these financially-backward children to pursue their dreams, the programme aims to turn them into well-rounded individuals—confident, poised and practised.

Their programme named 'Design of Life' has the objective of blending art, activity and music with the other subjects of the school curriculum. Learning becomes fun and memorable through this programme. 'Joyful Choir for Children' is meant for children on the autism spectrum. The children get some moments of sheer joy when they come together online and perform in a joyful choir. In the annual gathering of SMA, they come, perform and spread cheer. The SMA also partnered with some special schools like Samantha, Colours and Samaritan Trust for the specially-abled.

'Archive to Alive' is an extremely important programme through which SMA brought to the world the rare compositions of the great maestros of Carnatic classical music. Apart from the archival value, the purpose of the programme is also to make those immortal compositions available for all. 'The Special Courses for Senior Citizens' shows that learning music doesn't need any age bar, and it is never too late to start. One of the biggest banes of modern society is the loneliness of elderly people and this programme has become a source of joy in the lives of those people. The SMA Samaj is a trust that runs contests from time to time to find good lyricists, talented singers and musicians. The winners come together to produce music videos that spread social awareness. Shankar composes music from the lyrics and then they get the students and teachers, and Shankar himself, to sing and launch the song. Once, the winner had come up with a song 'Humari Zameen' that spoke against plastic use.

Many SMA Sangam shows happen in Bangalore and many others take place in National Centre for the Performing Arts (NCPA) in Mumbai. There have been occasions where distinguished guests like Kaushiki Chakraborty, Hariharan and Shreya Ghoshal came to inspire the young learners to fulfil their dreams. In one such SMA show in NCPA, Shankar announced the programme 'My Country My Music'—the initiative that came as a result of the collaboration between SMA and Connect India. It aimed to connect rural India to the world through the medium of music. The way Shankar comes to the level of these bubbling children, sings with them and shares fun and laughter with them only shows how his inner self comes alive when he stays unarmed and unpretentious with these kids. The SMA Sangam happens quite frequently now, where students from all around the globe wait for an opportunity to perform with and meet Shankar. With an unfading smile and infectious enthusiasm, Shankar respects each one of those selfie-seeking students and allows them to have some rare moments of supreme joy.

'Aman Ki Asha'

The SMA is not only an endeavour to spread happiness through music, but it is also a means to promote the immense treasure of our country's music. Shankar has always been the flagbearer of promoting the culture of India to the world via his music. Ever since he was a kid standing in front of the mic to sing 'Nanha Munna Rahi Ho' in school functions, Shankar became synonymous with singing songs that showed his love for India. After *Breathless*, Javed Akhtar and Shankar collaborated once again in a non-film album *Nine* in 2003. Shankar sang nine songs on nine emotions of humans, known as the *Navarasa*.

One of those songs, 'Oh Sahibaa', celebrates the most precious of human emotions—joy. Shankar sang this up-tempo number that speaks of the happiness of life. The music video of this song, made by Shaad Ali in the wonderful locales of Rohtang Pass and adjoining villages, portrays the vignettes of a happy India. In his mirthful and ever-jubilant voice, Shankar addresses his listeners as *'sahibaa'* and urges everyone to look around the country filled with smiles, laughter, fragrance, energy and vibrance. The concept of the video was to bring out a sense of happiness and positivity when one looks around the country. In one of the sequences, a young Siddharth was also seen laughing gleefully on top of a lorry.

This spirit of nationalism reverberates again in an inspiring song that Shankar sang with Sukhwinder Singh when *The Times of India* launched the 'Lead India' project in 2007. It was aimed to inspire the youth of India to get mobilized and initiate the movement of changing India for good. Shankar's voice in his usual trademark style, singing 'Tum Chalo To Hindustan Chale', was like a war cry for all the individuals to break the shackles of inertia, come forward and lead the country to excellence. On the occasion of India's 72nd Independence Day, Shankar lent his voice to another song titled 'Ye Desh Meri Jaan' for Doordarshan.

In 2010, *The Times of India* and the Jang Group of Pakistan jointly started a campaign for imparting mutual peace and spreading the message of solidarity and bonhomie between the two neighbouring countries. The series of commercials, directed by Angello Dias, under the name 'Aman ki Asha', wanted to promote the message of love across the border and propagate the idea that though the two countries have been separated by a line, they are always united by one tune. Shankar composed a soul-stirring song and sang it along with the talented Pakistani artist Rahat Fateh Ali Khan. It stands for the spirit of one nation resonating in the heart of every person, be it on any side of the border. The twin voices of Shankar and Rahat Fateh Ali Khan were like the harbingers of peace across the barrier.

∽

Before the ICC Men's Cricket World Cup in 2003, Pritam's debut solo album was released for the film *Stumped*. The film was set against the backdrop of the Kargil War and the Cricket World Cup in England. Along with a host of singers, Shankar sang an inspirational anthem on Indian cricket 'Humko Hai Pura Yakeen'. There was an interesting twist to SEL's songs having patriotic flavour when they gave an instant hit with the 2011 ICC World Cup song 'De Ghumake'. It was the time when audio CDs had gone into the pages of history, and the number of YouTube hits became the benchmark of a song's fate. This ICC theme song quickly hit the charts within two days of its YouTube release. Shankar used the phrase *'de ghumake'* to bring in the freewheeling spirit of the song. They wanted to make a fun song on which people could dance.

Before the start of the 2023 ICC World Cup in India, a poll was conducted on X (formerly known as Twitter) regarding the country's favourite World Cup anthem. An overwhelming number of the audience fell back on 'De Ghumake', as for them no other anthem could express the emotion of the millions like this song did.

The song reminded Shankar of the time when the young boy from Chembur, with no ambition of becoming one of the best voices in the country, would play with gay abandon with his friends and use this phrase whenever his teammate would go for huge shots during the days of *gully* cricket. It doesn't speak of anything deeply patriotic, but it is so ethnic in its essence that every Indian can relate to it. In a country where cricket is a religion, this song acted like an anthem which built up the excitement even before the tournament had started. Shankar picked a highly talented singer from Mumbai, Divya Kumar, from a popular reality show, to sing the song.

Shankar sang another song on cricket, 'Chal Jeet Le Yahaan', in 2019 along with the actor–singer Aushim Khetarpal and singer Madhushree. The song is dedicated to the lives and struggles of para cricketers.

∽

Gulzar has done several anthems with Shankar. There was one for the Indian commandos. They had gone to Punjab and Delhi, where they performed the song with the commandos. Gulzar and Shankar had done one anthem with the Indian Air Force and one for the Indian National Flag. Gulzar says that whenever there is an anthem required, Shankar's voice is the best for a call. Pt Ravi Shankar's compositions for 'Saare Jahan Se Accha' and 'Jana Gana Mana' were always chosen for All India Radio. Similarly, for any nation-related song, one goes to Shankar because everyone feels that only he will do it justice.

In 2017, SEL composed and Shankar sang one Gulzar composition 'Vaadi-e-Kashmir' to promote love and support for the people of Kashmir and spread the message of oneness and love for the brethren of the Valley across the country. Directed by the noted filmmaker Pradeep Sarkar and conceptualized by Praveen Kenneth, the music video is shot in picturesque locations across Kashmir.

Shankar participated in a socially powerful initiative of bringing in millions under one umbrella. On the eve of Republic Day in 2012 at Aurangabad, he led close to one million people singing the national anthem in unison. The roads leading to the stadium were filled with people, students, families, youngsters and elderly people. The stadium itself was full. Speaking about the event, Shankar was choked with emotion, as he always felt that the national anthem 'is the most beautiful and emotional piece of music'. It was a never before experience for him. He said, 'Every time I hear "Jana Gana Mana" my mind, body and soul are enraptured. Every time I go abroad, I am always fiercely proud to represent my country and sing for my country.'

On the eve of Independence Day in 2020, Ludo King released a patriotic song 'Hindustan' on their official YouTube channel. The song is composed by Meet Bros and Shankar and the lyrics are written by Kumaar. The Ludo King game, developed by Gametion Technologies, has become the first Indian game to cross 100 million downloads on Google Play. The patriotic song 'Hindustan' is a salute to the frontline workers like the doctors, police and everyone who fought relentlessly to keep India safe during this pandemic and helped the countrymen march ahead into a glorious future.

Unrelatedly, in 2022, a song on the glory of the Indian Navy was released on the occasion of Indian Navy Day at Vishakhapatnam. The lyrics were penned by Prasoon Joshi and composed by SEL. On the occasion, in front of the august presence of President Droupadi Murmu, Shankar sang the song with Ehsaan and Loy standing by his side. The Indian Navy Band gave the instrumental support when he sang the song.

Ditties of a Devotee

Not just the songs that were meant to promote nationalism and patriotism, Shankar was inspired to sing any song that would showcase India and its culture. Indian soundscape is studded with devotional songs of all types. Shlokas, bhajans, kirtans, aartis and mantras are deeply embedded in the psyche of most Indians. This genre of music never saw a dip in popularity despite the overwhelming presence of Bollywood music. Devotional music, which once enjoyed the patronage of temples and religious gatherings or an assembly of a particular sect or community, now enjoys a secular presence. Commercial markets are always flooded with albums and despite the mediocrity that comes as an offshoot of mass production, the number of mobile downloads of such albums have never been on the wane.

As mentioned earlier, Shankar grew up listening and imbibing the mantras and shlokas chanted by his father every morning. It was a norm in almost every South Indian family to wake up to the strains of M.S. Subbulakshmi. His early association with Srinivas Khale and the concert experiences with him opened a world of Marathi *abhangas* and *bhakti sangeet*. His formative years were passed in the proximity of T.R. Balamani, whose teachings of Carnatic classical music made him more acquainted with devotional songs. There are compositions of the saints like Thyagaraja and Purandara Dasa which were part of his learning. His strong devotion towards god and spirituality come across from the very personality he carries. Every show of Shankar's, be it a SEL show, or a jazz fusion show of SILK or Shakti, starts with

Shankar chanting 'Vakratunda Mahakaya'. The audience soaks in the divine energy that his chant brings on stage.

Shankar catapulted into great heights with the differently arranged bhajan, 'Shree Ganeshaya Dheemahi', composed by Ajay–Atul in 2005. The highly energetic 'Shiv Tandava Stotram' has a trance-like madness to it. The high-octane beats, the peppy rhythm and Shankar's exuberant Sanskrit chants in a relentless crescendo leave a stunning effect. It has been a hot favourite even among the generation-next, who use it as their caller tunes and ringtones. The stage gets fired up when he chants the fiery mantra with up-tempo drumbeats. The sheer energy with which he sings the song is highly infectious. The energy of the song that binds everyone in the concert goes beyond any religious sect, and proves the secular virtue of music in bringing it all together with its rhythm.

Shankar recorded devotional albums in various languages. When Shankar recorded the traditional bhajan 'Om Jai Jagdish Hare' with only a tanpura and flute backup, it sounded surreal. In many traditional songs, he often employed different musical arrangements with piano and guitar with a more familiar soundscape of temple bells. The modern arrangements with bass–guitar–keyboard create a unique vibration. The devotional appeal of the songs is never compromised. Tabla, santoor and other usual sounds are subtly blended with Western instruments. The devotional songs do not sound alien, but they get a contemporary twist. The 'Krishna Bhajan' was recorded with this modern arrangement, as if the medium of film music is used for the traditional chant, but he sang those with intense dedication keeping the devotional spirit alive.

When one thinks about 'Venkateshwara Suprabhatam', only the voice of M.S. Subbulakshmi comes to mind. Generations of South Indians have woken up to this chant in her immortal voice. For Shankar, it was a matter of great honour to recreate the *stotra* in his album *Venkateshwara Suprabhatam* in 2006. He recorded the 'Hanuman Chalisa' in two styles, one is a soothing and calm rendition and the other one is a completely antithetical breezy 'Breathless'-mode song. The 'Padipattu' in praise of Lord Ayyappan is also sung in a similar 'Breathless' style. The 'Krishna Mahamantra' gets a beautiful makeover with a catchy tabla rhythm, with flute and santoor playing in the backdrop.

☙

Shankar always fondly remembers the first time he sat in front of the microphone in a studio. It was nothing short of divine intervention when he, an 11-year-old kid, recorded veena pieces in the august presence of Lata Mangeshkar and Pt Bhimsen Joshi. Later, he sang the 'Shiva Aarti' with the legend herself for the album *Har Har Mahadev* when Lata Mangeshkar was pushing 80.

The kid who used to ramble through the by-lanes of Chembur during Ganesh Chaturthi, singing devotional songs during the weeklong festivities in different neighbourhoods, now holds Ganesh Puja at his mansion in Navi Mumbai. The Ganesh Chaturthi celebrations at his residence becomes a gathering of not only his friends and family but everyone from the music industry. There are endless nights of bhajans and shlokas. Singers and colleagues from the film industry come and regale the audience with impromptu jam sessions. The doors are always open for anybody to come in and soak in that ambience. The sangeet mehfils, the bhajans and prayers create an unforgettable aura.

☙

Shankar, as always, kept dabbling in different levels of music simultaneously. Very often, he would go back to his early days of singing in sabhas and kutcheris. He would never miss it when he would be called in to sing devotional songs in any sabha. Shankar spoke about a particular show where he had an unforgettable experience. Once, his friend and organizer of classical shows, Shashi Vyas had asked him to sing in his annual cultural programme called 'Bolava Vitthala'. The programme had great artists like Jayateerth Mevundi, Ashwini Bhide-Deshpande and many more, and Shankar was to perform last. He was sceptical of singing after these stalwarts, as he was not very confident to pull a 45-minute-long show. Abhangas are generally composed on the *bhajani theka* that goes '*dhina dhin dhin na tinna tin tin na*'. From the beginning of the show, this went on for two hours. Shankar knew that it is a human tendency to grow fatigued if the same rhythm goes on for long.

During the break, Uddhav Thackeray, who was sitting in the audience, gifted Shankar a book which was about a project on aerial photography on the *warkaris*. Every year when *ashadhi ekadashi* approaches, these warkaris walk towards Lord Vitthala temple in Pandharpur, singing and playing the ektara. On flipping through the book, reading the account of warkaris and seeing their photographs, Shankar was amazed.

Inspired and encouraged by this, when it was his turn, he went on stage and did something unimaginable. He asked the musicians to stop playing all the instruments except the ektara. The images he had seen in the book were floating in his mind. Shankar wanted to create an atmosphere that felt just like the warkaris, who sang solely for themselves without looking for applause, cheer or accolades. He kept singing whatever came to his mind, starting with the antara of some abhanga, taking an alaap in between, singing only two lines from another one or sometimes singing a whole abhanga. Thus, he sang a non-stop medley of devotional bhajans instinctively for 45 minutes only with an ektara. There was an awe-inspiring silence when the performance ended before the crowd broke out in incessant cheer.

Shankar planned and repeated the same concept in the Sawai Gandharva Bhimsen Mahotsav in Pune in 2011, where he gave tributes to Khale Kaka, Pt Bhimsen Joshi and Kumar Gandharva in a similar way. The Sawai Gandharva Bhimsen Mahotsav has been an annual gathering of classical musicians since 1953. The festival aims to promote and uphold the great cultural and musical heritage of India. This is equivalent to events like Woodstock, where every year there is a large turnout of people. People come to the Mahotsav with mats, tiffin boxes and beverages to get absorbed in classical music. In 2011, to the delight of the masses, Shankar performed at that event. He sang like a devotee verbalizing his devotion for his deity. He said that it wasn't the place to flaunt his skills but to worship Lord Vitthala at his pantheon. The audience of the festival, after almost 40 years, gave a standing ovation to an artist on that night.

Chittagong

For SEL, the scope of composing music on the Indian freedom movement or songs glorifying the valour of the immortal freedom fighters came when they composed music for *Chittagong* in 2012. This was their first time working on a period film. The splendid soundtrack of this film, set in the 1930s, makes optimum use of traditional Bengali folk instruments like *khol* and *mondira* and has strong *baul* influences, but with a contemporary twist.

Nobody ever imagined that a low-budget film on the national uprising in Chittagong would fetch a slew of National Awards—one for the director Bedabrata Pain, the second for the lyricist Prasoon Joshi and the third one for Shankar for the melodious number 'Bolo Na'. It is a raga-based semi-classical song that comes as a brief interlude to a sustained atmosphere of tension during the freedom movement. The soothing tune is a respite from the relentless sense of fear and foreboding. Shankar was in his element when he sang this beautiful number based on the Bageshree Raga, a very popular raga in the Carnatic style of classical music.

Chittagong came at a time when SEL was receiving barbs from the music critics because they 'failed' to keep up the hits. Though it was not an out-and-out victory in terms of being a chartbuster, the soulfulness was a respite for them from the hullabaloo of commercial releases and the expectations that they carried. *Chittagong* came and disappeared, as was expected from such a low-budget production. But what remained were some songs of great value. There were no known 'stars' to back the film, and the music companies withdrew themselves from promoting such songs that lacked any star value. It did fetch Shankar his National Award but there was no hype surrounding that. But that is how the three of them are, content and happy. With *Chittagong*, they struck gold with something intrinsically personal. Though *Chittagong* was not a commercial success, it received critical acclaim from all corners and even went on to win the jury award for best film in the Caleidoscope Indian Film Festival.

∽

Unlike *Chittagong*, the next period film that came their way was bound to generate huge expectations because of its larger scope, production value and promotional clips that showed an intense Farhan Akhtar impersonating the legend Milkha Singh while sprinting in the picturesque valley of Ladakh. There was just a glimpse of what sounded like a hard rock song in a raw, never-heard-before voice playing in the background. It was the first feature film where SEL collaborated with their long-time friend, Rakeysh Omprakash Mehra.

Rakeysh's association with Shankar started even before SEL came into being. It was from the jingle-making days. Rakeysh had made a documentary, five years before his first film *Aks* in 2001. The documentary was called *Mamuliram: The Little Big Man*, where Shankar sang songs under the music composer Rajat Dholakia.

Rakeysh fondly remembers his first meeting with Shankar. He said:

It was for the song 'Ek Boond Se Boond Mila Toh Boond Bane Sagar'. I distinctly remember he turned away from the mic and faced the wall. The mic was behind him because he was expressing himself in full flow and when we heard the voice for the first time, it was like God's own voice. It was mesmerizing. It reverberated with me much after the recording and you see now that after 25–26 years I still remember what happened.

Coming across the autobiography of Milkha Singh, a celebrated athlete and also a victim of Partition, Rakeysh conceived the idea of fulfilling his long-cherished dream of making a biopic. After running from pillar to post to find a producer, Rakeysh even thought of mortgaging his home to produce this movie before Viacom 18 Motion Pictures agreed to the proposal of producing one of the first sports biopics of Bollywood, *Bhaag Milkha Bhaag.*

Bhaag Milkha Bhaag

The idea of *Bhaag Milkha Bhaag* started when Rakeysh had just finished *Delhi 6*. He met Shankar in Delhi, where both were watching the same play and staying in the same hotel. The play went on till late and they decided to get back to the hotel and have dinner together. As Rakeysh had just finished *Delhi 6*, they were talking about the film and the music. Rakeysh shared an idea for a new film that he had been thinking about for long. He recalled:

> I told Shankar that I have this film where I want to talk about the partition of India and this whole hatred we store in our hearts as an after effect and we are still not able to move on and live as peaceful neighbours. So, I wanted to address that the demon is within us. Shankar heard me with pin-drop silence, totally understood my thoughts and felt that this was indeed a good subject to do. I don't know how, but all my ideas started pouring out to him—right from my thought of wanting to do it around the life of an athlete, to it being more of a brother-sister story, to having just a flash of romance. I think that was the moment I started writing the script in my mind, there, sitting with Shankar.

The film shows the story of the legendary sportsman's rise to becoming one of the most worshipped athletes in the country, along with the romantic subplot. Besides this, the film portrays an emotional tryst of the man with his lost motherland. Thus, the film offered the composers a huge canvas to create music for the varied ranges: love songs; motivational songs on the sportsman's relentless struggle to rise to glory; and a heart-warming yet riveting background score that brings out the pain and pathos of the main undercurrent of the narrative, the Partition.

Prasoon Joshi's words in Javed Bashir's 'Mera Yaar' conveys a deep love for the beloved and immense happiness on being close to her. Keeping in mind that the man was uprooted from his ancestral home in West Punjab, there is a liberal use of regional dialects and a distinct sufi strain to recreate the essence of the 1950s. But SEL blended hard rock elements with this sufi-based folksy song. The chorus lends elements of trance music too. The violin that envelopes the song makes it very earthy. Sonam Kapoor, who portrays Milkha's love interest, is seen fetching water in a bucket when the song is used in the background. The guitar and a raw voice that sounds like a vocal whiplash of 'chhapak' coming in the refrain, bring out the effect of water spilling out of the bucket in waves.

Ehsaan shared a very funny incident that led to the making of the song. Javed Bashir was called in the studio to record 'O Rangrez'. After the recording, when the unit went for a lunch break, Shankar and Ehsaan were mulling over the prospective singer for 'Mera Yaar'. They were toying with the idea of using sufi folk music, and Shankar suddenly broke out into an instantaneous tune to mimic the style that was traditionally heard and had been rehashed to death. His reaction was very tongue-in-cheek and he made it very clear that he did not wish to follow the same beaten track. But Ehsaan pounced on the tune and asked Shankar to build on it because the melody of that small ditty hooked him. Shankar was surprised but readily agreed. Within no time they were ready with the tune, and Bashir had no clue why he was being asked to finish his lunch in a hurry. He entered the recording booth and came out with this winner.

'O Rangrez' is a beautiful melody composed by Shankar and brilliantly adorned with Ehsaan's guitar chords throughout. This tune is based on the Khamaaj Raga, a much-preferred raga in thumris, ghazals and light classical songs. If the guitar strums make it sound modern, the voice of Javed Bashir and the sufi strain in his singing gives the song a vintage feel. The contrasting voice textures of Bashir and Shreya make it all the more sonorous. A very evocative sarangi takes one back to the days of yore. With the rhythm of the tabla and dholak, one gets the feeling of witnessing a sufi performance in a *dargah* or *mazaar*. The lyrics have the word '*rangrez*', which is a Persian word for a cloth dyer, very often used by sufi poets. If the buoyant tune of the sarangi, interlaced in layers with the sound of clapping and dholak, make it sound like a song soaked in the colours of love and romance, the sad version pierces the heart with its poignancy and pathos.

'Slow Motion Angreza' is another brilliant example of a composition bringing topicality to the film's narration. The setting of the song is Australia where Milkha Singh and other Indian contingents went to participate in a championship. Shankar–Ehsaan–Loy sourced the Western Bluegrass Country songs to create the milieu of an Australian pub. The scene is also that of a pub where Milkha and his fellow Indian participants encounter local Australian ladies (*gori mems*) in a manner they had never experienced before.

As the setting was Australia, SEL were looking for the kind of music that would reflect the energy of the place. They narrowed down on bebop, country and Western styles. Shankar wanted a phrase to make it catchy, and on further research they found the phrase 'wooloomooloo wanda', which is a street in Sydney. When they were in Sydney, they had driven passed that street. It had the looks of old black-and-white Hindi films where one of the many songs would get picturized in a dance bar, or even the old Texan classics where the jaunty merry-makers saunter in the softly-lit pubs, flaunting leather jackets and cool cowboy hats while breaking into a freewheeling jig. Reminiscent of those films, the on-screen musicians are seen playing the instruments used in the song's original arrangements thereby giving an authentic touch to the picturization.

Shankar–Ehsaan–Loy made brilliant use of fiddle, concertina and old acoustic guitar sounds to give the right feel to the song. It brings in the colonial flavour with Loy breaking into funny-sounding lyrics like *'wooloomooloo wooloomooloo wanda'* and the blending of desi tunes with English lyrics like 'whoo hoo hoo, love you lady' produce an ambience of joie de vivre. It creates the base of a cheerful vibe which is utilized to a great impact by the infectious joviality of Sukhwinder Singh. The earthiness in his voice, and the pulsating finger-styled rhythm guitar that plays alongside, take the song to an exhilarating height. The change of chord patterns in the crosslines, the crescendo on snare drums and its sudden withdrawal make it exceptional. Especially in the second antara of the song, when the setting shifts to a sunny white sand beach where Milkha Singh does push-ups with the lady on his back, just the rhythm guitar amplifies the deliriously sweet-sounding lyrics, *'Kaanch si hai tu naazuk, saans lena sambhal ke* (You are as fragile as glass, breathe with care).' Then, the song goes back to its previous pattern with a delightful solo violin run. The entire effect is scintillating. Rakeysh remembered that actually it was Loy who had composed the song, and it was great fun to make a shy musician play a cameo in the film.

Together with Tubby, SEL composed some of the best background pieces for this film. The film went beyond the periphery of just a period film and became a timeless sports film. When Farhan, as Milkha, appears on the screen with the background music of a sensational guitar riff, there is an exciting ambience of the Olympic race, but the music sounds like a hard rock guitar concert.

Many old movies, especially those from the 1970s, shows the transition of the hero from childhood to adulthood, with the child running and appearing within a few seconds as the grown-up hero—the best example being Mayur Verma growing up into

Amitabh Bachchan in *Muqaddar Ka Sikandar*. The transition of Milkha as a child, sprinting and transforming into a brash youth, is not only reminiscent of the old movies but also has many more layers. A protected child, who, post Partition, learns to survive in the harsh environs of refugee camps and becomes fearless, needed a song that could capture this vital transition.

The song created to be used in the background was 'Zinda', with the word itself depicting survival of the fittest. 'Zinda' saw the debut of Siddharth Mahadevan in Hindi film music. The rock guitar sets off the melody and slowly goes underneath, giving way to successive base drum thumps. Siddharth fluently takes the song from a zappy and zingy staccato of *'Zinda, hain toh, pyala, poora bhar le* (If you are alive, fill your cup to the brim)...' to a mellifluous passage of, *'Zindagi ka ye ghada le, ek saans mein chadha le* (Take this cup filled with life, and drink it at one go).'

Then comes the assertive punchline that shoots off with a bang along with the layer of hard rock guitar. Ehsaan wrote this part before the actual mukhra. Once the transition is complete, the guitar flows throughout the melody in different tributaries, and in parts, it sounds insane and electrifying. Siddharth's powerful singing perfectly complements this and makes it a one-of-a-kind rock anthem fit for a sports movie. Rakeysh speaks about 'Zinda', saying, '"Zinda" was treated as a background track and then we made it into a song. It was not thought of as a "song". It was thought of as a thematic fusion of the two worlds which is the contemporary space of sound that you hear today, what you have been trained to, and going back in the past.'

Ehsaan developed the opening riff randomly, when they were shooting for the ICC Men's Cricket World Cup song 'De Ghumake'. They thought to use the riff for any Punjabi rock song later on. The opportunity came soon when they were writing music for 'Zinda'.

Siddharth won the Filmfare R.D. Burman Award for new music talent for the song. It was a proud moment not only for

Shankar as a father but also for SEL as composers when the debutant's talent was recognized. Siddharth singing 'Zinda' was Ehsaan's suggestion. Life came full circle for SEL when Siddharth's award invariably reminded them of their own R.D. Burman Award when they got it after *Dil Chahta Hai*. Siddharth narrated his experience in an interview, saying, 'It was all because of Rakeysh uncle I got to sing "Zinda". I had sung a song for him earlier in a video for Greenpeace organization. He was confident that I could pull off this energetic song as well. I am grateful to Rakeysh uncle for this amazing break.'[13]

The film's title song is used twice, once in a folksy pattern when Milkha takes to the track to prove his mettle, and once at the end of the film when he is hailed as 'The Flying Sikh' and wins the hearts of the millions despite losing in the grand finale. In the slower version, with just a string instrument backup, Arif Lohar sings like a wandering minstrel coming from a distant land.

The version used at the end of the movie, sung by Siddharth, has an electrifying effect. The high energy in the debutant's vocals has shades of the intensity and spirit of his father. The guitar–bass–drums–keys arrangements slowly rise towards the hook line. Darshan Doshi goes all out with rumbustious drumming and Ehsaan's guitar riffs simply take your breath away. It leaves the listeners gasping for more. Siddharth takes the intensity of the song to the hilt. Growing up in a household that eats, breathes and sleeps music, with Shankar Mahadevan as father and Guru, the way Siddharth's music sensibilities were shaped was not surprising.

∽

After a long hiatus since their advertising days, Shankar and Rakeysh met for this film and had a blast in every music sitting

---

[13]*The Score Magazine*, May 2014.

they had together. Rakeysh shared a very interesting anecdote in his book *The Stranger in The Mirror*:

> Shankar has this instinct to improvise. There was the scene from the race where Milkha during his run hurt his leg and was bleeding. An idea struck him that we must use a line from the Gurbani in Daler Mehndi's voice because only God can get you through such situations. We immediately called Gulzar Sahab later in the day. He heard the situation and then suggested a traditional prayer. This inspired treatment of the scene remains one of the finest moments of the film.[14]

His thoughts on the vibes he shared with Shankar throw light on the fact that two people with similar wavelengths will definitely connect. This connection goes beyond the constricted barrier of professional commitments. Rakeysh said:

> The collaborations with the different music directors are very personal. He is an early riser, he believes in early mornings. I wake up very early, for me *Brahma Muhurat*, 4.00 a.m., is sacrosanct. That's the most productive time for both me and Shankar. We normally speak at 6.00 a.m. or 6.30 a.m. and even if there is nothing we just talk about things. Our music sessions were more about meeting each other and talking than actually focussing on the job at hand. In the morning, we discuss what are we having for lunch and also about doing a song. And all our songs have happened like this. I will be sitting next to him on that sofa in Purple Haze and we would just talk. I will talk about the situation in the film, the characters, what we do and like why am I making this film, what difficulties I am facing in terms of storytelling and all. Suddenly, he is taking the mic there

---

[14]Mehra, Rakeysh Omprakash, and Reeta Ramamurthy Gupta, *The Stranger in the Mirror*, Rupa Publications, 2021.

and starts humming the tune and we would have a song like that here in five minutes out of nowhere. Songs like 'O Rangrez' or the title song happened like this.

The end of *Bhaag Milkha Bhaag* was the beginning of the next film that came from Rakeysh. And it took three long years to create its music because Rakeysh had a completely new vision. The film didn't meet with success, but the soundtrack that SEL composed became another significant landmark in their career. The soundtrack for the film *Mirzya* in 2016 redefined the music of SEL once again.

2 States to Kill Dill

After the resounding musical success of *Wake Up Sid*, Dharma Productions roped in SEL for another film that had a debutant director. Abhishek Verman created a cross-cultural film based on the extremely popular novel of Chetan Bhagat. The film vis-a-vis the novel generated contradictory responses from the critics and audience. But the songs were unanimously loved because of their freshness. For the first time, SEL used Benny Dayal, an A.R. Rahman discovery and a Salim–Sulaiman favourite, who shot to fame with 'Pappu Can't Dance', 'Rehna Tu' and then with 'Badtameez Dil'. In *2 States*, 'Locha-E-Ulfat' is a catchy and peppy song that took SEL back to their favourite domain of youthful college romance.

The film *2 States* satisfied the unfulfilled desire of a young lyricist to work with SEL. The young Amitabh Bhattacharya came to Mumbai from Lucknow with a dream of becoming a singer. Somehow, he became a lyricist when 'Emosanal Attyachar' became all the rage. It brought him closer to SEL, as Sajid Khan called him up to write two songs for *Houseful* in 2010. He wrote 'Papa Jag Jayega' and 'Loser' and even sang the latter of the two. But he was asking for more and *2 States* gave him the opportunity. Speaking about working with SEL, Amitabh spoke straight from his heart, saying:

> Shankar Sir composes music in a supersonic speed. Before you realize it, the song is done. If you give him a newspaper article, he will make a song of it. With SEL, I made the most impromptu music. Before I think of a word, they would start

creating a groove. They are the most spontaneous kind of music composers I ever worked with. Shankar Sir gave me a tune. I stepped out of the studio, put on my earphones, sat in the lobby and then I came up with something and then I went back. The song was made instantly, *garmagaram*. 90 per cent of the song I do in Bollywood is that I get a melody from the composers and I write on that at my home or at my time and then present it to them. With Shankar ji you give him a situation. He will take the mic, the guitar will start playing, the pad will start playing and he will start singing the lines. The beauty of it is that it is catchy, simple but original. SEL music and Shankar Sir's melodies are original. You won't hear it anywhere.

The 'Locha-E-Ulfat' song comes in a very amusing way. They were stuck, and were looking for the right kind of phrase. Shankar was looking for a phrase and the director Abhishek Verman wasn't getting anything up to his satisfaction. Then, Amitabh came up with an interjection *'offo'* with two phrases, *'isse daant ke bhagaun/ yaa seene se lagaun* (should I reprimand and send him away, or give him a warm hug). They loved it. However, with these words, they made another song. So, the original song was still lacking a phrase. Then Amitabh proposed something that he had oft-heard from Taufiq Qureshi, *'locha-e-ulfat'.* Shankar loved it and put it into the song.

Shankar–Ehsaan–Loy tried working with newer voices, as many singers were peopling the musical scenes, thanks to the TV reality shows. But of all the voices, one voice that came to stay and rule Bollywood was Arijit Singh. He was mentored by Shankar ever since he came to the limelight through a music reality show. Perhaps, SEL waited for the best opportunity to bring Arijit into their fold. However, since he came, in he has worked with them on almost every film they composed. 'Mast Magan', the song that fetched so many awards for SEL, is wonderfully lyrical. Since the film's narrative speaks of a love story between a South Indian girl and a North Indian boy, Shankar weaved Carnatic percussion instruments like nadaswaram and thavil in the interludes.

About the 'Mast Magan' song, Amitabh said that the phrase was on his mind for quite some time before one day he asked Shankar if anything could be done with that. Shankar–Ehsaan–Loy never rebuffed any idea thrown at them. Shankar instantly took the keyboard and started singing this phrase. The song was born, then and there. Amitabh was amazed at this streak of genius.

2 States was one such movie, where, after a long time, songs are lip-synced and the sound of the songs is much like the traditional Hindi films. One of the most melodious songs of the album is Mahalakshmi's medley of some all-time popular songs performed on-screen by Revathy. When with Tamil lyrics, are merged with her own yesteryear hit 'Saathiya Tune Kya Kiya', it brings a gush of nostalgia and feel-good vibes. Mahalakshmi said:

> This song has more than 12 crore views on YouTube. They have been told to make something that can make the mother or Revathi ji look very good. She is the mother who is asked to perform on stage. They didn't do something casual, they created something which is so beautiful and to this day I get innumerable requests in my FB inbox and Insta inbox. That says it all about these three people, they have never taken their work for granted, even if it is a small piece. If they have to enhance something they will take the pains and they will create something worthwhile. They will have the audience rooted to the screen making it very interesting.

2 States was, in a way, a return to their earlier turf—music written for soft romantic films like *Armaan, Kuch Naa Kaho, Kyun! Ho Gaya Na, Dil Jo Bhi Kahey* and some more. After a long gap, they made a sort of comeback to composing music for mushy romances that exude joy and excitement.

∽

Another director who roped in SEL for her debut project was Devika Bhagat. After having a successful stint as a screenplay writer for quite a few movies, she tried her hand at direction in *One by Two* in 2014. The film tanked and so did the songs, but SEL were at their experimentative best.

One of the songs that stand out is Shankar's 'Khushfemiyan'. His effortless journey with notes takes us to a feel-good state. 'Shehar Mera', sung by the jazz singer Thomson Andrews, sounds exactly like a true-blue jazz song. Gino Banks' syncopated beats on drums and a mellowed saxophone solo of Ryan Sadri created the charm of a typical old-world bebop jazz. Amitabh Bhattacharya's Gulzar-esque lyrics, Shefali Alvares's backup vocals and, on top of it, Shankar's whistling simply enamours the listeners. With the whistling imitating the lines of bebop musicians on a piccolo or a muted trumpet, the listeners are levitated to a dreamy groove.

The song that tops the list of all SEL compositions as far as Shankar's whistling is concerned, is the title track of Shaad's *Kill Dill*. The song is a throwback to the days of Ennio Morricone's Texan landscape or the 1970s Eastmancolor Bollywood of a *Khote Sikkay* or a *Kala Sona*. The very beginning of the song reminds one of the theme music of Morricone's 'L'arena' from *Il Marcenario*, where the gritty Franco Nero ambles with a laconic smile while lighting up his cigar. The prelude of 'Kill Dill' carries a similar verve and helps in building up the characters and telling the story of three vagabonds.

The trumpet adlibs; the vocal dummy words; the sound of bullets and church bells; Ehsaan's guitar; and then the drum pick-up synced with Shankar's wild Western kind of whistling, trigger a sound that leaves the audience breathless with excitement. The whistling in the prelude of the song creates an orchestral foundation from where there is a steady progression of tunes with two of the finest vocalists of the time—Shankar and Sonu—

juggling notes like two dribbling strikers piercing the melee of defenders with short magical wall passes and finally reaching the exhilarating hook line of 'Kill Dill'. Gulzar pens for the three non-conformist, lawless youth, painting the earth red with their irresistible bohemian urge to seize the day. The tempo with which Shankar and Sonu take the tune to a stratospheric height and then fade out with tremors on cymbals, leaves the audience gasping for more.

Shaad threw light on what led up to the composition of this song. He said:

> The title song of *Kill Dill* is not a song for a singer, it is a song for a performer and the only two performers who were there were Sonu and Shankar. There was no third name at all. And they were just performing it. While recording the song, Sonu was freaking out. He was having fun. And both of them were Kishore Kumar fans. So, the yodelling came just so easy and natural to them. With SEL in the end, it became more about spending time together. For *Kill Dill* I think, the studio recorded 110 days of music sittings that spread over time. No song took too long but just the way we were going about it, designing the music and putting it together, it took a while. I think the title track took the longest time comparatively. Shankar had a bad voice and a bad throat when we started composing. He was composing the tunes in whistles only as he had a bad throat. So, the song shot from there.

Kill Dill was Shaad's third film on the trot with SEL after *Bunty Aur Babli* and *Jhoom Barabar Jhoom*. If the use of muted colours and pastel shades recreate the old mood, SEL's background score with triangle–guitar–piano–accordion–violin ensemble lends it a typical retro groove. Shaad had even chosen the familiar old film tropes of a *mohalla*, the moving trains beside it and the transistors beaming songs of old films. Adnan Sami's moody crooning of

'Sweeta' is a brilliant melody and the piano–accordion–bongo arrangements teleport one to the black-and-white era of the 1960s. One wonders at the effect of just a pithy span of a 2-minute-long song that is filled with Gulzar's trademark images, which are traditional yet contemporary.

One of the genres where SEL excelled in their experimentation is rock qawwali. The verve and high energy of a traditional qawwali were not compromised, even when they took liberty with the use of instruments and chorus. Minimal instrumentation with the synth patches, riffs of rock guitar, flurry of strings, drums and tabla pick-up of 'Sajde' make it a very urban and sophisticated qawwali. Shaad experimented with the traditional dream sequence of lovers, discarding regular sweet love songs at the backdrop of picturesque landscapes and making it intense and passionate with surreal images. Arijit's voice and style of singing are utilized to the fullest effect as the vagabond lover yearns for an isle of idyllic bliss. Shankar's appreciation of Arijit's immense talent goes on to show how he could highlight the pent-up passion of a lover. Shankar said:

> Arijit is not just a singer, he has tremendous musical depth and knowledge. I don't know anyone other than him who hears the tune and writes down the notation. He can sing anything from rock-n-roll to ghazal because he listens to everything and can modulate accordingly. He is a '*lambi race ka ghoda*'. Take the song 'Sajde'. It's a monster of a song especially when the hook comes. He sang the opening part first and did not stop till he got it right. Only then did he have lunch and sang the rest. He understands the aesthetics of a tune perfectly, and then has his way with it. His voice is touched from above like Kishore da's.

Shaad shared the story of the making of 'Sajde'. Nihira Joshi came to sing for the song 'Bawra'. After she was done, Shankar asked her to try 'Sajde'. The song may stand out to be one of the Arijit classics, but Nihira's vocals were brilliantly used to give it a silken edge.

Being a huge admirer of Gulzar, Shaad kept looking for the opportunity to use Gulzar's recitation in his films. Shaad said, 'I couldn't use his voice like that in any film. And here I thought I had a chance, so let me use it. It is one of those childhood dreams. His voice will always remain in my album.' So, at the beginning of three songs, Shaad used Gulzar's voice as the prologue to three tales. Shaad might be referring to the albums like *Marasim* and *Sunset Point.*

∽

Shankar–Ehsaan–Loy and Nikkhil Advani were a team for a long time, and every film they worked on boasts of a great soundtrack. But one rues to the sad fate of some of the best SEL compositions made for Nikkhil Advani's powerful and well-made film *D-Day*. Those songs were lost because they were left out of the film. The film had a classy album of four brilliant gems including a heart-wrenching 'Alvida', a rock-induced high-energy 'Dhuaan' and a mind-blowing thumri by Rekha Bhardwaj 'Ek Ghadi'. It is a pity that the songs could not see the light of day. A song like 'Ek Ghadi' doesn't come every other day and it deserves more than just YouTube viewing. About the song, Shankar recalled:

> I composed this song in Bhoop Raga but I programmed a groove in *rupak tala* which goes '*dheen dheen teena teena, teen teen na dheena dheena*'. There was no one in the studio apart from the sound engineer. After programming the groove for around 45 to 50 minutes, I went on singing whatever came to my mind while playing harmonium and the sound engineer Abhay went on recording. And from this whole recording, whatever I found best, I assembled and the song was ready. The song was a dedication to Begum Akhtar and that era so I thought that the perfect person to sing this

was none other than Rekha Bhardwaj. Rekha worked hard on the song rehearsing for many hours, taking a particular antara and singing it repeatedly when the rhythm was on. I did not stop the recording deliberately. I knew that when one is in a creative flow wonderful ideas take place.

After hearing this song, Amitabh Bachchan sent Shankar a huge bouquet and called him up asking if he could put this in his blog. In the blog, he had written about this song beautifully and mentioned that it was his favourite.

Dil Dhadakne Do

A music composer's job, according to Shankar, is to gauge the predilections of the directors he works with and write music according to their sensibilities. Abhay recalled the time when Purple Haze was just like the 'doctor's chamber', swarming with directors and producers who would wait for the sessions with SEL. Within a day, there would be directors looking for different types of music and it was Shankar's forte to present them the scratches of songs of varied tastes in a jiffy. Farhan and Zoya were two of the filmmakers with whom SEL always enjoyed a great rapport.

When SEL wrote music for Zoya's *Dil Dhadakne Do*, the feel-good, sophisticated and urban vibes of *Zindagi Na Milegi Dobara* continued. The title of the film was picked up from the song that was used in the title sequence of *Zindagi Na Milegi Dobara*. The joviality and mirthfulness of the title song carry with it the unmistakable rock-n-roll vibes. With the mixture of visuals introducing the ensemble cast of the film, the drums, piano, guitar and clapping bring alive the ambience of evergreen Hollywood musicals of Elvis in 'Viva Las Vegas' or Cliff Richard's freewheeling jigging with his ubiquitous 'Put on Your Dancing Shoes' in *Summer Holiday*.

The retro sound of the 1960s and '70s is back again in a vivacious duet by Sukriti Kakar and Siddharth called 'Pehli Baar' and Sunidhi's chirpy and upbeat 'Girls Like To Swing'. Brilliantly picturized and choreographed on two incredible actors Ranveer and Anushka, 'Pehli Baar' just sizzles on screen. The enthusiasm of the singers and the spontaneity of the dancing couple resonated

with the spiritedness of the track. Sunidhi narrated her experience
of singing the 'Swing' song, saying:

> I have a very fond memory for the song 'Swing'. The
> hangover of 'Bol Beliya' [*Kill Dill*] was still there. I was
> always excited to sing for SEL because they always come
> up with new styles of songs. Hearing it I felt that this is a
> fast rock-n-roll kind of song and I haven't done that type of
> song for long. When I sang the song, I just thought I was
> having fun singing the song on stage. Javed Saab was there
> and he told me that Farhan had come to watch you sing
> the song and I was very happy to have him there. I had a
> blast singing that song and I was dancing while singing the
> song and within no time we had finished the recording.

'Gallan Goodiyaan' was the only chartbuster of the film. It has
a lounge bhangra feel, much unlike the bhangra used in other
SEL films like *Kabhi Alvida Naa Kehna* and *Kal Ho Naa Ho*.
On persistent bass woofs, the bhangra crosses beyond it being a
Punjabi folk song.

∽

There is a certain relationship that goes beyond individual
boundaries. Individual identities cease there. Together, they form
a bond that earns an identity of its own. One such bond was
what Shankar shared with Javed Akhtar. In most cases, the filmy
situations or occasional non-film ones like *Breathless* or *Nine*, the
camaraderie resulted in commercial superhit releases that broke
records in popularity. But there have been occasions where they
came together for the expression of their souls.

There are some evenings in one's life that give one the happiness
of a lifetime. The content of those evenings often get blurred in the
repository of memories, but what remains is the essence of it. The
essence has a timeless appeal. In 2021, Shabana Azmi hosted a show
called 'Jashn-e-Rekhta' in fond memory of her father, the legendary

poet, Kaifi Azmi. Javed Akhtar designed the show where he chose and selected some poetry of Kaifi Azmi and decided to string it along with Shankar, Zakir Hussain, Dilshad Khan, Purbayan Chatterjee and Soumil. The show in NCPA took a special place in everyone's mind. Shabana shared her thoughts, saying:

> We hear most of Shankar's film work but one understands his real calibre when he is taken away from that and you know when I told him that this was fantastic, he very humbly said, 'Oh come on, come on. It's not that great.' He takes his name, fame and success so lightly on his shoulders. First of all, his singing takes it to another level altogether and I cannot stop marvelling at how effortlessly he does it. There have been instances where I have watched him when he is taking a swaram. He will walk down from the stage and continue with the swaram. He comes downstairs with the audience and goes back. I think even for talking it needs some strength in our breath but he doesn't do that. It is quite amazing.

The camaraderie shared by Shankar and Farhan give the Akhtars immense joy. Shabana said with contentment:

> When I see the next generation, that is his sons, or Farhan, I feel very happy, I also get sentimental. You know in old Hindi films there was always this that old close friends would always want their children to get married to each other or associated with each other. I can fully understand that emotion because it thrills me that these kids, although they are so young, are already working with our kids, it makes me so very happy.

∽

Dil Dhadakne Do was arguably SEL's last outing for quite a few years (barring the sequel of *Rock On* which leant heavily on rock band songs) where an urban sound was heard. Situations then demanded more earthy, folksy and traditional sound. In fact, in the last few years, there has been yet another paradigm shift in the Hindi movie-going experience. The international and diasporic audience, to whom the Hindi movies had been catering, started to gravitate towards the films being more Indian in their ethos.

Bollywood movies had already started shedding their larger-than-life stature. Save for the exception of Salman Khan films, films with ensemble casts were more the order of the day. At that time, blockbuster films on single heroes namely *Bajrangi Bhaijaan, Sultan* or *Rustom*; or titular characters like *Padmaavat, Bajirao Mastani, Tanhaji* or *Manikarnika* were the ones getting famous. There was a spurt of sports biopics and each character was a flagbearer of Indian culture. Films like *M.S. Dhoni: The Untold Story, Mary Kom, Paan Singh Tomar, Dangal, Saaho, Sarbjit* and *Soorma* had innately Indian stories. Last but not least, the stupendous success of *Bahubali* franchise opened the floodgates of South Indian movies that simply took the nation by storm. And South Indian films have mostly been based on regional folk sound.

Apart from the old timers who stuck to their same team, there was hardly any particular music composer to fall back on. Rarely did any particular composer stand out to be ruling the day. At this point, came some of SEL's best compositions based on traditional and Indian music. Films where SEL worked were not identified as musical blockbusters, but they continued to offer moments of bliss. Three albums in particular, one from the Marathi film where Shankar made his debut as an actor, *Katyar Kaljat Ghusali,* and two Hindi movies, *Mirzya* and *Raazi,* carried the great SEL legacy ahead.

Nine

Asmaan ke par shayad aur koi asmaan hoga...

Katyar Kaljat Ghusali

The month of Shravan is an emotion for the Maharashtrian. The incessant showers, the dip in the temperature and the greenery around have inspired many writers, poets and musicians to make this season a theme for their creations. A cup of tea, a favourite book and Khale Kaka's magical composition 'Shravanat Ghan Neela Barasla' playing in the background form a slice of heaven for the Marathi *manoos*.

Shankar's first non-filmi Marathi album, composed by Kedar Pandit, formed a beautiful pitter-patter of musical raindrops in the minds of the listeners. The album, a combination of his vocal proficiency with an infectious rhythm, was very trendy. He went on to record several bhakti geet like 'Pasaydan' and 'Majhe Maher Pandhari', which were originally sung by stalwarts like Lata Mangeshkar and Pt Bhimsen Joshi. But the devotional song that made his voice echo in every household, especially during Ganesh Chaturthi, was 'Shree Ganeshaya Dheemahi' composed by Ajay–Atul.

Maharashtra has always been a culturally rich state in terms of music. A typical Maharashtrian household wakes up to bhakti geet with the voices of Lata Mangeshkar, Asha Bhosle or Pt Bhimsen Joshi echoing throughout the house. Another genre called *bhaav geet*, which means songs having emotional expressions, is more popular than film music with brilliant compositions and poets coming together in independent albums. As mentioned earlier, living in a cosmopolitan suburb like Chembur, Shankar had many Maharashtrian friends in their close-knit group called The

Originals. For a musically inclined person like Shankar, it was natural to be influenced by these amazing genres of Marathi music. Hence, right from an impressionable age, he developed a certain comfort with the language and music.

Shankar entered the Marathi *chitrapat sangeet* scene with the soft and earthy 'Man Udhan Varyache' composed by Ajay-Atul for the film *Aga Bai Arrecha!* in 2004. He sang several songs for Marathi films under eminent composers like Kaushal Inamdar, Ashok Patki, Salil Kulkarni and many more. Two famous Pt Hridaynath Mangeshkar compositions—Asha Bhosle's 'Tarun Ahe Ratra Ajuni' and 'Ye Re Ghana'—were revived by SEL for the film *Anvatt* in 2014. 'Tarun Ahe' in Shankar's vocals was used with lesser percussion and made softer for the romantic situation of the film. This was something which the trio had never attempted before and it was a high-risk situation, as this song is so deeply rooted in the psyche of the average Maharashtrian. Getting the audience to accept another voice along with the recreated music was going to be tough. But they did well and it was a way of reviving the classic for the new generation.

Shankar sang 'Gajananaa Gajananaa' for the film *Lokmanya: Ek Yugpurush* in 2015 based on the life of Bal Gangadhar Tilak. The high-energy song is an important part of the narrative, as it was Tilak who started the *saarvajanik* celebration of the Ganesh festivals as a means of bringing together the revolutionaries when public meetings were banned by the British. As composers, SEL, after their revival of two classics for *Anvatt*, co-composed for *Mitwaa* in 2015 with Nilesh Moharir, Amitraj and Pankaj Padghan. Speaking on Marathi songs, Shankar said, 'I love singing Marathi songs because of the raw, emotional and unpretentious quality of songs. They can preserve their innocence.'

For both Shankar and SEL, the significant milestone of their careers in Marathi film industry was the film *Katyar Kaljat Ghusali* in 2015. The film also marks the memorable debut of Shankar as an actor.

⌒

The music of iconic sangeet *natak* or musical dramas like *Manapman* is deeply embedded in the psyche of an entire generation of Maharashtrians. One can say that it stands to be almost as sacrosanct as Rabindra Sangeet is to a Bengali. Actor, writer and producer, Subodh Bhave, attempted to try his hand at direction for the first time, and *Katyar Kaljat Ghusali* on celluloid stood out to be the very best. The play was originally written by Purshottam Darvhekar and it attained cult status among the classics.

The play had the music composed by one of the stalwarts of Hindustani classical music, Pt Jitendra Abhisheki, who also lent his voice along with the eminent Dr Vasantrao Deshpande and Prasad Sawkar in the songs whose popularity and appeal were timeless. Dr Deshpande's grandson, Rahul Deshpande, revived three of his grandfather's classic musicals including *Katyar Kaljat Ghusali* in 2010. The extremely talented Subodh Bhave took the responsibility of directing the play and essayed the supporting role of Sadashiv in the play. The play was well received by the audience and, in a way, it revived the interest of the people in these musicals which had been lying dormant for quite some time. This response further encouraged Subodh to think about putting it on celluloid.

The story centres around a clash between two musical *gharanas* with a lesson that art does not stay with someone with pride and arrogance. The two main characters were: Pt Bhanushankar Shastri, the royal singer with a kind heart and extreme devotion to his music; and the other one, Khansahab, who is extremely talented but cannot accept defeat and gets increasingly narrow-minded. Subodh cast Shankar as Pandit ji and Sachin Pilgaonkar as Khansahab. About working with Shankar, Subodh said:

> I have always been a huge fan of Shankar and it was my
> wish that he compose music for any film of mine. I had

approached them to compose for another film, but for some reason that got shelved. After that, I thought of doing *Balgandharva*, for which Nitin Desai came in as producer and I expressed my desire to rope in Shankar for the music. But I think he was extremely busy during that time and we were in a hurry to shoot the film. So, unfortunately, the collaboration did not happen then. But it stayed at the back of my mind, that I do want his music in my film. So, after *Balgandharva* when we started thinking about KKG [*Katyar Kaljat Ghusali*], again I approached him and I said before this I had tried twice but for whatever reasons we could not collaborate, but it is my earnest desire if he could compose for KKG.

Quite naturally, Shankar was dithering a bit. To him, the very thought of touching such a classic was like building another 'Taj Mahal in front of the original Taj Mahal'. However, he agreed to Subodh's proposal in the first meeting itself.

Upon hearing Shankar infusing soul to the theme of the combative jugalbandi of two gharanas in a royal durbar, the mind gets transported to a realm of sheer bliss. The presence of two of the biggest names of Marathi classical music—Rahul Deshpande and Mahesh Kale—make it a stunning tapestry of classical music which sounds surreal in the time of modern-day music. An opportunity came to SEL to search for the roots of Indian classical music for the first time and with Shankar at the helm of it, both as an actor and singer, SEL marked another landmark in their career. For the singer Shankar, *Katyar Kaljat Ghusali* came at the juncture of his life where he employed all the skill that he had gathered in the 35 years of his musical career. Every bit of learning that he had received from Khale Kaka and his interactions with other maestros over the years left a collective impression in his mind, and the essence of it took shape in every single song that he sang in the movie.

Shankar–Ehsaan–Loy faced a virtual acid test when they embarked on the project of reinventing the songs. Recreating Pt Abhisheki's compositions was an extremely sensitive issue. The purity of the compositions had to be intact. At the same time, it had to appeal to the younger generation who have short attention spans. At first, Subodh thought of using all original compositions. But later on, he decided to keep some of the old songs of Abhisekhi and create some new compositions so that the newer generation could connect and be aware of the great tradition as well. Subodh was particularly impressed by the way SEL bridged the gap. Their adaptations of the original compositions left their mark and also kept the sanctity of the original songs intact. He said:

> The way Shankar composed the songs is to suppose a young boy who doesn't know about the original or Pt Abhisheki, either will feel that all of them have been composed by Pt Abhisheki or that all of them have been composed by Shankar ji. (sic) The assimilation of the old songs with the new has been done so incredibly that one cannot make out which song is composed by whom.

Shankar took it as the biggest compliment. The original compositions like 'Ghei Chhand' and 'Surat Piya Ki' went beyond 10 minutes in the original play. They were shortened to 4–6 minutes for the film. Along with the iconic *natya geets* from the original, SEL added several original scores which include *bandishes*, devotional songs and qawwalis. The film had a whopping 17 songs. Both the film and the music were huge commercial successes. It is considered one of the highest-grossing Marathi films. Mahesh Kale won the National Award for the best male playback singer for the song 'Aruni Kirani' at the 63rd National Film Awards. The music of this movie made people sit up and appreciate the multi-talented side of SEL.

Quite understandably, Shankar was in two minds about accepting the offer of acting. Watching him play the role of the royal singer and sing some of the best songs he had ever sung, one feels that the role was perhaps meant only for him. Regarding his acting stint, Shankar says:

> When you are delivering hits, making the crowd swing with your performances and content with the gifts God has given you, you ask yourself what else you need. When you push yourself over, it reveals a part of you that you didn't know about. It's like I used to live in this house and never knew about a room that existed. It has been very liberating.

When Shankar was approached to act in one of the key roles of the film, he took a couple of days to finally decide in the affirmative. He might have starred in some music videos and a TV serial long back, but fleshing out a character as significant as Pandit ji wasn't a cakewalk. In Shankar's own words, 'I could relate to his character, his belief in the purity of music and the fact that he was true to himself. It struck me that this may be a role of a lifetime that I may never get again.'

The character of Pandit ji in the film was an embodiment of purity, innocence and goodness. That was the time when Subodh used to meet Shankar almost every day for music sessions. Subodh says how his search for the person to impersonate the role of Pandit ji ended one day when a sudden realization came to him. He said:

> I was looking out for Pandit ji in the outside world, and in this world daily I was working with Pandit ji here. One day I felt that the one whom I am searching for is the one whom I am meeting every day. So why not ask him to do the role? If Shankar ji does the role of Pandit ji I felt there was no acting needed to show his goodness or purity of heart, as that is what is inherent in him. (sic) The

one who has such a clear pure heart doesn't need to act to show these qualities. So, I just told him you don't have to do anything, you just have to wear a different costume and you have to just play yourself, for me you are Pandit ji in body and soul.

When Shankar played the character of Pandit ji singing 'Sur Niragas Ho' and worshipping Lord Ganesha, it is not just the character but Shankar himself becoming an ascetic in the continuous quest for a note that connects him with the divine. Every musician seeks it but not everyone is blessed with it. The ascension of notes that come in succession in the invocation of the Lord goes beyond time and space. It springs out of a soul that finds a state of ultimate spiritual bliss. At this point, the character that Shankar played became the fictional embodiment of what Shankar carried with him all his life—the pure, unadulterated soul of a child that stems out of divinity. The most striking feature in Shankar's personality is an air of candour that gets associated with him wherever he goes, whenever he talks and in whichever way he sings. That is why when he ventured into the new arena of acting in movies, unlike other singers–actors, Shankar opted for a glamour-less character that outshone others through his simplicity.

တ

Walking through the passage of life, he dallied in various avenues, dabbled in the music of various forms, essayed himself in the menagerie of electronic sounds and Western ways and juggled his unfathomable talent in numerous forms. Even with all his dexterous flirtations with musical notes, deep down in his being, he is a seeker—a humble worshipper of music. He invokes 'sur' to be innocent and pure, free from all bias and prejudices. Shankar reaches the pinnacle of his talent in this movie. As the elderly Pandit ji—who metaphorically epitomizes gentility, humility and innocence—Shankar ambles across the screen and dedicates himself at the altar of music. Through his depiction, the fictional character and the quintessential Shankar Mahadevan become synonymous.

While facing the camera for the first time for *Katyar Kaljat Ghusali*, he said that while singing for the last 20 years he never had any anxiety or nervousness, but for this he had the jitters. He realized that it was not just about delivering dialogues but a tremendous amount of work with the mind that an actor had to do. He had to lip sync, remember where to stop, take care of the lights, react to something and at the same time remember his dialogues. The scene where Pandit ji loses his voice was a very emotional and challenging one for him, as he had to put himself in a situation where he is losing his own voice. That was quite a torture for him because the biggest thing for him has always been music. He said that acting is a mind game and that a good actor has to place himself in the character's shoes. Shankar did that scene in one take.

In the sequence of 'Man Mandira' where Pandit ji takes his young disciple, Sadashiv, near a river with a lamp in an enchantingly dreamy sequence, Shankar embodies his character. The disciple is surprised when the lamp is not handed over to him as a mark of the continuation of the gharana. The boy is baptized as the person bestowed with the gift of carrying the legacy forward in a ritualistic ceremony when a holy thread is tied around his wrist. The 'guru' in Indian culture is the most respected and revered figure, placed even before parents. A guru is someone who takes one from ignorance to enlightenment—metaphorically speaking, from darkness to light.

Shankar, as Pandit ji, takes his young disciple to a dark forest and through this song which talks about enlightening the temple of the mind through *sadhana*, shows him the brilliant luminous light of the numerous fireflies. The sequence shows the beautiful love and respect between the Guru and the young *shishya*. The dark forest, illuminated by the innumerable fireflies, is akin to the

Guru illuminating the young disciple's mind with the invaluable light of musical knowledge.

Shivam Mahadevan (who sang Sadashiv's part) takes the tune from his father with great reverence and lets it flow in the world. When Shankar sings, '*Swaynprakaashi tu taaraa / chaitanyaachaa gaabhaaraa* (You are a self-illuminated star, you are a whole world of divine consciousness)', he sends the message that there is no need to hand over the lamp as a mark of handing over the baton. The shishya himself is a self-illuminated star whose effulgence will shine through. The deeply meaningful lyrics of a father encouraging his son with '*Bhar pankhaatun swapna udyaache/ Jhep ghe re paakharaa/ Ujalun ghei saadhakaa* (O free bird, take a huge leap and fly towards the open sky)' sounds highly apt for Shankar and Shivam. The purity with which Shivam warbles in the path shown by his father is one of the high points in Shankar's singing career too.

Subodh shared a great anecdote about the picturization of the song 'Man Mandira'. He said:

> The sargam for 'Man Mandira' was already recorded because we wanted to picturize it. In the original recording, it was very short. When we went about to shoot it, seeing the entire atmosphere, Shankar just left that recorded sargam and sang live there and that was picturized on the spot. If there had been some other actor, I would not have had this invaluable moment.

ॐ

From 'Kajrare' to *Katyar Kaljat Ghusali*, it was a long journey for Shankar where he kept on exploring various genres of music. He would bring in all his multi-layered and interdisciplinary dimensions of singing while performing at concerts. He would easily put himself in a different avatar the moment he shifted from one space to another. So, in his recording, he would be

at his casual best, composing music with Ehsaan and Loy in a
fun way. Looking at the lyrics, he would instantly break out into
a new tune and record the scratch. The very next moment he
would get inside the recording booth and play a nice little groove
on any percussion instrument. His evenings would either be at
a Marathi bhav geet show where he would be the first among
equals, singing in praise of Vitthala. He would also spend time in
his own recording studio discussing and exploring ways of folk
fusions with Siddharth and nephew Soumil—the chief keyboardist
whenever Shankar had a solo public show.

In the solo public shows, he often blends one beautiful bhav
geet with a bhajan. He can easily break into a difficult Pt Bhimsen
Joshi abhang 'Maje Maher Pandhari' with as much ease as he can
soulfully render Vasantrao Deshpande's 'Baglyanchi Maal Phule'
composed by Khale Kaka. At a huge Bollywood concert, with
more than 10,000 people, he would sing an abhanga. The purpose
has always been to draw audiences towards different genres of
music and to make them feel that mainstream music is not the
only music in our country. He said, 'When I have been blessed,
I have dealt with so many genres and can easily blend them and
present them, I decide to do shows where I can showcase all the
genres on one platform.'

The score of *Katyar Kaljat Ghusali* was considered for the
United Nations Educational Scientific and Cultural Organization's
Fellini medal for its outstanding achievements in music. Subodh is
now coming up with another old Marathi play called *Manapman*.
It is ages old from the time when Balagandharva and Deenanath
Mangeshkar worked in this play. The album of *Manapman* was
the biggest hit of all time. So, Subodh is trying to revive this
100-year-old classic of Marathi theatre and convert it into a
musical fairy-tale love story. He said:

> If today I have to bring it to the people then again I have to
> combine the original stuff with the new stuff and none other

than Shankar ji can do justice to this. I want this because I want his positivity to be with my film. That will be like his blessing to my film. For me, Shankar ji is an angel sent to this earth by God.

Manapman has gone on the floors in October 2023 and should probably be released by next year.

Folk Rock

Though SEL blazed the trail of creating a rock genre in the confines of Hindi film music with *Rock On*, the chances of composing band music did not come very often except in some sporadic films like *London Dreams*. When *Rock On 2* released, it did create a hype among the listeners. The super successful prequel of *Rock On 2* quite naturally created an expectation for the audience, who flocked to the theatres hoping to find something suiting their taste. However, the film tanked. The intensity of *Rock On* never actually got replicated.

The gulf of years between the sensational denouement of *Rock On* and the reappearance of 'Magik', the band in the movie, took away a bit of magic in the chemistry among the band members as well. What remained was the spark in SEL's music that continued from where it had ended. The songs could well have been an independent rock album. Farhan's 'Jaago' has that venomous intensity of Suraj Jagan's 'Zehreelay'. The guitar flicks that slither around the initial guitar loop making it a thunderous rock song in the same league as any hard metal song. Javed Akhtar wrote lines that acted as a wake-up call from the deep slumber of the social and cultural ennui. Ehsaan's guitar sounds are like hammer blows that break the wall of outdated creeds and ideas. The film's failure took away the scope of the song being a cult protest number. Independent albums from the trio never happened, but the song had the potential to be an Indian rock counterpart to Pete Seeger's classic 'If I Had A Hammer' in its concept.

Lyrically, the catchy and colloquial 'You Know What I Mean' is like a continuation of 'Pichle Saat Dino Mein' with its everyday parlance and images taken from the normal conversations of day-to-day life. But the hook line—'you know what I mean'—is how Farhan speaks in his real life and is an integral appendage of his expressions. The strain of this melody was heard in an English song in the prequel of this film, where Purab Kohli is seen uncovering the band's magic caravan. Ehsaan sang the tune there. 'Manzar Naya' is a soft rock ballad, one of the many inspirational songs that SEL and Javed Akhtar wrote together. Farhan croons with just an acoustic guitar backup and soliloquizes the essential messages of the dynamism of life.

Farhan's band, Farhan Live, was started five years after *Rock On*. This was in response to the terrible Nirbhaya rape case that had happened in Delhi. Farhan started a foundation after that called MARD (Men Against Rape and Discrimination). So, Farhan wanted to take that message of MARD to colleges across India. Soon, Farhan joined SEL in many concerts and he had a tour to the US with SEL as well. It was called SELF (SEL with Farhan). They played in almost six to eight cities. Farhan said that it was just like hanging out with friends, and that it didn't feel like anything new or forced. One of the funniest moments on stage was the live dub smash in Atlanta, where Shankar sang 'Breathless' standing at the back with Farhan lip-syncing the tune.

Dibyajyoti, the bassist of some of the songs of the album, spoke of an anecdote during the recording of the song 'Ishq Mastana' of *Rock On 2*. He said:

During *Rock On 2* recording at the studio, they wanted to record a song with the band together. We were setting it all up. Shankar bhai called one of the members. We asked him, 'If you have the song, we can listen to the melody and try to work out something.' He said, 'How can I send the melody? I am on the way and will compose it sitting in the car.' So, by the time he reached the studio he composed half of the song and he sang the melody and the arrangements were done.

Shankar always felt that as a responsible musician, the onus is on him to preserve the folk tradition, and that inspires him to compose film songs based on traditional instruments or tunes. The most striking feature of the album is the way SEL sourced elements from the folk songs of the Northeast and assimilated them into the film's album. They collaborated with local bands in Assam and Meghalaya to promote and bring the topicality of the film. 'Hoi Kiw' is the Naga rock where the Naga parlance is blended with Hindi lyrics. The singing vocals of the local Naga band Summer Salt, Pynsuklin Syiemiong, is reminiscent of Remo Fernandes singing Goanese folk in Hindi film songs. Usha Uthup carried the song to a whole new level! Northeast India has always been one of the main hubs of the Indian parallel rock music scene. Shankar–Ehsaan–Loy made the best use of the local ethos dating back to the past, yet the rock vibes of the song made it a modern-day fusion rock.

☙

Over the decades, on countless occasions, Bollywood film songs leant heavily on regional folk songs. Starting from S.D. Burman using strains of East Bengal's *bhatiyali* in many of his boatman's songs; Salil Chowdhury using Assamese *bihu* song in 'Chadh Gayo Papi Bichhua' from *Madhumati*; Naushad using UP folk music in 'Nain Lad Jai Hai' from *Ganga Jumna*; C. Ramachandra using Gujarati folk in 'Are Ja Re Hat Natkhat' in *Navrang*; Shankar–Jaikishan and Manna Dey immortalizing the cult Bhojpuri folk song 'Chalat Musafir' in *Teesri Kasam*, are few of the several instances of composers borrowing folk elements in mainstream film music.

The tradition continued with modern-day Hindi film songs as well. For instance, a Marathi wedding song celebrating the hopes and desires of a newlywed bride, 'Navrai Majhi', found a place in *English Vinglish*; the Chattisgarh folk song 'Dadaria Dadaria' transformed into a very popular 'Genda Phool' in a humorous situation in *Delhi 6*; Arif Lohar's sufi version of a Punjabi folk song expresses the trials of a lover in 'Jugni' in *Cocktail*; and one of the most famous Rajasthani folk songs of all time 'Kesariya Balam'—originally composed to hail and welcome the triumphant soldiers back home—was used earlier in *Lekin* and then in *Dor*. Even SEL culled elements from Kashmiri folk songs for 'Bumbro' and 'Rind Posh Pal' in *Mission Kashmir* and later for 'Dilbaro' in *Raazi*.

Music comes as part of the celebration of life, and the deep rootedness of folk tunes always seems to perennially carry human emotions. Shankar has always been fascinated by this cultural multiplicity and the presence of multi-layered folk elements in every nook of the country. The cross-pollination of the folksy elements and modern parlance happened in many of his non-film albums, among which *Tandanu* is a noted instance. Since film songs are predominantly made according to the demand of a situation, the scope of using folk songs in them is limited. However, the non-film albums have given singers and composers opportunities to make use of their more democratic scopes.

Tandanu is a 2014 album produced by the folk-rock band Indian Ocean, whom Shankar had met some time back at the Storm Festival. When Shankar heard the lead singer Rahul Ram singing this song, he felt excited to record it. During the freedom struggle, Rahul's aunt used to sing folk songs with her sisters. He had heard the song first when he was probably a 3-year-old and it had stayed in his head all these years. Shankar's improvisations while recording the song stunned him. In an impromptu take on the song, he doubled his rhythmic beats. The vibes of the band was so infectious that Shankar felt the need to excel each time he went on to record one line. Shankar said that 'Tandanu' was like a plant that slowly blossomed into a tree. In the creative process, the musicians kept modifying and the original song veered in different directions. Like the proper definition of a folk song, this Kannada folk number had an amorphous quality where they could develop an 8-minute song into a 20-minute long one with expansion of stanzas. Shankar incorporated some of his own impromptu inflexions and brought a unique flavour to the music.

Shankar used the powerful vocals of Rahul Ram in a high-energy rock song 'Dhuan' from *D-Day*. The husky and throaty Rahul Ram and the young, raw voice of Siddharth Mahadevan are brilliantly juxtaposed with the operatic and dreamy vocal backup of Alyssa Mendonsa. Shankar himself sang a brilliant folk rock song 'Uhe Baatiyan' under the music director duo Bishakh–Kanish's debut venture *Babloo Happy Hai* in 2014. In the guitar–drums–bass–piano groove, Shankar's classical singing, layered with his own alaap and sargam, and Rahul Ram's backup vocals, sound scintillating. Songs like these are generally heard either in rock concerts or in the Coke Studio set up.

This kind of sourcing from traditional folk music, while assimilating it with his indigenous stuff and making the final output his own, happened several times with Shankar. In a Leslie Lewis production, the traditional Bihu song of Assam and Maharashtrian *koli* folk song of fishermen are blended where Shankar paired up with the Assamese singer Tapan Gogoi. The old koli folk song got a new dimension when Shankar transformed it into something that sounds uplifting and rejuvenating.

ᕟ

As a celebrity RJ, Shankar once hosted a weeklong radio show 'Musical-E-Azam' interacting with Zakir Hussain, Sonu Nigam,

Ghulam Ali, Shaan, Ehsaan and Loy to promote the treasures of our varied music.[15]

Shankar was like the wandering minstrel imbibing and spreading the unfathomable wealth of Indian traditional folk music wherever he went. Bringing in original folk songs and merging them with his popularly acclaimed film songs is nothing but a musical acknowledgement of the immeasurable depth of Indian folk music. Being intrigued by the iridescent sonic landscape of India, he has always been on the quest to bring the best of Indian folk sound to the discerning audience. His campaign of staging shows on Indian folk music comes under the project 'My Country, My Music' where he dons the role of the flagbearer of Indian folk music, along with a host of contemporary musicians from different parts of the country.

---

[15]'Shankar Mahadevan Brings Together Musical Guru's for "Musical-E-Azam"', *RandMBiz*, 29 December 2006, https://tinyurl.com/ym77xhk3. Accessed on 6 December 2023.

My Country, My Music

Shankar had a firm belief that our country's youth could be drawn to folk music. He wanted to bust the myth about the youth not being interested in folk music through his concerts. With time, he realized that the onus of popularizing folk music lies on the musicians who had mastered their craft and had earned a name. He found immense possibilities in this art form which has its roots deeply ingrained in time, tradition and psyche of the masses.

Bollywood music can be all too powerful because of its reach but if the diverse strains of earthy folk tunes are blended with the popular songs and modern instruments, a different identity of folk music can be explored. Folk music, in its original form, might not have gone beyond the periphery of its respective locale and culture. However, it has certain intrinsic elements which are time-tested and which have the potential to penetrate the psyche of young people as well. Shankar took the essence of it and presented it in a new format, with the glitz and glamour that would be attractive to the audience while remaining rich in content as well. Shankar conceived this idea for a recital known as 'Kaleidoscope: Musical Heritage of India' in 2015 that premiered at Esplanade–Theatres on the Bay in Singapore.

He jammed for two days at a stretch with artists from across India as if madness and sheer hysteria possessed him, and he transmitted this energy on stage. Later, the concert was renamed as 'My Country, My Music' when it premiered in Mumbai. With the music of various parts of India brought into one melting pot,

Shankar virtually travelled pan India through sound. Shankar said, 'You just close your eyes and you can see India in the show.' Folk music has been the bedrock of Indian culture and it has its significance in every occasion of life— from cradle to grave.

In his undying endeavour to enshrine and spread the rich cultural heritage of our country, Shankar brought hidden talents from various parts of India to the limelight. He started collaborating with folk artists from Tamil Nadu, Kerala, Andhra Pradesh, Maharashtra, Rajasthan, Assam and West Bengal and amalgamated their songs with his interpretations. 'My Country, My Music' is a celebration of music that Shankar drives all over the country. Often, he takes it to the stage of Bacardi NH7 Weekender, a programme earmarked for the youth. Often, NCPA hosts shows where Shankar brings several musicians from all over the country. Shankar keeps exploring raw talents and curates them for the shows and as it is him running the show, the concerts have been a large draw among the different sections.

Instead of singing the traditional songs as they were sung in the past, Shankar embellished them with modern idioms and made them relatable to the youth fed with the MTV and Coke Studio culture. The fluidity of folk music encompasses all genres. So, in the Bacardi NH7 Weekender concert, the young crowd got to see a spectacular presentation of musical tableaux on stage. The predominantly young people are accustomed to seeing the guitarists bending their bodies over the strings and twitching their contours while pulling the whammy bar; and the pony-tailed musician clad in 'Led Zeppelin' T-shirts flaunting muscular tattooed upper arms, shrieking their songs of protest in a throaty husky voice. But there are also singers and musicians in their traditional, regional apparel playing some unfamiliar string instrument, with Shankar belting out his sargams or blending a thumri with the songs sung in the regional language.

To bring together folk musicians from all parts of the country, Shankar connected with Rajappa Iyer from South, Mame Khan

from Rajasthan, Rasika Chandrasekhar from Kashmir, Dr Ganesh
Chandanshive from Maharashtra, Anindita Paul from Assam and
many more.

Shankar's very presence on the stage drew instant euphoric
expressions from the audience. But here, he was not the chief or
only vocalist like in other shows. He took the role of a *sutradhar*
or a coordinator. The pageant rolled out. Chandanshive brought
a slice of rural Maharashtra in his folk song, and Shankar
complemented it with an improvised melodic line. Then he took
his audience in a vocal sing-along with catchy Tamil hook lines.
He had his audience jigging to the ever-popular 'Ekla Cholo Re'
and swinging to the hypnotic Bihu folk of 'Chadh Gayo Papi
Bichhua' sung by Anindita. When he engaged in an absorbing
vocal sawal-jawab with Mame Khan, the audience went berserk
and soon yells and screams of approval filled the entire venue.
The dholaks that one got to hear in the rural neighbourhood
of Northern India threw the young audience in raptures. The
melodic see-saw of his alaap and Rasika's flute and the bassist's
guitar held the audience in awe.

He took any folk song and let the unfamiliar notes traverse
an uncharted terrain and gradually morph into SEL's popular
'Bawra'. This happened again when a Gujarati folk song got
metamorphosed into his ever-popular 'Albela Sajan'. His
impromptu sargam underwent an unconscious and spontaneous
change, and the traditional Bihari folk sound evolved into the
familiar tune of 'Chalat Musafir'. Rasika shared her experience
of working with Shankar on this project, saying:

> We were at the rehearsals and during the break, we were
> having chai. Shankar ji was also sitting with us but his mind
> was somewhere else. I saw him continuously shaking his head
> with a beat on his hand. So, in literally 15 minutes, in his mind,
> while we were all taking a break, he had already composed a
> new tarana. And on the way back home he had figured out

the lyrics for it and had completed the composition in the Raga Sindhu Bhairavi. That was like magic.

Shankar helped the audience relate more to these folk songs by singing his popular songs. So, 'Mano Ya Na Mano' from the *Breathless* album came as an instance of North Indian folk sound. The folk rap 'Man Mohini' of *Hum Dil De Chuke Sanam* is sung to demonstrate the richness of the Gujarati culture. 'Bumbro' is sampled to show how he makes use of Kashmiri folk elements to churn out a chartbuster. Thus, the audience got a rare opportunity to witness something new being born on stage.

In many of his jazz fusion shows abroad, with the most unlikely backup of double bass and tenor saxophone, he merged kirtans and bhajans to give the international audience an idea of the richness of Indian culture. As Shankar has always envisioned, the youth of the country comes to the concerts to feel the energy, to dance and sing. But when they return home, they carry with them the soul of their motherland and feel proud of the music that the country has. Dr Ganesh Chandanshive reinstates the basic purpose of these shows, saying:

> India is a melting pot of culture. The language changes every 12 km. Every state has a different language. But the music from my free state states that it is a soul. (sic) Music is a soul. Every state is a soul. Together the soul of every state makes this nation India. This is what we want to see via 'My Country My Music'.

Mame Khan adds to this sentiment saying that Indian folk music has immense potential to unify the religious differences of the countrymen. He says, 'We Manganiyars [he belongs to the renowned folk musicians of the Thar Desert and they are hereditary musicians] are Hindus, Christians and Muslims. We sing songs about all religions. All I would like to say is let music have its own religion.'

Shankar is always keen to collaborate with diverse musicians. Speaking about the successful collaboration that Shankar had with artists of different genres of music, he thinks that the key to such fusion of genres lies in the concept of theatre. He says, 'For me singing with someone is only about love. It was never about one-upmanship.'

When someone wants to take a step forward, he quietly takes a backseat. He smiles to himself and never once embarrasses others. He just allows himself to be what he is in front of others as a normal listener of someone else's craft. His confidence in his own art makes him so sound that he wears the virtues of simplicity as the best of his ornaments. Shankar knows that he has the undivided attention of the audience when he sings solos and improvisations. That is what brings the appreciation of his rendition during a classical concert.

Shankar partnered with the streaming platform JioSaavn, record label Warner Music India and smartphone maker One Plus, to release the 6-track album *Dil Ki Dhun* in 2022. Shankar spoke of the concept of tying the nation with one thread of music, saying, 'Right from the heartbeat to the rustling of leaves, to the chirping of birds, to the clanking of railway tracks—we find rhythm everywhere.' The song triggers among the listeners a desire to explore music everywhere and then asks the listener to finally go inward and listen to the *dhun* of one's heart that harmonizes all the diverse rhythms of life.

Once, Shankar was having breakfast in a restaurant when he happened to listen to a musician playing flute on the pavement. He was so pleased with the misnomer's flute that he posted it on social media and also went on to have an instant jugalbandi with the flautist.

တ

Shankar was invited to take India to the doorstep of the world once again after SILK, when Indian tabla exponent Ustad Zakir

Hussain, English jazz double bassist Dave Holland and American saxophonist Chris Potter formed the band Cross Currents in 2017. With their original compositions, Western jazz standards and Indian classical pieces they presented shows on cross-cultural continuum. Indian jazz guitarist Sanjay Divecha, the godfather of Indian jazz Louiz Banks and his son Gino completed the formidable line-up. Cross Currents' idea was to bring together two different flows of music—American jazz and Indian classical music—as they have so many connecting points. The band keeps travelling all over Europe and the US carrying the message of how the basic spirit of music remains the same and how music has bridged the cultural differences between the two continents. Sanjay Divecha shared his experience of working with Shankar on stage in these shows, saying:

> Shankar always has a smile on his face and what a beaming smile it is. Zakir bhai used to say that his smile entered with him. I have never seen him complain about anything. He will find a way to deal with whatever situation he faces. His eyes are always bright and lit up. He creates a situation on stage for us to play freely and he loves that.

Shankar got the scope of unearthing the treasures of folk music with the next film that came his way. Rakeysh Omprakash Mehra's dream project *Mirzya* was ambitious in its scope and premise. Even though it didn't get commercial success, the film's soundtrack remains one of the most significant milestones in SEL's career. If in Rakeysh's earlier films like *Bhaag Milkha Bhaag* they used Punjabi folk elements, in *Mirzya* they resorted to using Rajasthani folk sound.

Mirzya

In 1999, when Gulzar wrote '*asmaan ke par shayad aur koi asmaan hoga* (there might be another sky beyond this one)' for *Rockford*, SEL were just a film old. They hadn't even met Gulzar when he wrote the lyrics. When Gulzar's quest for another sky continued in 2016 for *Mirzya*—'*asmaan khol ke dekhne do, uss taraf shayad ek aur bhi ho* (let me open and peek through the sky, there might be another sky at the other end)'—SEL had completed 20 years in Bollywood. The amount of mutual respect among them had grown boundlessly. Their oeuvre encompassed music of all genres in these two decades. The more they matured, the more they fell back on one of the oldest forms of music—folk.

The rich heritage of Indian folk music inspired them to explore the immense possibilities of using this genre in mainstream film songs. The legendary love story of Mirzya and Sahiban offered them the opportunity to assimilate Rajasthani folk songs in their compositions. The huge expanse of the film gave them the chance to unleash their best. Gulzar took time to write this magnum opus, as he came back with screenplay writing for movies after 17 years (he last wrote for his film *Hu Tu Tu*). The end of the story, where Sahiban betrays her lover, intrigued Rakeysh so much. He wanted to find a proper justification for Sahiban's action. When he asked Gulzar about this, the latter replied in his characteristic humourous style, '*Ab ye toh Sahiban se hi poochna tha! Aao saath milkar jawaab talaash karte hain* (Now this should have been asked to Sahiban. Come, let's find out the answer together).' Rakeysh's unfulfilled desire of making a *Devdas* with Gulzar got fulfilled through this film. The poetry of the bard makes the film a spectacle of lyrics.

Alongside the development of the story, the songs became a parallel film within the film, as just watching the songs is like watching a movie. Three layers of storytelling are interlaced with one another. If on one end there is a modern-day love story of a girl, her lover and her suitor, there is a constant parallelism of this story with the timeless mythical characters. Additionally, there is also the story of vagrant dwellers in the desert brought in medias res.

Music is the key to going back and forth from the time of the legendary folklore filmed in the white desert of Ladakh, to the modern-day love story based in Rajasthan. Shankar–Ehsaan–Loy composed on a wide canvas of music, where one can trace music of the past evolving into contemporary sound. As the narrative overlaps from the past to the present and vice versa, musical notes keep journeying from one era to another in a single sweep. Naturally, even though traditional Rajasthani folk music forms the mainstay of the film, the songs can't be classified into one particular genre. If the story and the looks of the film are at times Shakespearean in their approach, SEL is Eliot-esque in bringing in references to all that they had assimilated in their music over the years. Their defiance against being straitjacketed reaches new heights in this movie. Though the compositions are largely based on folk music, SEL thrived in all possible avenues of music.

'Mirzya Theme: Broken Arrows' binds the three layers of the film. The very high-pitched searing cry of Daler Mehndi takes one to that imaginary land which, to quote Rakeysh, was 'surreal and captivating'. The violin ensemble and a sinister-sounding string instrument make an ominous and terrifying soundscape of a tragedy. The expansive sound of Western symphony properly creates the backdrop of a period which is timeless—a period difficult to place in the timeline of civilization. The score that accompanies the scenes of that time enhances the breathtaking appeal of the visuals. The distance from the present to this undefined past brings in a romantic charm. Daler Mehndi's voice sounds as vast and powerful as the mountains. It issues out of the universe and envelops it. In the title song of *Mirzya*, Pakistani sufi singer Saieen Zahoor, Balochi folk singer Akhtar Chanal and the Nooran sisters create a *qissa* style feel on which the legendary love story is based.

Shankar–Ehsaan–Loy are at their experimental best when they used Western classical symphony to picturize scenes of the past. In the wordless sequences, the intense sound makes the vastness of the arid white desert even more surreal. The tale of contrasts comes at every step. The sarangi or sitar, commonly used to portray the mythical stories of the Indian subcontinent, is replaced here with Western symphony.

The way 'Ave Re Hitchki' becomes a part of the storytelling makes one feel that the lyrical dialogues almost spontaneously transform themselves into a song. The song grows in the mind, and the entire feel is like a dream throwing one in a trance. The gradual build-up of tunes and the blending of wonderful chorals; the slow introduction of Eastern percussions with violin; and a very soft piano running in the background, create a magical mood. Mame Khan brings in folk elements along with the use of the sarangi. The languidness of the song is infectious and deeply aphrodisiac. Shankar outpours his emotions by staying on-key for each note. The lyrics act as a commentary on the narrative just like the way rustics take the role of the chorus in an ancient classical drama. Gulzar's lyrics harp on one of the most popular superstitions that whenever there is a hiccup, someone (probably a beloved) remembers his lover somewhere. 'Ave Re Hitchki' was the favourite track for each one associated with the film.

Each song is like a chapter in a book that Rakeysh had visualized. Often disoriented from the film, the songs may have slackened the pace of the film but they offer the audience a separate space to explore. The stasis of the lovers enamoured in each other's arms is juxtaposed with a lively dance sequence. The tune that comes alongside is synced with the choreography of the vagrant dwellers in a chiaroscuro variation. The blending of electronic beats and folk tunes make it modern as well as archaic.

Shankar has a very fond memory of this song. One morning, when Gulzar Saab called Shankar over to discuss this song, Shankar recalled the memory of a certain phrase that he had heard somewhere in Rajasthan. In the Rajasthani folk song, where a person is remembering his loved one, he used the phrase '*ave re hitchki* (getting a hiccup)'. That phrase is retained in the composition and Gulzar Saab wrote the lyrics around it. But the way he composed the song was even more interesting. Shankar kept on singing tunes without thinking of any particular form of a song. It was like a stream of musical consciousness. Gulzar Saab was instantly putting words on the tune. That is why the antaras of the song are asymmetrical because Shankar just let the notes flow and take a shape of their own. With the wordsmith sitting beside him, those progression of notes were automatically taking the shape of a song.

'Doli Re Doli' is a kind of rebellious song in which Rajasthani folk song is placed on a jazz canvas. Shankar delivers the lines that bring out dormant emotions with a rare finesse. The gentle piano, melodica (played by Shankar himself), upright bass and Victor Garcia's muted trumpet sound like a true-blue jazz piece. In this song, folk is blended with jazz to such a mesmeric effect that one needs to be in a different groove to savour it. Jazz keeps flitting in and out and blends marvellously with Shankar's classical vocals. It ends in a sensational amalgamation of Eastern classical vocals against a Western symphony. Kaushiki's 'Kaaga' shows sheer musical prowess and is a reflection of the ages of classical training that goes into making a voice of that calibre. 'Kaaga' is an out-of-the-world classical piece interspersed with the dramatic orchestration of a Western opera and musical.

'Chakora' is an amazing blend of folk with an infectious beat of electronic dance music. Mame Khan's and Suchismita Das' vocals are complemented by Akhtar Chanal's full-throated chants. Gulzar's lyrics are again a distant commentary on the action of the movie. Elements from traditional myth are used to portray a modern-day love story. Like every song, this too takes the story forward. The lyrics drive home the idea of star-crossed legendary lovers, where pain and tragedy in love are celebrated and unconditional pure love is described as the fire of desire that consumes the ill-fated lovers.

'Ek Nadi Thi' is wonderfully lyrical. It gives the impression of a folk track, with Taufiq's superb finger snaps and claps used as percussion. And then the strums of the guitar take it to another level with the Nooran Sisters. Abhay remembers that whenever the Nooran Sisters would come for recording, they would come with a group and to their greatest delight there would be an ambience of huge fun when they would sing many sufi and folk songs. The soft vocals of K. Mohan complement the high-pitched vocals of the Nooran sisters. Unfortunately, just a strain of it is picturized but the tune instigates the listeners to look for more. The only song that sounds like one from a film album is 'Teen Gawah Hai Ishq Ke', sung by Siddharth and Saieen. The song starts with the high vocals of Saieen's *doha* and has got the Salvation Singers' chorus adding their special touch.

Apart from Siddharth and Shankar, there are no regular film playback singers in the entire album. Speaking on this unusual line of singers, Rakeysh said:

> We sought traditional folk and offbeat singing voices as the narrators who serve as balladeers to supplement this. Daler Mehndi from Punjab, the sufi musician Saieen Zahoor from Pakistan, the folk singer Pathanay Khan from Balochistan, on the borders of Afghanistan, and the famous sufi singers the Nooran Sisters all rendered the folklore. The present-

day voices were those of the contemporary genius Shankar himself, Siddharth Mahadevan and the classical singer Kaushiki Chakraborty.

The song-making of *Mirzya* continued for more than two years. They kept evolving before they took final shape. The most abiding memory of *Mirzya* for all of them was the presence of Gulzar in the studio. Rakeysh recalled, 'In *Mirzya* a song might have got over in five minutes but Shankar dressed it up, took it, cast the singer and did the programming and it took a year. It is incredible.' Gulzar found similarities between Shankar and R.D. Burman, as both of them used to 'nourish' their tunes repeatedly. *Mirzya* remained one of the most precious memories for Shankar as well. He said, 'When the greatest writer in this country Gulzar Saab says that working on this album reminded him of the way he used to work with Pancham Da, I think we cannot get a bigger compliment than this.'

Speaking about the experience of creating *Mirzya*, Rakeysh went introspective and narrated how the film was a realization of his long-cherished dream. He said:

The art of cinema is very unique, it's different from any other art form and it is a collaborative art. Different colours will make the painting beautiful. As a director you are a brush, you are applying the colours. We are all in it together. *Mirzya* is like an experience we all will cherish, to work along with Shankar and Gulzar bhai is like a dream come true. Gulzar bhai is like my foster father. He indulged me. In *Mirzya*, it was like we had gone in search of Antarctica and it was like an exploration trip and we were just exploring, and it was very clear that there was no destination. We had found the purpose to create a musical, an attempt or a semi-attempt to make a musical film. It gives us a lot of wings to make my next musical because there is so much learning from there.

Mirzya turned out to be one of the most glorious failures of all time. It followed suit of *Razia Sultan* or *Heer Ranjha* where the songs outlived the films. But the album is widely regarded to be one of the best, if not the very best of SEL. Shankar himself thought the same. Failures never really surprised them because they deliberately bungee jumped from their usual fares. As Loy perfectly introspected, 'No composer, no director, no singer or even cricketer has a 100 per cent success record. We are here to create art not just deliver hits.' This work of art is like possessing a collector's item to decorate the most treasured corner of one's home. Rakeysh's worldview sums up the concept with which this magnum opus was made. Rakeysh said with a smile of satisfaction:

> The first thing I told SEL was let's give ourselves permission to fail, only then we will achieve something. So, let's not chase a hit or a miss. We will just pour our hearts out. The music will stay forever. Films will happen. I am not the first person to make a film and will not be the last person to make one. We are just a small link in the chain, not just in India, but the entire world. If you can make that thing, just like a favourite book, then you read it maybe even after 20 years. This was our experience with *Mirzya*. We know that even after 25 years when we look back, we will wonder how it happened.

Ten

Dil mein jo geet hai gungunaa lijiye...

Home Is Where the Heart Is

On a December evening in 2015, Shankar was singing at a private party of a minister's daughter's sangeet ceremony in Delhi. After the show, he felt unease in his chest and was rushed to the hospital. He had to undergo immediate angioplasty. To the relief of the anxious millions, no major arterial block was detected but it gave a sudden jolt to all those who were close to him. Anupam Ghatak, one of the key percussionists of his band of musicians, spoke of the time when he got to hear the news of Shankar's hospitalization:

> When he had that heart attack I must have cried for more than half an hour in our studio in front of god. I sent a message to Sangeeta bhabhi that don't worry he will be alright. I requested her when he gets well and comes back home to go to Siddhivinayak temple and offer prayer to him. Then after he came back we had a party for KKG [*Katyar Kaljat Ghusali*] at his farmhouse. There were so many people but I just could not stop myself from just going and hugging him.

With god's grace and prayers from music lovers across the world, Shankar was back in the studio after a swift recovery. His first song after recovering from the heart attack was for the Tamil action thriller *Motta Shiva Ketta Shiva* under the music direction of Amrish. The song, a duet with Sadhana Sargam, is a remix of an old superhit MGR song 'Aadaludan Paadalai Kettu'.

The heart attack did give Shankar a rude reminder that

overwork, and more importantly indiscretion in choosing the right kind of work, told upon his health. As giving and accommodating a person as he is, be it on stage or off it, it was barely possible for him to say a blunt 'no' to any proposal or request that came his way. By his own confession, 'Before the heart attack I used to do a lot of work, what is needed and what is not needed. I used to sing songs that live and impact and those that did not. I could never say "no".'

It is a no brainer that a transition from being a complier to any request to a naysayer didn't come easy. The Originals, as always, stood by him in rain or shine and sometimes they had to administer bitter pills to see their Jaadya not get taken for a ride. Umesh, his childhood buddy and also his schedule manager, said:

> Shankar is so gullible. He trusts anybody and everybody and people often take advantage of him. It is not that he doesn't understand this but despite that he lets it go. Then I have to be the bad cop. He tries and adjusts his schedule to accommodate maximum people. He comes up with suggestions as to how to do it. Then I step in. But the biggest boss is Sangeeta. We report to her. She is the pillar. She is very sweet, extremely helpful but sometimes she has to be practical. She brings us to our senses.

During our talk, Umesh went back to those frolicsome days, when he used to be the short-tempered one among his friend circle too. Even their friendship started in a filmy way when both of them had a brawl over something trivial. He recalled with a smile, 'We had a fight where both of us hit each other. At heart, he is still the typical middle-class *madrasi* keeping very safe and protective about his family.'

The home was where Shankar sourced his positivity. Staying under the glare of fame, he was never swayed by its ephemeral existence. Home has always been his pantheon of peace and after day-long activities of hopping from recording studios to reality-show sets, he seeks the most reassuring presence of Sangeeta and his kids. This is the reason why apart from being one of the most gifted musicians of the time, he is regarded as an exemplary family man. He can effortlessly put aside his robe of popularity and fame and become a doting father and loving husband just like any other regular guy. Finding time for family comes quite naturally to him. Quite unabashedly, he shares that if someone tries to 'make time out' for family depending on the work schedule he will never have time. But on the contrary, if someone builds up a work schedule around his family this will never be an issue.

Despite this way of living out of a suitcase, Shankar is always present for his kids and Sangeeta. He loves to book flight tickets all of a sudden and sweep Sangeeta off her feet, and take her for a birthday brunch in Dubai. Or on a quieter weekend, he drives down with her to their farmhouse on the outskirts of Maharashtra. Together with their sons he would swim at the farmhouse, cook their favourite dishes like steamed fish, Thai curry and Indian delicacies and sing songs for hours. He would sit with his sons with a harmonium. There would be people gathering in his home and the great hosts that they are, they would make sure to have a fulfilling vacation with food, fun and music. The house would come alive with music and love flowing in profusion. No wonder they had named their home 'Sahana', after Shankar's favourite raga. This was to be their daughter's name if they ever had one.

Shankar's heartfelt words sum up how he has valued his family more than anything and everything:

> Family is most important for both of us and we always look forward to the times when we are together, with each other and with the children. Nothing, not even music, gives us the high [that we get from] spending time at our farm house or just doing simple things like cooking at home and being with the kids, or stepping out to watch a movie and going for dinner or maybe just shopping, without a plan in mind.

I can vouch for her also that it is the biggest high for both of us. That is priority number one. Then comes music, then comes your fame and popularity and the success and the money. All these things are important. But if family is not there, all these things don't make sense.[16]

About Sangeeta and Shankar being the best hosts among their friends and his ubiquitous gastronomy, Umesh spoke at length, saying:

Shankar is a big foodie and loves cooking. Even in restaurants if he likes a particular dish he will talk to the chef and ask him about the ingredients, discuss with him with so much passion. All the cooks at his home are excellent and have been personally trained by him. He is a total culinary expert. Whatever work matters I have to discuss with Sangeeta, we do it over lunch at his house to have dishes cooked by Shankar. Shankar is such a person who loves to feed his near and dear ones. Sometimes, when I am around during lunchtime, he says, 'I have ordered butter chicken from your favourite place, you don't like South Indian food with veggies that's why.' He is so warm and caring. Even when my son goes over, he makes it a point to feed him his favourite things. He cares about everybody. Even during parties, he makes it a point to make every guest comfortable. He personally attends to their needs, even making their drinks and bringing it to them. Both Sangeeta and Shankar are the best hosts.

Salim, of the Salim–Sulaiman duo, shares his birthday with Shankar. Salim spoke of the birthday celebrations they have had together, either in Shankar's place or his farmhouse in Karjat. He said, 'Two birthday parties we celebrated at his place, once

---

[16]Mayani, Viren, 'A Conversation with Shankar Mahadevan', *khabar*, September 2010, https://tinyurl.com/mrx5mr8m. Accessed on 6 December 2023.

in Karjat, at his farmhouse. It was a historic party because Zakir bhai was there. We cut his cake also because his birthday is on 9 March. So, we cut three cakes and the who's who of the music world was there.'

There was once a family gathering and puja in Shankar's farmhouse in Karjat where his very dear friend Hariharan was present. After the puja that day, someone unexpected arrived. Shankar wasn't agreeing to meet the guest, as he knew that at that time only local people would be coming with the crops of their land. On other days, he would love to meet and talk with them but that day chatting with Hariharan was too engrossing. But Hariharan himself insisted that Shankar should go and check who had come in.

Shankar opened the door only to get the biggest shock of his life. At the other end of the door stood the man whom he had idolized ever since his boyhood days—Ghulam Ali. It was Hariharan's plan to bring Ghulam Ali, as he knew what he meant to Shankar. Ghulam Ali came and sang in his house. They did not have a mic at home. So, somebody ran into the village and got a microphone and somebody borrowed a harmonium. Ghulam Ali performed for about three hours in front of only 15 people.

∽

Every year, Shankar's work calendar comes with some dates crossed beforehand. Apart from Diwali, Holi, Christmas, Ganapati puja and New Year, the most cherished occasions have always been the birthdays and anniversaries in the family. When millions of people scream at him with song requests, swing to his tunes and have unbridled joy listening to him singing, he feels as if he is connecting to his extended family. Sometimes he is advised to start charging more for the shows, but he brushes off the idea. He says if he quotes a higher price and if people stop calling him for shows, he will get bored to death.

Even while being at the peak of this professional world for

so many years, the banes of commercialism never touched him. He took money extremely lightly. He never stays back late after a show, as he can never deny the autograph and selfie seekers. He quietly sneaks out of the stage and gets inside his car to get back to his family. People, with whom he has personal and professional relationships, adore this facet of his personality. Ehsaan spoke of an incident that only underlines his undying love for family. He said:

> Once we had gone for the IIFA awards to Malaysia. It got over pretty late. The thing was that children were not allowed inside the venue. So, Siddharth was in the room only watching TV. He was maybe 12 or 13 at that time. Sangeeta stayed with him in the room. After coming back Shankar took Siddharth to play video games late at night just so that he didn't feel bad that he was left behind. That was amazing. Siddharth probably didn't feel bad but Shankar would do that. He is very much grounded with his family. For him, family is before everything. And then food, and then music.

On normal days, when he would be busy with recording, he would round off the day's work by the evening to go home to his sons. His kids gradually taking to music as their prime moving force happens to be his biggest delight. He never impressed on his sons that they have to follow the path laid out by him. He said that he was ready to see his sons taking up the profession of pilot if they choose. He wouldn't mind them taking to agriculture either, if that was where they wanted to flourish. Perhaps, this freedom of choosing their path helped his sons instinctively listen to the call of music.

The children could let their imagination soar high to any horizon, but the four walls that reverberated with music at all times was the ultimate refuge for anyone who grew up there. The tradition of having the musical adda in their 500 sq. ft home continued during Siddharth's infancy. The constant presence of music in their house created an ethereal vibe in their home. When Siddharth grew up and started frequenting Purple Haze, he would watch musical ideas bouncing from one to another and how they shaped into a full-grown song in the process. Back home, he would sit with his cousin Soumil and try his hand on any percussion instruments. Those instruments would be kept scattered all over the room. Siddharth would take a djembe and Soumil would play any harmony on his keyboard. The immediate influences were, of course, the SEL compositions.

Later, when Shivam came of age and joined the party, the band increased at home also. Savouring time with his kids would be the most desired moments of the day for Shankar. Either he would don the chef's apron catering to the demands of his sons or sit casually to chat. Though their discussion usually started with something else, it would invariably veer into music. Sometimes, Shankar would sing with them the tunes he had composed with Ehsaan and Loy. They would jam together with a harmonium and percussion instrument. It was during this casual musical adda that Shankar would teach his boys valuable lessons of music.

Siddharth had an impeccable sense of timing and pitch from a very early age. His passion was to play rhythm instruments and noticing this, Shankar and Sangeeta gifted him red and black congas for his fifth birthday. When Shankar saw Siddharth and Soumil jamming for hours, he got them basic programming software. Siddharth and Soumil would put tunes together and were slowly taking baby steps towards becoming songwriters and music producers. It was a moment of huge pride and pleasure, when the little kid Siddharth grew up so much that he got a vintage Chevrolet 1961 flown from abroad as an anniversary gift for his parents. The car now dons the entrance of their home in Navi Mumbai.

Siddharth and Soumil composed the music for the Marathi film *Swapna Tujhe Ni Majhe* where Shankar sang a song. He shared his experience, saying:

They invited me as a professional playback singer, gave me
the lyrics, explained the tune, its context and just made me
sing it. They took no creative input from me to help them
make the tune. It was entirely theirs. I was proud that day.
They also got singers like Shreya Ghoshal and Rahul Vaidya
to sing in the same film. If I am not mistaken they must be
the youngest music director duo for films in the country.

Shivam's debut had a striking similarity with that of Shankar. Ever
since his musical skill came to be known to others, he used to
be asked to sing in any social gathering. Lata Mangeshkar's 'Ram
Shyam Gungan' was the first song where Shankar had debuted
as a veena player. Similarly, Shivam also made his recording in a
devotional album of Ganpati Bhajan. He sang Lata Mangeshkar's
'Tuj Magato Me Aata'. Shankar's love for Ghulam Ali inspired
Shivam to stay hooked to the ghazal maestro as well. While
his elder brother was getting drawn to the groove of Western
music, Shivam was following his dad's footsteps more closely and
gravitating towards the wealth of classical music. While Siddharth
would swing to the rhythm of Linkin Park and Bruno Mars,
Shivam would immerse himself in Lata Mangeshkar and sing
along with Shankar on his improvised alaaps during their jamming
sessions. The first concert for Shivam was a bhajan show on Lord
Vitthal. When the kid took his seat beside his father in front
of the harmonium, the audience felt as if a young Shankar was
singing along with the maestro.

Farhan shared a very amusing anecdote on Shivam. Like many
of Shankar's closest allies, Farhan saw the kids growing in front
of his eyes. Acknowledging the talent with which Shivam and
Siddharth were born and how they are growing up as 'incredible
musicians in their own right', he remembered an incident with
great fondness. He said:

We had gone to promote the music of *Karthik Calling Karthik*
on one of those reality shows where Shankar was the judge.

So, Deepika and I had gone. We went on stage, spoke about the music, performed a bit and then we came and sat down. There was this really tiny kid Shivam sitting next to me. He looks at me and smiles and I say 'Hey how are you' and all. He said, 'I really like that song in this film, that "Uff Teri Ada" and he started singing and sang it perfectly. He got transported just like when his father started singing. And then he suddenly said 'But I don't like that part' and he said 'that part could have been like this' and I said 'I have got to tell your Dad this'. So, I met Shankar later and said, 'The way you are, your son is like miles ahead of you.' Shankar says, 'He is my biggest critic. He keeps telling me this can be that and that can be this.' He was on the tour with us. Sid came and sang 'Zinda' and stuff. Shivam didn't sing. Both of them have this music in their blood. Shivam just reminds me of Shankar.

Siddharth recorded 'Zinda' when he was 19 and none of them knew that his voice was ultimately selected by Rakeysh among many other versions sung by other singers. And Shivam was nine when he sang 'Man Mandira' in *Katyar Kaljat Ghusali*. It was especially a matter of pride for Shankar because unlike most of the singers, his repertoire of songs in the concerts boasted of several numbers sung by his sons. About the bond that he has with his kids, Shankar says:

> I can actually go on stage and sing my kids' songs. That is truly a blessing. The bond we share is like, we are buddies. We discuss things openly. I end up learning a lot from them, as they are totally glued to the current musical trends, the current songs and what is happening in the world in various genres of music. I learn a lot from their advice and their songs matter a lot to me because they are both aesthetically very good musicians.

In 2017, some months after his angioplasty, Shankar had one of the most treasured occasions of his life when one of his long-cherished dreams was fulfilled. At a concert at Shaikh Rashid Auditorium in Dubai, he was joined on stage by Siddharth (24) and Shivam (15). Shankar took the opportunity to present his two sons in a show which wasn't meant for any particular genre of singing. As always, besides taking part in mainstream SEL concerts, Shankar was using the stage to showcase the musical diversity of India.

The concert was named 'Songs of Krishna Concert' and though Shankar presented the Indian deity through music, the audience got a chance to experience diverse elements of Indian music. Since Krishna is presented in different forms all over India, Shankar presented Krishna through various forms of Indian music. From Carnatic pieces to qawwalis; from bhajans to jazz; and from abhangas to sruti—Shankar brought a broader aspect of Krishna to the audience. Siddharth composed a rock piece for the concert and the young Shivam sang a song representing Balkrishna. He sang 'Main Nahin Makhan Khayo', a Hridaynath Mangeshkar composition in Marathi.

Infallible Partners: From Rakeysh and Farhan to Shaad

Like all art forms, even music keeps changing gears to match the taste and convenience of the listeners. Going hand in hand with the changed cultural milieu, a good number of virtual online musical platforms like YouTube, Wynk Music, JioSaavn, iTunes and Spotify have mushroomed, overshadowing CDs, records and cassettes. While consumers are fed with multiple options to access music just through a few clicks, musical scores have become largely amorphous and the composer has to strike gold in the opening bars to draw the attention of the upgraded listener who lacks both patience and time. The laid-back musical breaks in the drawing rooms have shifted to the interiors of speeding cars with stereos blaring. While infectious bass and thumping beats give one an adrenaline rush, the invisible wings of music transport one back to their personal space—anytime, anywhere.

So, more often than not, the songs have a breezy element to hold the listener's attention inside a moving vehicle whizzing away in a sway. The visuals of *Dil Chahta Hai* have that intrinsic appeal. It continued through *Zindagi Na Milegi Dobara*. Some songs stuck out among the hundreds that come and go. Rahman's 'Safarnama' and 'Maahi Ve', Pritam's 'Ilahi', Vishal–Shekhar's 'Hairat', Amit Trivedi's 'O Gujariya' and several SEL numbers have that dynamic feel that instantly struck a chord with the listeners.

One such song 'Kaash' was released when Arijit sang with Alyssa in a much forgettable fare, *The Zoya Factor*. It brings instant reminiscence of multiple SEL numbers of the past. The likeability of this song comes from the rhythm and seemingly easy singing of Arijit and Alyssa.

There was another movie where an Arijit–SEL combination came forth. It has the magic often overlooked by listeners looking for a jazzier groove. *Mere Pyare Prime Minister* is a charming story of some street kids embarking on a playful adventure of meeting the prime minister to get home their message of needing a toilet in their area. Shankar's delightful whistling matches Arijit's falsetto and Gulzar's verse in the title song of the film: '*Tuhi government gaushale bhi de de, Chaali lagi hai shauchalay bhi de de* (You are the government, please give us a bathroom/ Give us a toilet too).'

Mere Pyare Prime Minister was the result of the creative team of Rakeysh–Gulzar–SEL that didn't always thrive on the largeness of Bollywood films. The issue of open defecation became the central motif of quite a few other movies including, *Toilet: Ek Prem Katha* and *Halkaa*. There is a heart-warming Rekha Bhardwaj classic 'Kanna Re Kanna', where a mother sings a lullaby to her child. The song stands out as one of the most honest and sincerest Shankar compositions.

There is a lovely recall of the golden days of Indian classics when a C. Ramchandra song was recreated to bring in the celebratory ambience of the *mohalla* where the story was set. Here, the song sounds conventional, like what it was in the past. Rakeysh spoke of how his love for this old song led him to use it in his film:

The Holi song is one of my favourites from a V. Shantaram movie *Navrang*. He is one of the masters whom I have learnt from. 'Are Ja Re Hat Natkhat' was originally by Asha Bhosle. I said this is my song because it is a colony and it is a holi festival. They sing and dance to the songs and this song is from a loudspeaker supposedly playing in the colony. So, we thought 'Let's make it like this'. So, Gulzar bhai was sitting there and he started writing, '*baja baja baja baja dhol baja re*' and the song was intertwined with the original *Navrang* song so beautifully.

Shankar–Ehsaan–Loy did another reworking of the original O.P. Nayyar classic 'Babuji Dheere Chalna' in *Salaam-E-Ishq*. The cult cabaret number has a lounge touch there.

Rakeysh introspects a good reason as to why his bond with Shankar has always been so productive. He said:

> First my connection with Shankar is human being to human being, not a director to a composer. So, if we connect like that automatically the genius inside will come out, and work will happen. I have never given him a reference, never said that a song should be like this or like that. I have only spoken about the feelings I am going through and what he gives me I accept that. It is like *prasad*. For me, working with Shankar is the human connection. What is very important for me, nobody knows if we will be born or not, but we all know we are to die. That is the reality. It is the work which will stay in perpetuity. Working with Shankar you are assured of that.

Rakeysh and SEL teamed with Javed Akhtar for the first time in *Toofaan*. It was an unusual hiatus of six long years between two films—from Zoya's *Dil Dhadakne Do* to Rakeysh's *Toofan* in 2021—where Javed Saab wrote the lyrics and Farhan played the titular character. The film was made to premiere exclusively on Amazon Prime Video when the quarantine days of Covid-19 shut the doors to the outside world.

The film generated excitement because it was released at a time when entertainment was more of a luxury. The day it was premiered, India registered nearly 40,000 Covid cases with numerous deaths reported. The story of the resurgence of a lost warrior in the boxing ring aimed to instil hope and confidence in that trying and turbulent time. The attractive promos showed an intense and focussed Farhan, heralded by Siddharth's passionate singing of the verse: '*Tooo faaan parvat ko tod de, Tooo faaan dariya ko mod de* (Toofan, break the mountains; Toofan, bend the river).' Strains of the songs that came in the promos brought flashes of the old association of SEL and Javed Akhtar. Of all the songs, Arijit's soulful love ballad 'Ananya' stands out to be one of most soothing melodies of the day. The acoustic guitar-backed song starts as a groovy one, like the matured, introspective Leonard Cohen singing his reflections on Suzanne Verdal to himself. The gentle keyboard patches and a poignant cello bring out the pathos of a fleeting love story.

People who have been privy to the creative process in Purple Haze witnessed the creative vibes when SEL interacted with Javed Akhtar. Both Javed and Gulzar have an amazing sense of humour and they have been witness to so many laughter-filled sessions in the studio. Gulzar would recall anecdotes from his early days with R.D. Burman, or Javed would talk about other music composers of the past. All of them would just sit and listen to them mesmerized. Mahalakshmi says:

> They can talk about economy, philosophy, theology and what not. Shankar's knowledge of technology, science and astronomy, or Ehsaan's interest in the occult or what lies ahead make it an absorbing discussion. You can have fascinating conversations during the recording. Nowhere else I saw these kinds of sessions. If it was possible, I would want to be the fly on the wall for all their sessions just to stay and listen.

Abhay throws very interesting insights into the relationship SEL had with the Akhtars, 'With them, it was like a family get-together with more food and other things than work. Shankar would draw the day to a close by declaring "today's picnic is over".'

Speaking about the ambience in Purple Haze, Farhan said that he always found the sessions with SEL to be the most relaxing time in any filmmaking process. They make others feel so comfortable with their easy-going attitude that filmmakers feel privileged to have their company in the studio. Farhan spoke of an undying curiosity with which Shankar approaches anyone in the studio. He said:

> He is interested in hearing what you want to say and is curious about people when he meets them. I have seen him when singers come to Purple Haze for example, the amount of time he gives them, and in a very positive way he does the critique, like 'your voice is good, but you need to work on this, go back focus on this'. He has never shied away from using new voices.

Shankar–Ehsaan–Loy used a reality-show finalist Himani Kapoor's voice in *Toofaan*. In another sports drama, *Panga*, Shankar sang a beautiful ballad 'Jugnu' with a reality show winner Sunny Hindustani.

Rakeysh feels that the songs of SEL have won the test of time and the newer songs that they have composed are dynamic dots in a huge spectrum of their creative canvas. He said:

> The beauty about SEL is that they haven't remained static. It is like flowing water. But at the same time, if I would have taken the beautiful song in *Mirzya* that Kaushiki has sung with Shankar to Bade Ghulam Ali Khan or a master or a Rashid Khan, they would have done the same, irrespective of which year it happened. His strokes are very bold at times and very delicate at times. So, it covers the canvas.

On his experience of teaming up with Akhtar and Gulzar, Rakeysh said:

> With Javed Saab when I go for a sitting, my main objective is the lunch which will be served in his house. With Gulzar

bhai we sit for hours. We go in the morning. He invited me for tea and till evening 4–4.30 we just sat and talked, discussing how he dealt with Hrishida because he was a master. And then he says, 'I forgot we have to do this song also.' He says, 'We will do the song. You tell Shankar to make the tune, I will write it.' I then told him back, 'Shankar was saying you write and he will make the tune', and finally Gulzar Saab assured me, 'No worries we will do it over the phone.' It's about hanging out, it's enriching, so it's really lucky to work with them. They are the soldiers of cinema.

∽

As time went by, the scope of music further diminished in films, and music composers gradually got a curious identity as music supervisors. In the film posters, where once along with the name of the director–producer there would be the credits of music composers, now they barely get a mention. Some of the old masters still manage to sneak in when they work with their successful partners, with whom they had delivered not just hits but also some landmark films. Shankar's camaraderie with Shaad is one such partnership that always bore fruitful music.

They worked together on *Soorma*, a biopic on the hockey player Sandeep Singh. Shaad had first named the film *Flicker Singh*. For songs to be a part of the biopic, there was an inherent love story rolled with the real-life hockey story. Shankar sang the title song in his inimitable style, befitting the milieu of a sports drama. Then there was Diljit Dosanjh's 'Ishq Di Baajiyaan'. The word '*baajiyaan*' carries a double meaning of '*baaji*' (the front rolls that the hockey players are made to do for freshman training) and 'baajiyaan' (referring to the high stakes for the love story), implying the motivation behind the protagonist playing hockey.

Shaad fondly recounts:

It was never uncomfortable, either for him or for me not to do any work. I think that's when the relationship becomes bigger than the profession. It is just like how you are with your wife, even if you guys are not talking to each other in a room doesn't mean that you are fighting, it just means that you are comfortable with each other's silence. So, I can be taking a nap here, Shankar can be just sitting and doing nothing for 2–3 hours. I will not think as a producer–director that the metre of the studio is running. Similarly, he will not think there is no work being done and we are just sitting. There is no pressure on both of us. That is when I think work automatically becomes good. When I am in his company it is like I am in a spa, I am just spoilt and pampered. I just have to hear beautiful music. So, what more can you ask for? You feel like Akbar because Tansen is singing for you, it is that kind of a feeling.

○

People like Shaad, Farhan or Rakeysh—with whom Shankar has a cherished and deep-rooted friendship—often speak about a common vibe that they all have. They all swear by their love for food. If music hadn't bound them together, gastronomy would surely have had them savouring pleasures from delicacies of all kinds. When the studio atmosphere is more of a fun-filled, closed-door, intimate musical soirée rather than a professional place, food is an integral part of their creativity. After a long stint of nerve-racking sessions of finding the proper tune, Shankar often stuns the others with the declaration that the best part of the day is still remaining. When everyone is looking for the next part of the sentence, Shankar lowers his voice and says, 'Food will be served now.' Rakeysh, in his tongue-in-cheek manner, said with a chuckle:

After our life when our ghosts are also travelling they would be looking for food. The ghosts will meet again in some restaurant only, not in a film studio or a music studio. We will be looking at the menu, with nobody to take orders because they don't serve ghosts. But we will meet there and we will figure out what to do.

Sanjay Divecha spoke on Shankar's passion for food. He said, 'In the Cross Currents tour two biggest foodies were Louiz Banks and Shankar. Even before the plan for the next day was done, plans for taking which food and where were always on the list of priority. Once, we found a Korean barbecue place and Shankar was extremely excited about it.' Sanjay also said that Shankar would make sure that everyone in the team is well. His generosity comes across in everything he does with his teammates.

Both Shaad and Gulzar spoke of a concert that was held in Dehradun in 2019. It was the 82nd Foundation Day celebration of Welham Boys' School where Shaad had studied. So, he booked SEL well in advance knowing that most of the calendar dates are chock-a-block with appointments. Shankar–Ehsaan–Loy and Gulzar Saab came and performed till the wee hours. Shaad said, 'The biggest memory I will take home to my grave was the 25th-year reunion of the school group of my boarding school. The school in its years of existence had not seen a programme like this and SEL just blew everybody's mind.' Gulzar remembered, 'Once we went to Dehradun with Shaad to his alma mater. They had organized an evening of music with SEL. What a memorable evening it was! It was such a wonderful experience being with them on stage, enjoying the compositions that they did for Shaad.'

...and Meghna

Mirzya left an immense impact on Meghna Gulzar. After debuting with Vishal Bhardwaj and after working with several other music composers like Anu Malik and Pritam, she worked with SEL in her espionage thriller *Raazi*. The day she finished writing the script of *Raazi*, she approached SEL. On the script listening session itself, Shankar was blown away. Meghna seemed to have inherited the bond that her illustrious father has with Shankar. Since then, they have worked in three critically acclaimed movies, *Chhapaak* and *Sam Bahadur* being the other two.

Raazi is the story of a spy caught in the quagmire of love for her motherland and loyalty to her beloved. The songs in this movie highlight the innermost turmoil of the protagonist. Based on the true account of a R&AW agent, the narrative naturally demanded songs on patriotism also. Patriotic songs have become very rare in Hindi films nowadays. The way Arijit owned the song and rendered it, sets 'Ae Watan' apart from the jingoistic patriotic songs. The easily hummable tune came straight from his heart and it evoked love for one's country and a feeling of pride in the listeners.

Shankar said that the film is based on a true story, and Meghna wanted to stay true to the script. Hence, they couldn't bring in elements of rock and pop. They had to adhere to the period and the feel of the story. Stressing the sentiments embedded in the line *'Main jahan rahoon jahaan mein yaad rahe tu* (Wherever I am in the world, I will remember you)' Shankar wanted to bring in a universal emotion for one's own motherland. As he said, 'No matter where you go, no matter whichever country you are in, you can still sing the song and can feel emotionally connected to your nation.' Loy shared a very interesting analogy comparing this with something that he had read during his school days. He said, 'It reminds me of an old English poem "The Dying Soldier".' An English soldier who is killed somewhere in Europe is saying, "The place where I have died will be forever England, as I keep England in my heart".'

'Ae Watan' was composed in the blink of an eye. Shankar composed it when he was reading the lyrics for the first time. The production did take a longer time because the situation was unlike the regular song sequences that come in Hindi films. Meghna made her own observation about the time the tune was composed. She said:

> The first music sitting of *Raazi* was very special because we managed to run through three songs. It was the title song, 'Ae Watan' and 'Dilbaro'. It was so spontaneous because even today if I try to think back, did the lyrics come first or the tune come first, it is very difficult to draw the line because the synergy with which SEL work with Papa is so special. I kept teasing them that I felt like an outsider. Like I have come and busted this squad of theirs but that was very short-lived. I was welcomed very quickly and since then it has been an extremely fulfilling musical relationship with them.

Sunidhi's version of the song has a slightly different music arrangement. The chorus here are children from SMA which gives a simplistic charm to the version. Archana, a teacher at SMA, narrated her experience:

> In the song 'Ae Watan', Shankar ji wanted the students of the academy to be part of the chorus. So, I was appointed to teach the selected students. It all happened in a matter of

4 to 5 hours. I got a call from Shankar Sir that there is such and such song and I should select students. I was travelling on the train at that time. I immediately coordinated with the students. The track was sent to me and I had to call all the students in our school at a particular time just an hour before the recording. I had just trained them a bit, taught them the basic melody and the students were prepared.

Meghna said:

> The situation was such that the character was singing a song which she was actually teaching children of a school in Pakistan but when she was singing it, she was singing it for her own country. So, we need[ed] a song which could be sung by a person from either of the countries and resonate just as deeply. 'Aee Watan' does exactly that.

Shankar–Ehsaan–Loy had composed an evocative bidai song 'Doli Re Doli' for *Mirzya*. In *Raazi*, they have 'Dilbaro' which starts with a traditional Kashmiri marriage song sung by Vibha Saraf and the whole melody takes over from here with Harshdeep Kaur and Shankar making a soulful appearance. The authenticity with which the tune brought out the topicality of Kashmir made Gulzar feel 'that the song now belongs to the Valley. That is what creativity is'.

Shankar composed 'Dilbaro' after delving deeper into the narrative of the film. They did their research on Kashmiri folk songs and the use of Kashmiri instruments. In that way, they brought out the social and cultural ethos of the place. To use his own words, Shankar wanted 'to infuse the entire aura of the time and place'. The same thing can be said about the title track of *Raazi* where they have used the flavour of Kashmiri and Afghani music. They used rubab and a little bit of santoor in places to bring in that Afghani kind of sound. The folk orchestration of 'Dilbaro' is based on Tapas Roy's rubab and Arshad Khan's esraj.

Meghna's *Chhapaak* touched on the social issue of acid attacks and was based on the biographical life of an acid attack survivor Laxmi Agarwal. Though the highly charged emotional drama could well have digressed into a melodrama, Meghna's portrayal of the topic was delicate, dignified and restrained.

The story of *Chhapaak* was such that it didn't need songs at all as part of the narrative. But songs came as an extension of the dialogues. Meghna was struggling to create song situations, but once she created the situations it felt that songs became an inseparable part of the film. They become a more effective medium to drive home the message which dialogues would have made loud and unrestrained. The title song of *Chhapaak* is sombre and poignant. The words complement the composition and describe what the process of living through an acid attack is and what goes through the mind of the victim. Without presenting any ghastly spectacle of pain, Gulzar's hard-hitting imagery brings out the anguish and psychological trauma that the lead character goes through. The precise and minimal use of instruments and Arijit's controlled singing help focus one's attention on the psyche of the victim.

'Khulne Do' is a song that they wrote after Meghna finished the entire cut of the film. Gulzar believed that the song had to reflect the feelings of the character and it had to be expressed musically. It was another unusual song as far as the film is concerned because it speaks of hope, resurgence and coming to life again. Meghna says, 'There is a surge in the way the melody just hits a crescendo and the way Arijit has sung it, the way the composition arrangement is, it is truly heart-warming for me.'

'Nok Jhok' is an interesting song. Meghna wasn't sure how to use it because the song came in a scene which had dialogues. Shankar–Ehsaan–Loy have always been popular among musicians in any recording because of the freedom they give everyone. Guitar was the main instrument of 'Nok Jhok' and Sanjay Divecha narrated his experience of the recording of this song, saying:

I got to the studio at around 11 and was told to do whatever I wanted. This is an incredible kind of trust and faith. So, I spent the first half of the day with Loy and went over the song and helped compose the harmony for the song. Then I recorded the song with both Shankar and Meghna sitting in the mixing console. I remember the incredible amount of freedom I got, and they eventually asked me to play a solo. I just basically played through the song in one take. And they kept everything that I played. This normally doesn't happen. I will never forget that session.

Gulzar always enjoyed when he teamed with the trio. Regarding their music-making process, he spoke in glowing terms, saying:

All songs were born just like that. The reason was that I wrote a line and, on that line, Shankar wrote a mukhra. He kept on developing the tune and then I put lyrics on that. Thus, an antara took shape. I kept following him. After that, it was just like putting words here and there to fit in the rhyme.

Shankar narrates his experience of working with Gulzar, saying:

I stay in Navi Mumbai. In the morning at around 9–9.30 a.m., it is a regular affair to receive a call from Gulzar Saab. He would just ask me whether I was on this side of the pool or on that side. This is because we are separated by the Vashi bridge. The answer would just give him an indication of exactly how long we can talk and discuss over the phone. If I am on the other side of the pool then I would have a pretty good amount of time before I reach Bandra, and in that case, our discussion would be lengthy too, and we would be discussing this and that, how line should be composed, what needs to get changed, etc. We discuss a lot and do a good bulk of work over the telephone. Whenever some ideas about a new song dawned upon the mind of Gulzar Saab, he would call me and even before saying 'hello' he would straightaway start telling me the lyrics of the song. It would take some two to three minutes for me to register which song he is referring to before I instantly get a hang of it and I remember the song soon after. So, he is amazing.

On the music sitting of *Chhapaak*, Gulzar once said that it was difficult to write songs with Meghna, as she kept asking him to change the lines several times. On being asked, Meghna replied by drawing a comparison with her childhood days. She said, 'You know it is like when I am asking him to change a line, suddenly I flashback to the 10-year-old girl who is asking for ₹100 more.'

The musical camaraderie between SEL and the father-daughter duo continues, as they are coming up with another film *Sam Bahadur*, a film based on the life of Field Marshal Sam Manekshaw.

∽

On SEL's ways of composing music, Shankar says:

It is like every morning we have a white canvas and the three of us have our sets of paints and brushes. What the other person paints becomes a trigger for the other two. And that is the most important thing we have to start working on each other's triggers. If Ehsaan plans to paint a horse I cannot say I want to paint a tree on top of the horse. We have to respect each other's triggers.

That is how the three friends keep making music like a band.

Friends Forever

After *Raazi*, none of the films saw commercial success so to speak. One wonders at the paltry number of musical blockbusters Bollywood has seen in the last few years. Shankar found one important reason for the recent downfall of Hindi film songs. He said that though the power seems to be in the hands of the creative people, in actuality, power lies with someone who has got the money. Incidentally, these powerful people are non-musical but the power of money prompted them to dictate terms even over the creative people. In this connection, Loy said, 'It is like music is a patient lying on the hospital table and a rich man is coming to operate on him, not because he is a doctor [but] just because he is rich.' About the outcome of a song, Shankar spoke about the factors behind the song becoming a hit, saying:

> We can never predict which song will be successful and if I had that magic I would instantly be rich and famous. I think ours is a creative job and we are creating something out of nothing. So, we keep looking for unchartered territories and move with the times. What is important is not to let mediocrity creep in. A musician has to just do his or her job and not wait or try to predict the outcome. But in the long run honesty and sincerity are what count.

This honesty is the bedrock of such a prolonged and successful musical camaraderie that the three of them have had for more than 27 years. Speaking about the paradox of remaining together for all these years, despite their inherent differences in approach, Shankar said that this is owing to the fact that they keep pushing the boundaries. In the process of creativity, disagreements and clash of ideas do occur but it only ends up creating something more beautiful. The difference in approach towards a particular tune is what made them stay together. They respect the differences and find strength in one another. Loy sums it up, saying, 'The core of our sound is very Indian and that is what roots our music and then we all have the other influences that we bring to it.'

The camaraderie between Shankar, Ehsaan and Loy has often set benchmarks in the industry. Mahalakshmi has a different take on why they work so well together. She said:

> Let me tell you that these three people have the most courteous sense of humour. Shankar–Ehsaan–Loy are those kind of people who will laugh at their work without any ego. They will write stuff and they will create music and they will ridicule their own work without any ego, and it is very magnanimous of these people to do that because in our industry so much is all about ego and one-upmanship and all that kind of stuff. And there are these three people who can sit back and look at their work and confess that they did not do a good job for a particular song. They are very large-hearted.

For them, their relationship is like a marriage where each one gives space to the other. They have got their own way of solving differences. 'We fight every day and we make sure we fight all the time,' says Ehsaan. Shankar says, 'We have boxing gloves just under the chair every day. We are not doing synchronized swimming here, as we are three individuals. So, we also fight.' Loy says with laughter, 'They have boxing gloves and I have the baseball bat so I always win.' It is interesting to look back at the time when they were unsure of getting any further assignments of writing music for Hindi films. When they received the R.D. Burman Award on

the Filmfare Awards night in 2002 for *Dil Chahta Hai*, the trio
said something funny. They said:

> It feels great to receive the Filmfare R.D. Burman award
> for upcoming talent in music especially since the veteran's
> name is attached to it. Frankly speaking, the award
> was unexpected. We waited and waited. When nothing
> happened until halfway through the show we thought,
> '*Chalo* let us just enjoy ourselves and go home'. Filmfare
> Awards had always been a TV affair for us. It was great to
> be invited this year and also get an award. In that sense,
> it has been a year of recognition for us. *Dil Chahta Hai*
> has changed our lives. We have finally broken into the
> film circle. But we will get the ultimate high the day we
> work in a film like *Daku Lakhanpal Aur Kali Shaitan* and
> make a success of it.[17]

Incidentally, nothing of the sort came their way to prove their
mettle. But, in retrospect, Amitabh Bhattacharya's words sum it all.
He said, 'I credit SEL with one thing. A.R. Rahman in Chennai
was found very interesting. But in the mainstream Bollywood
music it was SEL here who gave a makeover, a new millennium
makeover, a new facelift. That changed the game, changed the
face of it. That changed things for everybody.'

Shankar pointed out another very interesting aspect of their
music-making. It is all about how three individuals bring their
own personal and subjective views to the table and none of them
has any specific or defined role to play. He said, 'The way Ehsaan
looks at Indian classical music or I look at jazz music and Loy
looks at folk music makes it very interesting. For instance, Loy
observed Indian classical over the years and combined them with
jazz and then his [way of] composing classical was completely

---

[17]'R.D. Burman Award Shankar-Ehsaan-Loy, Dil Chahta Hai', *Filmfare Print
Edition*, April 2002.

out of the box. This brings the wow factor.'

Even though Shankar has left his incredible legacy in multidimensional fields of music, he believes that Bollywood music is the artery of the country because of its reach across the globe. Shankar says:

> When we would be driving down the roads of California and listen that our music is playing all over, we get a great feeling. I feel lucky that despite being a South Indian I have got an acceptance in mainstream Bollywood. If you see the history, it is extremely difficult to make a mark if you are not in the same line. There could have been putting me into a category of a classical singer saying that this is only what he is good at. Maybe I am an exception to be accepted in this way. I could have easily been branded but that did not happen and luckily I got this place with Ehsaan and Loy.

A sense of gratefulness is undying in him. Upon receiving the Padma Shri, he was ecstatic to call Sangeeta and graciously acknowledged the importance of Ehsaan and Loy in his journey.

The Transition

Many period films came to SEL from *Mirzya* to *Manikarnika* to *Samrat Prithviraj*. As all the films highlighted the life story of some historical or mythical characters of the past, songs became quite a natural precedent to create the cultural ethos of the period dramas. Shankar–Ehsaan–Loy sourced elements from the local folk tunes to make the story more authentic. Songs like 'Hadd Kar De' touched upon Rajasthani folk tunes. As both *Manikarnika* and *Samrat Prithviraj* were the valorous tales of two warriors, their songs were more like a war cry.

Manikarnika was set in the pre-Independence era based on the life of Rani of Jhansi. The song 'Bharat' is partly based on the Desh Raga. Prasoon Joshi's lyrics, *'Main rahoon ya na rahoon, Bharat ye rehna chahiye* (Regardless of my presence, India must forever be there)', evoked a feeling of unconditional love for the country. 'Bolo Kab Pratikaar Karoge', in the bold voice of Sukhwinder Singh starting with the sound of the tutari, is like a war cry meant to awaken a feeling of protecting the motherland. 'Hari Har' and Sunidhi's 'Yoddha' from *Samrat Prithviraj* and 'Vijayi Bhava' of *Manikarnika* where Shankar himself chips in with his trademark high-energy singing, have similar ebullience and passion of a war cry.

Shankar–Ehsaan–Loy left their mark where the songs became a tranquil refuge from the high-octane sounds of trumpets, tutari, bugle, nagada and daf. Pratibha Singh Baghel's 'Rajaji' is a very simple, playful song with a pleasant melody. The other one, 'Tak Taki', is a song that depicts the happiness as well as the underlying fear of welcoming a child into the world. But

'Makhmali' from *Samrat Prithviraj* stands out like one vintage SEL number which will take one back to their past. Backed up by precise and minimal instrumentation, Shreya and Arijit just glide through this wonderful lingering melody.

∽

Shankar underwent significant transitions in the entertainment industry. The voice that redefined Indian TV jingles in the Doordarshan days has now reached every corner of the nation in d2h days. The social dynamics have also changed. The entertainment world shrank when OTT arrived. Mobile phones with keypads became outdated. The rapid expansion of mobile phones brought a leap in network speed also. The digital explosion was nothing short of a Big Bang. The Internet penetration reached the forest and rural areas of the country. The entertainment industry has became young once more.

Budding talents started uploading stuff on digital platforms to showcase their skill. The platter was expanded. The traditional TV serials that seemed to have no ending were replaced with a wide variety of content qualitatively much superior and even fresher in approach. With the ease of access and the varied choice of content, the OTT platforms become a never-before consumer experience. The prolonged lockdown during the Covid-19 pandemic played a cataclysmic role in the enormous popularity of OTT. Proximity with smartphones, laptops and tablets grew and this helped OTT platforms gain acceptance and popularity. And everything happened within a demi decade.

Shankar–Ehsaan–Loy made their debut in the digital platform when they were approached to make scores for a musical, *Bandish Bandits*, that started a new genre in this domain of web series. The trio's foray into this untested domain was like Veni, vidi, vici. *Bandish Bandits* turned out to be a one-of-a-kind web series where the music composers, and not the actors, became the main attraction of the project.

Bandish Bandits

Bandish Bandits was like a platter of colours that SEL had culled from their entire oeuvre of work. The expanse of a web series, where the plot is spread across eight episodes, gave them scope to go all out in experimentation. With the male lead being a staunch follower of Indian classical music, and the girl representing the generation of millennials with predilections of selfies and EDM, SEL could use their entire gamut of song-writing befitting the varied characters and their choices. The convention of the clash of musical ideas, the opulence of Rajasthani gharana of folk music and the elements of a modern, youthful romance exact the versatility of SEL to its fullest extent. Completing more than 20 years in the industry and traversing several milestones of all-time superhits, SEL now had a scope to sprinkle everything that they had done in one single canvas of 11 songs and background scores. *Bandish Bandits* became the gallery of all SEL exhibits.

The songs based on the pure classical tradition remind one of what SEL did in *Mirzya* and *Katyar Kaljat Ghusali*. In 'Virah', Shankar reins in every note, from the lowest to the highest, with effortless ease. Shankar's singing has a hypnotic effect, as if an ascetic is offering prayer through musical notes to his deity. The poise in every note that he sings, expresses the longing for an unfulfilled love story.

Shankar excels himself in 'Dhara Hogi'. The ecstatic mood of rain is all-enveloping. He gets in the folksy groove and brings out the delight of rain. The song brings an instant reminder of the delectable Zakir Hussain composition on the same Miya Ke

Malhar Raga in 'Badal Ghummad' in *Saaz*. Once, Shankar sang a Monty Sharma composition 'Kaare Kaare Badra' for the film *Mirch*, where in an unrestrained exuberance of rock–folk fusion, he sang on the advent of rain.

'Garaj Garaj', another raga-based song on rain, is used twice in the series. While Ajoy Chakrabarty's version is poised and tranquil in its appeal, the duet of Farid Hasan and Md Aman is scintillating. In Ajoy Chakrabarty's version, the sarangi that was used was 150 years old. It has that vintage feel, where someone is absorbed in a musical meditation. In a true-blue jugalbandi mode, with just the basic instrumentation, Shankar composed a Megh Malhar-based tune that showcases the pure and unadulterated form of Hindustani classical music.

Memories of *Katyar Kaljat Ghusali* come again when Javed Ali sings a delightful thumri in 'Labb Par Aye'. In the theme song of *Bandish Bandits*, Mame Khan makes it sound like a continuation of *Mirzya*. Rajasthani folk tune is set in a modern high-sounding ambient soundscape. Shankar–Ehsaan–Loy experimented with fusing genres in many songs bringing the traditional song in modern formats. But the one that stands out, in its unadulterated and purest form, is the eponymous Rajasthani folk 'Padharo Maare Des'. Shankar sounds blessed and sings like someone who is holding the fortification of an ancient tradition with utmost care.

Shankar bent genres and fused songs of bubblegum romance with a classical bandish in the extravagant pastiche of sounds in 'Sajan Bin'. The outlandish juxtaposition of images like the trendy '*Yeh meme se hoti baatein, yeh video calling raatein* (A chat via the memes, and video calls at night)' with the traditional '*Sajan bin aye na, mohe nindiya* (I can't get sleep without my paramour)' in a single mukhra may sound incredulous. But the way SEL fused the two disparities—blending the lounge music with classical taranas—takes fusion music to a new level. Shivam sounds exactly like his father in the way he bends his voice and sings like a seasoned classical singer. But the youthfulness of

Junior Mahadevan keeps the juvenile spirit alive, as SEL takes a serio-comic approach to the classical bandish by mixing it with layers of vocal harmony and the processed voice of Jonita Gandhi.

The use of tabla within the layer of synth sound is an easy recall to 'It's the Time to Disco'. The gradual addition of layers leading up to the hook line is typical of SEL in their early years. In *Ghayal Once Again*, there is one college fest number 'Lapak Jhapak'. There is the same youthful band vibe with a blend of Hindi and colloquial English lyrics that bring out the juvenile feel of the song.

Shankar–Ehsaan–Loy were the ultimate go-to composer when the theme of the films would be based on the characters of musicians. Two versions of *Rock On*, *London Dreams* and *Katyar Kaljat Ghusali* only testified to this. So, when a song like 'Mastiyaapa' comes, where the leading lady is singing and dancing at a rock concert, SEL is at their belligerent best. Shivam steps into his father's shoes once again and sounds like the maestro in all his cheeky folksy inflexions of a pop song, when he sings this teaser of a song 'Chedkhaniyan'. The song is too brief and tantalizes one to yearn for more. Along with this song, the peppy folk fusion, an Arman Malik–Jonita Gandhi duet, 'Couple Goals', have that groove for the young listeners to get the kick for a jig.

With all of SEL's experimentation in the vast panorama of eight episodes, the success lies in the fact that it woos even the most non-musical people who love to binge-watch web series for the sake of it. Amid a host of crime and political thrillers, a love story based on music is a great variation. Along with the freshness of the couple and the presence of some of the doyen of Indian cinema like Naseeruddin Shah and Atul Kulkarni, the series crossed the bridge with style riding on the shoulders of the trio.

'Bending the Rules'[18]

The year 2020 brought an apocalyptic change in the world. In an interminable warfare with an unseen enemy, people were compelled to stay inside for months on end. In the days when survival was the key to success, entertainment was a luxury for the millions. Life limped back to normalcy but the scars Covid left bear the tell-tale marks of unprecedented gloom. Music has been the great healer in all senses of the term. Shankar's life was not untouched in this Valhalla of death. But as the messenger of hope and regeneration, he sang the days through.

Once, when asked about whether he listens to music for relaxation now, Shankar said that listening to music can't be a way of unwinding for him. The moment he listens to something interesting, he becomes alert and tends to learn it. This alertness takes away his relaxation. Then he resorts to something he has always enjoyed—the most primal passion of cooking. Donning the apron, he would toss multicoloured bell peppers and seasonal vegetables on a wok to create a salad. When he was not cooking, he would doodle on a piece of paper and discover his skill in sketching. Sometimes, he would loll on the lounger with his kids to watch movies. Often, he would be gardening a bit and sometimes he would take to origami as a stress buster.

Suddenly, it seemed that a pause button was pressed. Everything came to a stasis. The spectacle of gloom on the newspaper cover pages and in news channels made one feel claustrophobic. But here

---

[18]This is a Shankar Mahadevan composition in Shakti's latest album, *This Moment*.

is one man who has always been the poster child of positivity, for himself and everyone around him. Taking life as it came, he decided to look inward and sourced creativity to offer a silver lining to the millions. Flanked by Siddharth and Shivam, he took his harmonium and created something new. On some evenings, they would have fun on Instagram Live, catering to the demands of his admirers and sometimes he would impart his lessons of riyaaz to numerous students online. From the confines of his home, he would sing online with others to inspire the listeners with messages of hope and regeneration.

Composing music never stopped for him. He was busier than other times writing music in multiple languages. During the lockdown, he wanted to reach more people with his music. He said, 'I am so happy that through music we can communicate messages and inspire people. I think God has sent us here for a purpose during such hard times.'

During the Covid days, Shankar, Siddharth and Shivam composed a new single to release on the occasion of World Music Day. 'When I go on stage and sing with both my children like band members, it feels amazing. I can't explain how satisfying that feels. We jam, learn, create, record, discuss and argue. So, it's a wonderful musical team that we have,' said Shankar. His legacy will thrive and live on through his kids.

He performed innumerable online concerts to garner funds for musicians who were suffering during the pandemic. At the end of the day, what he cherished the most was creating music with his kids. He composed tunes and left them to Siddharth for production in his home studio. And his constant source of happiness is his involvement with his brainchild—SMA.

∽

The music curriculum of SMA has now been adopted by more than 65 schools including Akshaya Patra Foundation which has the world's largest non-profit mid-day meal programme. Shankar has been the goodwill ambassador for Akshaya Patra Foundation and has specially composed and sung a track dedicated to the organization. The song 'Gyan Ki Kahani', with lyrics by Javed Akhtar, was composed to mark the auspicious occasion of one billion meals served by Akshaya Patra Foundation across the country.

In 2017, Shankar took part in a two-day educational festival, hosted by the Rajasthan government and GEMS education, to create a stimulating experience among the learners and promote Rajasthan as 'the knowledge hub' of India.

In 2019, Shankar was awarded the Padma Shri. When he stood on stage to collect the award, he realized that this was a recognition of his music and his contribution to the country. Shankar said, 'It struck me that this is a huge responsibility of entertaining the citizens as well as using it as a social tool to empower them. Social relevance matters when I am chosen for this title. I feel more responsible, as I have this title and it is extremely important for me to keep its sanctity.'

For Shankar, SMA is not just a business venture or a diversified venture which is generally the case with a lot of celebrities. This is his way of giving back the love and respect to the society to which he owed a lot. Shankar could relate to the problems he had when he was a school student. He said:

> Imagine if all the difficulty in learning can be done through the music! A song can be made out of everything that a student finds difficult and every child would be singing that. If all the mathematical formulas, Pythagoras theorem are made into a song you can make music as a powerful tool. Music is not only about going and performing and trying to become a Mohammed Rafi or a Kishore Kumar. Music can be used as a tool that finds utility for multiple purposes.

The growth of SMA, with every passing year, is a step towards Shankar realizing his dream of building the world's biggest academy, to teach Indian music and explore various avenues of finding joy through this medium.

During the stressful pandemic, the idea of 'SMA Nirvana' was born. Shankar said:

> There are so many people who are very sick, dealing with terminal diseases just waiting to take leave from this earth. There might be no cure. They are in palliative care and old age homes. For these kinds of people, cancer patients and terminally ill patients, we started this programme. If we can give them joy for this one or one-and-a-half hours then the purpose of music becomes so huge. The kind of blessings we have been receiving is something we can't measure in terms of money. During Covid-19, I made a song 'Haara Nahi Hoon Main' to give a boost to the people, which was written by Amitabh Bhattacharya. Then through SMA Nirvana, we started giving online performances. We installed a huge screen in hospitals. By the end of the performance, all the patients, doctors, nurses and everyone was dancing and enjoying. The patients who were seriously ill also I remember they were doing the *garba* dance. When we saw this we thought that the power of music is so amazing. We can change lives through music.

The number of people that have performed through SMA Nirvana is more than a whopping 450,000. Through the Inspire India Project, of which they are extremely proud, more than 2,000 people have learnt music. So, the seed that was planted 12 years ago with just 15 students, grew up into a tree that has spread its branches and is giving its shade to millions of people. The Internet allowed them to go to many countries. Now, they are in about 90 countries, moving towards conducting 3.5 lakh classes. They have some 600 courses and about 3,000 students from all over the world. Indians are scattered all over the world and through his academy, Shankar tries to connect with them. In its depth and vastness, SMA is well and truly on course to becoming a Berkeley from India, as Shankar had once envisioned.

∽

As a part of The Shakti Foundation's annual fundraising concert named 'Gurucarana', for the medical aid of the underprivileged people in rural areas, Shankar took part in a show under the name of a different outfit—'Shraddha'. With Shankar, Loy, U. Srinivas and Sivamani, the band first performed 10 years back for the Shakti Foundation. Shraddha performed a unique brand of spiritual fusion music for social causes. Like Remember Shakti, Shraddha also received a huge blow when U. Srinivas passed away in 2014.

Shankar narrated a very amusing incident that happened in Rashtrapati Bhavan during the tenure of President A.P.J. Abdul Kalam.

> I got the opportunity to perform in front of Kalam Sir at Rashtrapati Bhavan with our band Shraddha. That time they used to hold such private concerts on the lawns. I still remember we were all having dinner on the lawn. The President was moving around. It was not as crazy security as it is now. He came and served gulab jamun. His favourite was vinyl records. And his favourite song was 'Endaro Mahanubhavulu', a Thyagaraja kriti. He said, 'Can you do one version of Endaro Mahanubhavulu and send it to me? Put it in a CD and I will market it.' I thought about how he being the President of India, thinks of marketing my song. But it was too sweet.

∽

During the Covid years, Shakti started recording the newest album, *This Moment*. Covid protocol barred them from assembling on a stage or coming physically into a studio atmosphere, but they kept sending music back and forth over the Internet. In the Zoom gatherings, they would discuss music and record it too. At the end of the dark days, the musicians became several years older without meeting one another. Zakir said, 'At this juncture when John is 80 and I am 72 years old I guess we are at a point where we both feel that we should go around the block once more while we still can and experience that incredible energy.'

By this time, Shakti touched the milestone of 50 years of existence. Zakir remembered the inception and the early days of the band, saying,

> One of the greatest moments of my life was sitting on stage with John McLaughlin, L. Shankar and Vikku flying high up in that sky, really feeling free and devoid of any worries or any issues. We were flying with wings and having such a great time with that music. That has always been there and now it is time to make that run one more time to impress that moment and hope that it will come again.

This idea of coming again to perform on a stage set out the concept of Shakti's fiftieth anniversary tour. The idea started before the pandemic but 2023 was officially the fiftieth anniversary of the great band, since it was in 1973 that Zakir and John began collaborating in New York and San Francisco. In their four-city tour in India (Bangalore, Kolkata, Delhi and Mumbai) they roped in the ace violinist Ganesh Rajagopalan. The Mumbai show saw a very hearty welcome of Vikku joining his mates of yore. Grins and embraces marked the historical reconciliation of the early bandmates. The packed venues of all four shows bear testimony to the exhilarating atmosphere they create.

Fifty years since the inception of Shakti, John McLaughlin and Zakir are still brothers-at-arms, inspiring generations of musicians with their global fusion music. On 16 September 2023, in Austin, Texas, their three-month-long sold-out concerts saw a grand finale.

∽

During this tour, on 23 June 2023, Shankar received the honorary doctorate from Birmingham City University for his contribution to music. Shankar never loses an opportunity to uphold the immensity of Indian classical music and in his speech, he once again reiterated the same. It was a moment of pride for Sangeeta, the lady to whom Shankar dedicated every single note that he had sung in his life. Sangeeta penned her heartfelt lines, 'Words are not enough to describe my feelings. My heart swells with pride witnessing you receive the doctorate for all your work in the field of music. Stay blessed my love with good health and music and happiness as always.'

The much-awaited album *This Moment* was finally released on 23 June 2023. The album stands as the most powerful documentation of the grand cultural cross-pollination of the East and the West.

Hyperactivity hardly makes Shankar weary and even if it often does, at the end of the day, home is one place that can assuage the exhaustion. His caring mother, without whose blessings, not a single day starts for him; his loving wife; his charming boys, Siddharth and Shivam; and the two fur babies Honey and Kiwi, the golden retrievers, make his close-knit comfort zone.

He feels proud and lucky to recount his glories in the innate musical creativity of his two sons. Shankar loves his city; his most frequented hangout, the Purple Haze studio; his childhood friend Umesh who keeps a tab of his daily appointments and schedules; The Originals; and no doubt, his musical partners Ehsaan and Loy. The trio—with a glorious run of 24 years of the brand name 'Shankar–Ehsaan–Loy'—has grown through thick and thin. Shankar Mahadevan is ready to conquer more hearts with music—his ever-constant companion.

Postlude

'Each time I pass through these tunnels here I feel excited that once I cross them, there will be blue mountains on the horizon. In the monsoon, they look so beautiful,' Ehsaan says excitedly.

'Yes, people should come here once in monsoon,' Loy agrees with Ehsaan.

As the car zooms out of the tunnel, both of them look at the distant hills which get closer with each bend. Thick dark black rain-fed clouds are swooning over the hills. The SUV glides on the glistening wet highway towards Pune. Rain again starts to patter on the windscreen. The wiper starts moving and the distant hills turn blurry. Shankar browses through the recent messages on his phone sitting in the back seat beside Loy. He too joins the chat.

'Bhatan tunnel! You remember how this tunnel is significantly associated with us?'

Without answering, Shankar, Ehsaan and Loy smile.

Their immediate response gives Shankar the answer. They two start singing together: *'Jagmagate hain jhilmilate hain apne raste'.*

Shankar joins them with the iconic vocal motif that comes after. All three remember the scene where the blue convertible Merc passed the Bhatan tunnel when this chorus was heard in the background. The three friends Akash, Sameer and Sid were going for a vacation in Goa. Today, Shankar, Ehsaan and Loy are heading towards Pune for an SEL concert to be held this evening. But thoughts of the conecrt aren't there in their minds at all. It is another of those wonderful joyrides that they are having, and the fun of togetherness is what always peps them up.

'Today we will order Kolahpuri chicken. I have been on this cheese and continental stuff for a week in Europe last week. Feel like taking some real spicy things, yaar,' Shankar says animatedly.

'What about Kutchi dabeli? You remember we had it that time. It was damn spicy and chilly man!' Ehsaan exclaimed.

'But you know, last week…'

Once their discussion veers towards food, there is no ending. Be it in the lobby of Purple Haze during breaks, or in the joyrides on the highway, the topic of food always spices up their fun. But music doesn't stay far away.

Shankar says, 'Whenever we have shows in Pune, two concerts come to my mind invariably. One was Sawai Gandharva, the year Bhimsen Joshi passed away. I came here to perform. I performed with no instrument backup but just an ektara. It was wonderful and the second one that we performed was in S.P. College Ground.'

Both of them immediately respond to him with an approving smile.

'It was 2011, no? Ehsaan?' Loy always trusts Ehsaan to be exact with dates and events.

'2010, November. There was no rain in the morning and no weather forecast for rain too. But suddenly it was like a rain cloud going elsewhere had lost its way and started falling on us from above.'

They recall the show they had in an open arena in Pune that day. Thirty-five thousand people were screaming and shouting at every song that SEL were performing. Halfway through the show came a sudden spate of downpour, flooding the stage in minutes, forcing the musicians to unplug their instruments in a hurry. Organizers ran helter-skelter to avert any further accidents. A big blue polythene sheet covered the stage.

From the wings, Shankar peeped out to check if the force of rain had decreased or not. All he could see was the entire arena still chock-a-block, with the audience eagerly waiting for the concert to resume. But there was no chance of setting up the sound from the beginning. As the intensity of rain died down a bit, Shankar stepped out on the stage to the huge roar of the audience. Shankar was overwhelmed by the ear-splitting sound and couldn't say what he had intended. When he saw the incessant waves of arms and eyes sparkling with excitement, he paused a bit and then agreed to the demands of the audience with a condition that they had to give non-stop rhythm with claps. The audience responded with glee and Shankar sang 'Breathless'. But what Shankar thought to be one consolation song didn't end like that. The encore and song requests continued.

Ehsaan came out of the dugout wrapping a band of his acoustic guitar. Loy picked up a tambourine and came out too. Out came Darshan Doshi with his drumstick. Shankar kept conversing with the crowd, flirting with the tune of 'Koi Kahe' and urging the audience to sing along. The jamming started and the co-singers joined the jamming. Who cares for an electronic ensemble? The show, which was to be aborted halfway, continued like that for another hour. Shankar was at his elemental best. The audience returned home soaked with rain, emotions and memories of a lifetime.

'I sang "Maa" for the thousandth time. But that evening, with no music but your acoustic guitar and those 35,000 people waving their hands with mobile torches on, we felt blessed to have composed the song,' Shankar says to Ehsaan.

'Indeed,' Ehsaan approves.

∽

The car stops near a toll gate. The rain has paused a bit but the sky looks like a mass of water drops lying suspended above. The fields around and the slopes of hills are looking dreamy in a new sheen.

'Chalo, let's have a cup of tea over there,' Shankar points out at a wayside tiny hotel overlooking the more fancied restaurants.

A small boy welcomes them, finding a very familiar face among them. Shankar pats his head lovingly and asks for three cutting chai.

'This cutting chai is such a Bombay thing, no? It reminds me of my childhood days with my Originals. You can't enjoy cutting chai unless you have it together. It is such a symbol of unity, bringing everyone together under one common place. So many relationships have started over a glass of cutting chai, no?'

'Have you guys seen Nupur's film on Amazon?' Ehsaan asks.

'I remember, when we were working with Nupur for *Modern Love*, we had nothing. No tune in the morning, not even lyrics. Lyricist Tanishq sent us the words, and Shankar came with the piece of paper and just sang it. Nupur came and sat, and by four in the evening, she had the song on WhatsApp. She went back to her office, hardly believing that only in such a short time she had come back with a song.'

'You know, the tune we wrote has something so fresh that it reminds me of our old *Dil Chahta Hai* days. I get déjà vu every time I listen to the song. It takes me to the time when we had no baggage or expectations. Every film could have been our last film. But every film had something so fresh and melodious that the journey continued,' Loy says with a smile of contentment.

'As if a road is rolled out before us and our car keeps moving on,' Ehsaan smiles.

'You know, I feel it was just the other day that I quit my job at Oracle. My manager was flabbergasted when I expressed my wish to drop the paper,' Shankar recalls.

'Music was your calling Shankar. It was meant to be,' Loy says.

'For all of us, Loy. When they say we are music directors, I feel angry. We are a band. We have always been like that. There has never been any signed agreement across the dotted lines.'

As Ehsaan is speaking, a muffled tune comes from the radio at the counter where a boy is counting cash. It is one of their old hits that brings them a smile of satisfaction.

As the drizzle starts again, they run inside their car and the journey starts again. Memories of *Dil Chahta Hai*, *Kal Ho Naa Ho*, *Lakshya*, *Bunty Aur Babli*, *Taare Zameen Par*, *Kabhi Alvida Naa Kehna*, *My Name Is Khan*, *Rock On*, *Zindagi Na Milegi Dobara* whizz past their minds like milestones. The car zooms through the Western Ghats with daylight slowly fading.

∽

The concert is to start within three hours. A call comes in Shankar's phone and someone informs him that the sound check is all done. He never feels like keeping any fixed playlist because everyone knows that he keeps changing it depending on the audience's reaction on any given day.

When it comes to connecting with the audience, Shankar is second to none. He is so confident in his craft that he knows the territory he is moving into. He can effortlessly glide on to any song anytime, taking a sudden R.D. Burman request from the audience and coming back to a SEL number seamlessly. That is the fun they have in every SEL concert. And fun comes from everywhere. With his juvenile mind, Shankar can make a prank out of anything.

In Florida, they did one show where the organizers, for some reason, had skimped on the budget and the lights were ridiculously low. In the middle of the show, Shankar said, 'I hope you are enjoying a *lovely laser light show* and the *beautiful lights* we have got. Please enjoy it.' The other day, they were doing a wedding of a corporate show. One guy wanted to sing 'Kajrare' and when Shankar took the mic back from that over-enthusiastic gentleman, he said to him, 'You know the lady who is there in the corner. She liked your singing very much.' His ways with filmmakers and clients are never formal. Even with the audience, the moment he gets on the stage, they are like his buddies.

By this time, the car has reached the outskirts of Pune. The shops, hotels and the billboards are showing the addresses of the town. Ehsaan points something to others through the windscreen. It is at the top of a building beside a bridge. The hoarding flashes these three best buddies smiling together wearing black T-shirts. The hoarding is for tonight's show. After the fresh rain, the hoarding was shimmering as the neon lights fell on them.

'Ok guys, before we reach our venue, let's play a game like what the guys did in ZNMD. They played funny and adventurous games but let's remember three of the funniest incidents in our career and relive the moments,' Shankar proposes and Loy almost pounces on the proposal.

'I will win the game hands down, but I will narrate at last. You guys start,' Loy laughs.

'Ok, let me narrate the incident that Loy missed, the one me and Ehsaan had in Washington. Once, we went to the National Aerospace Museum in Washington when we were touring. There was a cockpit of a plane and it simulated the way the plane turned. We could feel as if we were sitting in the cockpit. Only two people at a time were allowed. One person handled the weapon and the other navigated the actual flight. So, Ehsaan and I went in. I left the flying to him because he said he knows about planes but I wasn't prepared for what happened next.'

Shankar left it to Ehsaan to complete.

'I didn't know the stick was so sensitive. So, it was very difficult to control it because as you started going faster you touch the little tip and the whole plane would move and that kept happening and Shankar kept shouting at me like "What the hell are you doing, I told you to fly and we are upside down" and so on... we had a lot of fun.'

'Yeah, I still remember the look on Shankar's face when you two came out of the cockpit,' Loy laughs and says. Now, it is Ehsaan's turn.

'Ok let me go back to the early days once more. Once, a producer came to meet us, and Shankar and I were there. Loy, if you remember, was sitting on the other side doing programming.

So, we said we would do the meeting. The producer said, "I am making this film called Barsaat" or something like that.'

'Yeah, so I thought this filmmaker might have made that super hit film or maybe some old movie,' Shankar chips in.

Ehsaan continues, 'So, he was making a new movie and he wanted to show us the poster and production of his last film.' Before Ehsaan comes up with the punchline, all three of them start laughing uncontrollably. Ehsaan struggles to complete the narration, 'And we opened the poster and it turned out to be like one of those sleazy kinds of films and the poster was basically women half-dressed and all. Both of us cracked up laughing, but we couldn't insult the producer by letting him see that we were laughing so we were hiding behind the poster.'

Shankar finishes the story, 'I was holding the poster from this side and Ehsaan was holding it from the other side, just completely cracking up. And we couldn't put the poster down. So, he thought we loved what we were seeing. That was just so funny.'

Their stomach starts aching, laughing from the recollections. Loy said, 'It's impossible to maintain a straight face when you meet them. But I have the ace. My story centres around one of us. Guess guys, whose story is that!'

Shankar starts laughing before even Loy starts narrating. Ehsaan guffaws and screams, 'Oh gosh! Not again man!'

Loy says, 'This had happened 12 years ago when Cyrus Broacha used to host MTV Bakra. It was decided a day before that we were going to make Ehsaan the Bakra. Shaad came in the morning that day and set the hidden cameras in all corners. Remember it was during *Bunty Aur Babli* days. The Bakra team also came in time. We were all excited about something exciting to happen and were laughing inside. Shankar, you were damn natural in your play acting and that helped all of us. Shaad brought that guy and then told us that Adi wanted him to sing a song for us. Now, when the boy took the mic, I was watching your face you know Ehsaan. He was singing so awkwardly that all of us tried our best to keep calm. You say what you were feeling then.'

'It was very hard to control myself. When he started approaching me to touch my feet I felt "oh no not this"', Ehsaan smiles.

'It was really funny when I gave them a 'C' and asked him if the scale was okay and he casually replied, "*Haan wohi laga do*." Ehsaan was just flabbergasted. And to make matters worse Shankar said, "Let it be. It's ok." And then he started singing 'Kal Ho Naa Ho' in the weirdest manner possible,' Loy starts laughing uncontrollably.

'No Loy, then he asked me what I play and wanted me to play guitar with him. It was still bearable. I thought when all of us are getting angry, why you guys are not reacting? When he started singing that song, rather butchering the song, I lost it completely and wanted to leave.'

'Seriously speaking, we thought that you might be losing your cool,' Shankar says with a hearty dose of laughter.

The situation didn't worsen anymore that evening. When the guy was showing his mock anger and testing Ehsaan's patience, before it crossed the threshold, all the crew members rushed forth and spilled the beans. It ended with them hugging each other, peals of laughter and Ehsaan sportingly donning the crown of MTV Bakra.

∽

Shankar loves the screaming that can be heard from the wings of the stage. Taking the stage always gives him a feeling of coming back home with those thousands of familiar faces waiting for him to get some hours of absolute fun.

Like every day, he calls everyone together backstage. The musicians, the sound boys, the organizers and the backstage workers—all of them stand in a circle holding hands. Shaun, the guitarist, utters a prayer of gratitude thanking the universe for the show and all of them pray that the show will be a successful one. Each of them promises to give their best. All of them chant 'aum' and feel energized. Laser rays start creating patterns on the backdrop. The musicians start giving the rhythm. Shankar steps on stage in front of the roaring crowd, holds the mic and starts chanting 'Vakratunda Mahakaya'. There is pin-drop silence in the auditorium. But that erupts when the drum picks up, Loy gives the chord and Ehsaan's riff triggers excitement. Shankar greets the audience in his characteristic style.

The showreel keeps rolling on…

Author's Note

I went to see *Rock On* in a small multiplex in South Kolkata. I felt like watching this on the opening day because of its exciting poster, the intriguing promo and most importantly the names of the music composers. I remember the daze I was in after the end credits rolled in. The trail of '*Aankhon mein jiske, koi to khwaab hai*' was resounding in me. Getting out of the hall, I got my first caller-tune—'Sindbad the Sailor'. The discordant buzz around the mall couldn't penetrate through the spell of music that held me in a cocoon.

A sudden splash of August showers caught me unawares, as I stepped out of the mall and took refuge in a wayside shack where a family of three—a small girl and her parents—were serving *chapati* and curry to the customers. For someone who would always hesitate to speak his mind, on that day I was seized by almost an unusual bravado. I approached the girl's mother and told her not to engage her child in the shop. I added, 'Take my phone number. Do not hesitate to call if your child needs any help in her studies.' I was surprised with myself. Even a distant observer (to the point of being a pathological indolent) like me, broke through the veil of thought and execution in a jiffy.

Well, blame it on Shankar–Ehsaan–Loy.

I fell back on the music of Shankar–Ehsaan–Loy when contemporary music failed to please my music sensibilities. After R.D. Burman, Jatin–Lalit were the ones who got me hooked to Hindi film music. Shankar–Ehsaan–Loy were strikingly and defiantly different. Their music exudes a feel-good vibe, gives me a sense of wellbeing and reasons to smile to myself.

I met the cynosure of the trio, Shankar Mahadevan, at Purple Haze—their pantheon of music-making—when I went to interview him for my book on Louiz Banks. He immediately made me feel special. I got more than what I looked for: warmth, earnestness and an assurance that I may come back to him. It was so kind of him to come to the launch of my first book. What a reward it was for me when the first signature I scribbled as a writer was for the great Shankar Mahadevan! Just based on that, I proposed to write a book on him. And of course he said yes. Afterall, he is not one to dampen one's spirits.

Knowing Shankar Mahadevan is a delight. Rarely does one come across a personality who is so loved and admired by all who know him. The nation conferred on him the Padma Shri. The world saluted him with an honorary doctorate for being an inspiration among generations of musicians. But what overwhelmed me is how much he is admired by the common people. I met quite a few people who never stopped speaking about how their lives were touched by Shankar. Soumendu Kuber, the event organizer from Pune, was ecstatic about him. Kartik, a young singer who often tours with Shankar, spoke of a girl whom Shankar had inspired. After seeing her once in a school function, Shankar had opened up a new direction for the kid with his words of encouragement. A beaming Shankar greets everyone, from the courier boy to the plumber, with the same warmth reserved for celebrities of the music industry. He secures a place in the heart of even a casual onlooker with his gentle nod and a smile from the car window.

I found that the mystery of this essential goodness lies in Shankar's rare faculty to get completely involved in whatever he does. He knows the art of passionately living in the moment. Inside Purple Haze, his presence is simply electrifying. His grace and style, his method and mode, trigger sparks of magic. I was privileged to attend the music session of a film with him. Shankar nonchalantly took the mic, held the lyrics in his other hand and then effortlessly sang out the lyrics. It was incredible. Loy then started nurturing the tune with brief, lilting piano passages. Ehsaan joined from a certain bar and music started evolving. Shankar then went outside to take a call, and by the time he came back, all of us were jiving to the spontaneous groove. I met a group of folk musicians who came all the way from Gujarat, making an overnight bus journey, just to record a piece of music for them.

While being passionately involved, Shankar also has the saintly ability to detach himself. But whatever he does—from composing music and singing in concerts to meeting people and attending household chores—he is unfailingly driven by his single purpose of spreading joy and happiness around him.

Shankar Mahadevan, now at the acme of his career, is doubtlessly the biggest musical phenomenon of the present time. Shakti's latest album *This Moment* has received the prestigious Grammy nomination. This book only aims to explore the passage of his musical life till date. The song of his life starts with a prelude going back in time, and lands on a partially fictional interlude when the musician happens to meet two of his comrades for life. It is followed by a postlude showing a fictional representation of his life now—filled with concerts, laughter and joy. This is the story of an amazing musician, a great human being and a true-blue maverick.

Cheers to this life that the man embodies! Many more hits and melodies are yet to come! The journey continues!

Acknowledgements

Writing a book is so rewarding when you come across some wonderful people who offer support and guidance in abundance. They are the ones who helped my book see the light of day.

My heartfelt gratitude to one and only Louiz Banks, who put me in touch with Shankar ji. I came to know Louiz Banks through my fortunate association with the R.D. Burman Foundation, Euphony. He opened a vast new world to me.

My warmest thanks to two people without whom the research work would not have been possible, Shirin Shukeshwala, secretary to Shankar-Ehsaan-Loy, and Umesh Pradhan, Shankar's childhood friend and the one who handles his daily appointments. Had I been in their place, I wonder how I would have handled the continuous pestering over minute issues.

Meeting Ustad Zakir Hussain and talking to him was such a humbling experience. His brother Taufiq Qureshi and their friend Sridhar Parthasarathi are great raconteurs. Just spending time with them is a pleasure. Meeting John McLaughlin was an experience of a lifetime. Then, there were two delightful brothers who simply bowled me over with their stories—the giants of the Indian advertising industry—Prasoon and Piyush Pandey. Any book on music that I wish to write is incomplete without the intervention of the talented and much loved musician Sheldon D'Silva. My book is indebted to each of these legends for the valuable insights they shared.

No words of thanks are enough to express how I was benefitted from talking to Mahalakshmi Iyer, Vishal Dadlani,

Caralisa Monteiro, Sanjay Divecha, Suraj Jagan, Subodh Bhave, Amitabh Bhattacharya and Abhay Rumde. These people are the very backbone of the book.

My gratitude knows no bounds for people like Sunidhi Chauhan, Rakeysh Omprakash Mehra, Shaad Ali, Meghna Gulzar, Alisha Chinai, Clinton Cerejo, Alyssa Mendonsa and Shabana Azmi who were kind enough to find some time for me from their busy schedules. And then, there was the prized opportunity of listening to the charismatic Farhan Akhtar at his office. Speaking with legends like Suresh Wadkar and Sridhar Ranganathan, co-founder of the Shankar Mahadevan Academy, was an experience. Musicians from the SEL band, Dibyajyoti Nath and Anupam Ghatak, were so candid while speaking about Shankar. And so was the event organizer Soumendu Kuber. I can't ever forget the warmth and earnestness with which teachers of SMA, Archana Hegdekar and Kartik Raman, spoke of their mentor. I acknowledge the help that came from Rasika Chandrasekhar, Mame Khan, Kalpana Swamy (and her *Nostalgiaana*) and Deepti Sivan, the lady who made the great documentary on the maestro. I would specially like to acknowledge the pains three people took on my behalf: Avinash ji (secretary to Gulzar Saab); and Carol and Soniya Pant (secretaries to Javed Saab).

I loved talking endlessly to two of the best souls I have ever come across, Ehsaan Noorani and Loy Mendonsa. It was delightful to say the least.

I had huge fun talking to Umesh ji, Sudarshan Rao and Rajesh Pradhan, Shankar's childhood buddies. I am much obliged to Rajesh ji and Umesh ji for all the precious photographs they shared with me.

I am eternally indebted to Javed Akhtar for writing the foreword of the book.

I consider myself extremely fortunate to have spent an hour with Gulzar Saab at his residence to talk about Shankar. It was perhaps the best hour of my life.

Along with all of these names, I would also like to thank my near and dear ones who sincerely wished to support this book from its very inception. Debapriya Sanyal, my dearest friend, has been my mentor and guide since my college days. Debapriya, your choicest expletives at my errors only made me feel the warmth of our bond.

Gautam Bandopadhyay, my friend and colleague, went an extra mile to read the first draft of the book and point out the errors so meticulously. This is your book too, Gautam da.

Thank you Tanmayee for the support, and my student and steadfast companion Jayita for doing all the hard work. Just mentioning your name won't ever do justice. Thanks to Indranil Dam for diligently going through the book and his continuous support.

And last, but certainly not the least, I am much obliged to Dibakar Ghosh of Rupa Publications for having faith in me once more. Writing a book requires massive amounts of team work and the editorial team has been fantastic too. I would especially like to acknowledge the hard work of Sagareeka Pradhan, my copy editor, for making sure that my lapses were all rectified. Thanks Sagareeka, from my heart.

And to Hiya, here's another one for you to dust on our bookshelf...

Glossary

aarti	:	A Hindu ritual of offering prayer to Gods
abhangas	:	A devotional poem sung in praise of Lord Vitthal
Adda	:	A casual chit-chat session
Alaap	:	An improvised section of any raga in Indian classical music
Antara	:	second verse of a song
ashadhi Ekadashi	:	An important Hindu festival worshipping Lord Vitthala
azaan	:	Islamic call to prayer
baithaks	:	An old Indian tradition of musicians and dancers assembling and performing together
bandhani	:	Decorated tie-and-dye textile
bandish	:	A structured composition for singing in Indian classical music
bansuri	:	Flute
baul	:	A category of folk singers or songs from rural Bengal
besura	:	Off-key
bhajani theka	:	A particular style of playing tabla for devotional songs
bhajans	:	A category of Indian music meant for devotional songs
bhakti sangeet	:	Devotional songs
bidai	:	Farewell of a newly-wed bride from her home
chhapki	:	A particular style of playing rhythm on tabla
chitrapat sangeet	:	Film songs
dandiya	:	A folk dance form originated in Gujarat
dargah	:	A tomb of a Muslim saint
dhobi	:	Washerman
dhol	:	A musical instrument
dholak bol	:	Syllables used to mark the pattern of rhythm on dholak, a musical instrument

doha	:	A lyrical verse format used mainly in North India
Garba	:	A traditional song and dance form used in Gujarat
Gharana	:	A distinctive musical style belonging to a particular sect or region
gully	:	A lane
haldi kumkum	:	A traditional festival where married women exchange turmeric and vermillion powder, as a way of blessing one another
jugaad	:	A flexible and innovative way of solving any problem
jugalbandis	:	Vocal or instrumental duet in Indian classical music
kande pohe	:	Maharashtrian breakfast dish made using flattened rice and onions
karela gosht	:	A popular dish made of bitter gourd and meat
kathak	:	A traditional Indian dance form
katta	:	A place to hang out
keema	:	Minced meat
khamiri roti	:	Traditional Mughlai flatbread
koda	:	A musical ending of a song
konakkol	:	An old art from originated in South India where vocal percussions are used to practice rhythm
kriti	:	A form of musical composition in Carnatic music
kutcheris	:	Carnatic music concert
laddus	:	A type of sweets usually served as an offering to the Gods
majlish	:	A musical gathering or a gathering for making music
manoos	:	A popular Marathi term meaning people
mazaar	:	A shrine/tomb
Megh Malhar	:	A raga in Hindustani classical music
mehfils	:	A musical gathering
mohalla	:	A neighbourhood
mujra	:	A traditional dance form in India
mukhra	:	The first part of any song composition
murkis	:	An ornamentation in Indian Classical music
natak	:	A play
natya geets	:	Songs used in plays
navarasa	:	Nine emotions
pallavis	:	A refrain in Carnatic music

pandals	:	A temporary structure where pujas are held during festivals
puranpolis	:	A traditional, Indian sweet prepared in Maharashtra
qawwali	:	A Muslim devotional music
qissa	:	A traditional style of music that speaks of a fable or folktale
raga alapanas	:	Forms of improvisations in Indian classical music
saarvajanik	:	General public
saarvajanik Ganeshotsav	:	A Ganesh festival held in public
sabudana khichadi	:	A popular Indian food made using sago pearls
sadhana	:	Worshipping
sanchari	:	A style of music composition where a different tune is inserted between two similar sounding verses
sangeet	:	A ritual associated with marriage
sankirtan	:	A traditional style of singing devotional songs
sawal jawab	:	A style of improvisation where vocalists or instrumentalists engage in musical conversation during a performance
shishya	:	A disciple
stotra	:	A chant
sufi	:	A saint
sutradhaar	:	An introducer
swaras	:	Seven musical notes in Indian classical music
tarana	:	A tune
teelgul	:	A candy made of sesame seeds and jaggery
thumkas	:	A dance form
ukadiche modaks	:	A sweet dish mainly offered during Ganesh Puja
uttapam	:	A South Indian food
varnam	:	Fundamental form in Carnatic music
vibhuti	:	Sacred ash
vidwaans	:	Scholars
warkaris	:	A religious movement within the spiritual tradition of Hinduism, especially in Maharashtra

Bibliography

'Ehsaan Noorani || On The Inspiration Behind "Rock On" | The MJ Show', *YouTube*, 19 August 2013, https://tinyurl.com/3maaa4r3.

'How i became a musician, and tips for newcomers | Shankar Mahadevan || converSAtions', *YouTube*, 23 September 2014, https://tinyurl.com/5brewa7h.

'Shankar Ehsaan Loy - On music and more', *YouTube*, 1 August 2011, https://tinyurl.com/rsb67h84.

'Shankar Mahadevan in conversation with Sudha Ragunathan - Expressions Espresso S1 EP8', *YouTube*, 29 May 2020, https://tinyurl.com/4ar9a5tx.

'WATCH Shankar Mahadevan & His Sons In Candid Conversation With Rajdeep Sardesai', *YouTube*, 1 October 2022, https://tinyurl.com/mwf2mszc.

Basu, Dyuiti, 'Folk Music Is above Even Classical Music: Shankar Mahadevan', *DNA*, 23 September 2018, https://tinyurl.com/36jpw36d.

Bhattacharya, Roshmila, 'This Week That Year: Shah Rukh Khan, Sonu Nigam's Ode to Life in Kal Ho Naa Ho', *Mumbai Mirror*, 1 December 2018, https://tinyurl.com/r2utcmm9.

Chawla, Pavan R., 'Shankar Mahadevan on His Music, Musicality, and the Most Beautiful Piece of Music He Has Grown Up To', *Pavan R Chawla*, 31 January 2012, https://tinyurl.com/yc4jb5kz.

Chopra, Rukmini, 'We Have To Respect Each Other's Triggers While Making Music: Shankar Mahadevan', *Hindustan Times*, 23 January 2017, https://tinyurl.com/y6ynuak3.

Ghosh, Devarsi, 'Shankar-Ehsaan-Loy Interview: 'We Showed That

Bollywood Music Could Be Cool', *Scroll.in*, 13 July 2021, https://tinyurl.com/26y7jaf3.

Ghosh, Sankhayan, 'Song Sung True', *The Indian Express*, 2 September 2015, https://tinyurl.com/msd3uajn.

IANS, 'Khale a Maestro till His Last Breath: Mahadevan', *India Forums*, 4 September 2011, https://tinyurl.com/3pszefsp.

Jha, Vikas Kumar, *The Queen of Indian Pop: The Authorised Biography of Usha Uthup*, Srishti Jha (trans.), Penguin Random House, 2022.

Johar, Karan, and Poonam Saxena, *An Unsuitable Boy*, Penguin Random House India, 2018.

Kusnur, Narendra, 'A Folk-Rock Collective', *Mint*, 31 May 2014, https://tinyurl.com/y8h82ad4.

Mehra, Rakeysh Omprakash, and Reeta Ramamurthy Gupta, *The Stranger in the Mirror*, Rupa Publications, 2021.

Pandey, Anup, '21-Year Itch', *The Hindu*, 1 February 2017, https://tinyurl.com/4xrajnss.

Ramani, Hema Iyer, and V.V. Ramani, 'The Sound of His Music', *The Hindu*, 27 July 2017, https://tinyurl.com/35f56tzs.

Sivan, Deepti Pillay (dir.), *Decoding Shankar*, 2018.

Venkatraman, Deepa, 'Like Father, Like Son', *The Score Magazine*, Vol. 7, No. 3, May 2014, pp. 12–15.

www.ingramcontent.com/pod-product-compliance
Lightning Source LLC
Chambersburg PA
CBHW020441100426
42812CB00036B/3411/J